LIBERTY
of
CONTRACT

D A V I D   N .   M A Y E R

LIBERTY
of
CONTRACT

REDISCOVERING
A LOST
CONSTITUTIONAL
RIGHT

CATO
INSTITUTE
WASHINGTON, D.C.

Library of Congress Cataloging-in-Publication Data

Mayer, David N.
    Liberty of contract : rediscovering a lost constitutional right / by
    David N. Mayer.
        p. cm.
    ISBN 978-1-935308-38-6 (hardback : alk. paper) — ISBN 978-1-
935308-39-3 (pbk. : alk. paper)   1. Liberty of contract—United States. I.
Title.

    KF801.M29 2011
    346.7302—dc22

                                                          2010045597
Printed in the United States of America.

CATO INSTITUTE
1000 Massachusetts Ave., N.W.
Washington, D.C. 20001
www.cato.org

Contents

Introduction: The Myth of "Laissez-Faire Constitutionalism"

Is an employee in a bakery free to work as many hours as he and his employer agree to, in order to earn more money for himself or his family? May a female hotel elevator operator choose to accept part of her wages in the form of room and board? Is the owner of a new business free to enter a market and compete with established companies? Do homeowners have the right to sell their houses to whomever they wish, despite a city ordinance forbidding them from selling to someone of a different race? May parents choose to have their children taught in a language other than English, and may a teacher earn his living by instructing non-English-speaking students? Or are parents free to choose to send their children to a private school, whether a parochial school or a private military academy, and are such private schools free to compete with government schools?

At one time in American history, the United States Supreme Court answered yes to each of the above questions, protecting as a constitutional right something known as "liberty of contract." Exercising its power of judicial review, the Court declared unconstitutional various state and federal laws that abridged this liberty by denying individuals the freedom to bargain over the terms of their own contracts—maximum-hours laws, minimum-wage laws, business-licensing laws, housing-segregation laws, and compulsory-education laws—laws that interfered with individuals' liberty of contract in each of the above-mentioned cases.

For a period of exactly 40 years, from 1897 until 1937, the Supreme Court protected liberty of contract as a fundamental right, one aspect of the basic right to liberty safeguarded under the Constitution's due process clauses, which prohibit government—the federal government, under the Fifth Amendment, and states, under the Fourteenth Amendment—from depriving persons of "life, liberty, or property without due process of law." Because the Court

1

protected liberty of contract by evaluating how laws limited persons' liberty—the substance of the laws themselves, as distinct from the procedures by which laws were enacted or enforced—modern constitutional law scholars consider liberty of contract to be a form of "substantive" (as opposed to "procedural") due process.③Although the Supreme Court continues to use substantive due process to protect certain aspects of liberty—most of the rights enumerated in the Bill of Rights plus other "personal" rights—following its "New Deal Revolution" of 1937, it ceased protecting liberty of contract, a right it had first explicitly recognized merely 40 years before.④

No period in American constitutional history is more misunderstood than this 40-year stretch. Known as the "*Lochner era*," it is named for the best-known U.S. Supreme Court decision protecting liberty of contract, *Lochner v. New York*.⑤The Court's protection of liberty of contract during this period is often described as "economic substantive due process," both to emphasize the most famous line of *Lochner*-era decisions—those protecting economic liberty against restrictive labor legislation—and to distinguish the Court's use of substantive due process during that period from its use in the modern, post–New Deal era.⑥The phrase "economic substantive due process" is just one of the misleading labels commonly used to describe the era. Other, even more misleading, terms are used by modern scholars to describe both *Lochner* and the *Lochner* era.

Most modern legal scholars condemn the *Lochner* decision as an egregious instance of "judicial activism"—of judges making new law rather than interpreting and applying the existing rules of law: in other words, of judges reading their own policy preferences into the law. Indeed, *Lochner* is commonly regarded by legal scholars as the archetypal activist decision of the Supreme Court: "shorthand in constitutional law for the worst sins of subjective judicial activism," as Aviam Soifer puts it. "Nothing can so damn a decision as to compare it to *Lochner* and its ilk," observes Michael Les Benedict. The decision has even prompted some scholars to invent a new verb: "We speak of 'lochnerizing' when we wish to imply that judges substitute their policy preferences for those of the legislature," writes William Wiecek.⑦

Modern scholars also refer often to the early 20th century as the "era of laissez-faire constitutionalism" because they see it as a time when judges injected a radical libertarian, or laissez-faire, philosophy into their constitutional decisions. Indeed, the stereotypical view sees the *Lochner* era as a time when American judges, motivated by the desire to further the interests of rich capitalists, perverted the original meaning of the due process clauses in order to engraft a laissez-faire ideology—commonly caricatured as synonymous with the doctrines of "Social Darwinism"—on the Constitution.[8] This view so dominates modern scholarship that it is the orthodoxy of college textbooks, both the casebooks used in law school constitutional law classes and the textbooks used in undergraduate and graduate courses in constitutional and legal history.[9] The orthodox view is found in constitutional commentaries written by both conservatives and liberals[10] and even in opinions written by modern Supreme Court justices.[11]

The modern view originated in legal scholarship written during the Progressive Era in the early 20th century. Progressivism arose at that time as a reform movement involving a diverse coalition of Americans who shared the conviction that government at all levels should play an active role in regulating economic and social life.[12] Progressive Era scholars and jurists such as Roscoe Pound, Learned Hand, and Charles Warren were not neutral in their analysis of liberty of contract. Rather, as supporters of the Progressive movement, they were hostile to the individualist philosophy that they perceived in the courts' protection of liberty of contract, and their personal hostility to the philosophy colored their criticism of the jurisprudence.[13] Learned Hand, for example, was "a major ... figure" and "a true believer" in the Progressive movement, according to his biographer.[14] Indeed, as an advocate of maximum-hours, minimum-wage, and workers' compensation legislation, Hand was especially critical of judicial decisions invalidating such legislation; he even suggested total repeal of the due process provisions of the Fifth and Fourteenth Amendments to strip the courts of their power to protect liberty of contract.[15] Modern scholars who interpret *Lochner* or the *Lochner* era by relying mainly or even exclusively on the views of such partisans as Pound, Hand, or Warren have made the same kind of mistake that future historians would make were they to similarly rely on the views of, say, the National Right to Life Committee to interpret *Roe v. Wade.* [16]

Although propounded by Progressive-Era scholars, the modern view of the Supreme Court's *Lochner*-era jurisprudence can be traced back originally to a misconception by Justice Oliver Wendell Holmes Jr., in his famous dissent in *Lochner*. Holmes characterized the majority's opinion as having been "decided upon an economic theory which a large part of the country does not entertain," adding the oft-quoted pithy comment, "The 14th Amendment does not enact Mr. Herbert Spencer's Social Statics"—a reference to the most famous laissez-faire treatise of the time. He then explained,

> [A] constitution is not intended to embody a particular eco-
> nomic theory, whether of paternalism and the organic rela-
> tion of the citizen to the State or of laissez faire. It is made for
> people of fundamentally differing views, and the accident
> of our finding certain opinions natural and familiar or novel
> and even shocking ought not to conclude our judgment upon
> the question whether statutes embodying them conflict with
> the Constitution of the United States.[17]

Justice Holmes's dissent has been accepted unquestioningly by historians and constitutional scholars.[18] So pervasive has been the influence of his characterization of the *Lochner* majority, with its criticism of the majority's alleged judicial activism, that many modern commentators forget that Holmes was not condemning substantive due process per se. His declaration that "[t]he word liberty in the Fourteenth Amendment is perverted when it is held to prevent the natural outcome of a dominant opinion" has been so often quoted out of context that scholars frequently have overlooked what Holmes wrote in the rest of the sentence: "unless it can be said that a rational and fair man necessarily would admit that the statute proposed would infringe fundamental principles as they have been understood by the traditions of our people and the law.'[19] Thus, even Holmes recognized that certain "fundamental principles" might guide the courts in the exercise of their power of judicial review.[20]

The popularity of Justice Holmes's critique, as expressed in his *Lochner* dissent, has perpetuated yet another aspect of the orthodox view of laissez-faire constitutionalism: its association with legal formalism. According to the orthodox view, judges protected liberty of contract by applying, rather mechanically, formal rules of law that they regarded as objective and scientifically discoverable. The great treatise writers of the late 19th century—men such as Thomas M. Cooley, Christopher G. Tiedeman, and John Forrest

Dillon—typically are characterized as having provided a rationale, combining laissez faire with legal formalism, that "promoted an interventionist role for judges" who "treated law as frozen, with its principles and values set and its rules determined for all time.[21] In contrast to this formalist "declaratory jurisprudence," modern scholars have identified a different theory of law that had been embraced by the opponents of laissez-faire constitutionalism in the early 20th century: "sociological jurisprudence." As a leading constitutional history textbook describes it, this was "a theory of law that its proponents regarded as more realistic, democratic, and humane," viewing law as "not a body of immutable principles and rules, but rather an institution shaped by social pressures that was constantly changing.[22] Sociological jurisprudence viewed the law essentially as Justice Holmes had described it in his 1881 book, *The Common Law*:

> The life of the law has not been logic: it has been experience. The felt necessities of the time, the prevalent moral and political theories, institutions of public policy, avowed or unconscious, even the prejudices which judges share with their fellow-men, have had a good deal more to do than the syllogism in determining the rules by which men should be governed[23]

Hence, under the orthodox view, judicial protection of laissez-faire values has been seen as a product of formalist legal reasoning, shaped by conservative "prejudices," and out of touch with the "realities" of modern industrial society[24]

In recent years, however, several scholars have challenged the orthodox, neo-Holmesian view of the *Lochner* era, questioning a number of the assumptions on which it has rested. In reassessing the *Lochner* era, some of these revisionist scholars have traced the origins of liberty of contract to a variety of sources in early American constitutional thought: among them, the "original meaning" of the due process clauses of the Fifth and Fourteenth Amendments[25] a hostility to "special," or "class," legislation deeply ingrained in Anglo-American law and political theory[26] and the "free labor" ideology of the antislavery movement and 19th-century Republican Party.[27] Although the revisionist scholars disagree about the precise source of the doctrine, they basically all agree that the orthodox view errs in characterizing liberty of contract as, in the words of one scholar, "essentially unprincipled or rooted in extraconstitutional policy preferences for laissez-faire economics."[28] Rather, they argue, the doctrine was grounded in well-established constitutional traditions.[29] Other revisionist scholars have challenged the orthodox view by questioning other assumptions on which it rests: for example, that liberty of contract favored the economic interests of employers and those who were "well-off,"[30] that *Lochner*-era jurists were "Social Darwinists,"[31] or that laissez-faire constitutionalism generally was grounded in a mechanical, or formalistic, jurisprudence.[32] What emerges from this revisionism is a more complex, and far more objective, picture of *Lochner*-era constitutionalism—one that attempts more fully to take into account the worldview of the 19th century, a worldview vastly different from that of the 20th-century regulatory and welfare state.[33]

Synthesizing the new scholarship and presenting a coherent and comprehensive overview of liberty-of-contract jurisprudence, this book argues that the orthodox view of the so-called *Lochner* era is fundamentally flawed in a number of respects. Indeed, the orthodox view is wrong in virtually all of its assumptions, which were based on myths originally propounded by Progressive-Era scholars that have been perpetuated by modern scholars who similarly defend the policies of the modern regulatory state.

The most important of these myths concerns the terminology scholars have used to identify the jurisprudence of this era. Although generally regarded as synonymous with liberty of contract, "laissez-faire constitutionalism" is truly a misnomer. Judicial protection of liberty of contract never involved doctrinal application of libertarian, or laissez-faire, principles. Contrary to the orthodox, Holmesian view, judges did not read Herbert Spencer's *Social Statics*, or any other laissez-faire writing, into the Constitution. At most, what judges did in protecting liberty of contract was to apply something like a general presumption in favor of liberty—a presumption that could be rebutted by sufficient showing of "reasonableness" in justification of a given government regulation. Moreover, judges applied this presumption quite inconsistently, in large part because the definition of "reasonable" government regulation—and the definition of the proper scope of the government's so-called police power on which it turned—were undergoing significant changes in the early decades of the 20th century. Rather than limiting it to protection of public health, safety, or order, some scholars redefined the police power as designed to further "general welfare," an amorphous concept invoked to justify the activist regulatory agenda of the Progressive movement.

The courts' adherence to traditional limitations on the police power, through their protection of liberty of contract, thwarted the Progressives' attempts to enact a category of laws that modern scholars call "social legislation." As used here, "social legislation" is a term of art, referring to a concept first introduced into American law from Europe in the late 19th century but not recognized by the Supreme Court until 1940. As Ernst Freund, an early 20th-century legal scholar explained in a 1917 text, "The term came from Germany and there originated about the beginning of the [eighteen] eighties, . . . [referring to] measures which are intended for the relief and elevation of the less favored classes of the community," such as wage and hour regulations and other factory laws. A modern legal historian has observed that social legislation, unlike, for example, legislation for the safety of passengers on railroads, did not fall within the traditional scope of the police power to curtail liberty in the interests of public health, safety, or order. Rather, as legislation intended for the "relief" or "elevation" of particular groups of persons presumed to be the "less favored classes of the community," such laws were by definition unconstitutional under traditional standards.[34]

When courts eventually abandoned their protection of liberty of contract as a fundamental right after 1937, they did so because a sufficient number of judges had adopted the Progressive activists' reformulation of the police power. Thus, the orthodox Holmesian view has it almost precisely backward. Rather than focusing on pre-1937 decisions that allegedly read libertarian principles into the Constitution, critics of judicial activism ought to focus instead on post-1937 decisions in which judges unquestionably assumed the reasonableness of such "social legislation." The majority of the pre-1937 Court did not read into the Constitution Herbert Spencer's *Social Statics* or some similar laissez-faire tract, in *Lochner* or any of the Court's other liberty-of-contract decisions, but the majority of the post-1937 Court did follow the economic and legal theories of such proponents of social legislation as Henry W. Farnam and Ernst Freund in cases upholding regulatory laws under a new standard.[35] That standard, called the rational basis test by modern scholars, allows deprivation of liberty and property rights by laws that meet a minimal test of being "reasonable in relation to [their] subject" and "adapted in the interests of the community."(36)

The post-1937 Supreme Court did not completely transform the law of substantive due process protection for liberty rights, however. In a famous decision issued a year after it announced the rational basis test, the Court declared that it would follow a more stringent standard—what modern scholars call the strict scrutiny test—in protecting certain specific rights favored by liberal justices. The higher level of protection afforded these rights—including many (but not all) of the particular rights listed in the Bill of Rights as well as other rights such as voting and the right to privacy—has given rise to what many scholars today see as a "double standard" in modern constitutional law. It is in the creation of this double standard, under which economic liberty and property rights are devalued compared with more favored liberty rights, that improper judicial activism—what has been misleadingly branded "*Lochner*ism"—can truly be found.(37)

To develop those themes more fully, chapter 1 uncovers the historical foundations of liberty of contract, tracing the roots of the doctrine to two lines of precedents well established in early American constitutional law: first, the protection of economic liberty and property rights through substantive due process or equivalent constitutional provisions, and second, the limitation of state police powers through the enforcement of certain constitutional rules, both written and unwritten. As the third section shows, the ratification of the Fourteenth Amendment made it possible for courts to protect individual economic liberty and property rights against state legislation—and therefore to limit state police powers—through the United States Constitution.

Chapter 2 examines the philosophical foundations of liberty of contract. The first section discusses the broader jurisprudential context in which liberty of contract emerged by the late 19th century: the rise of contract law and what it revealed about the significance of individualism in American society. The second section examines two contrasting approaches by which a general right to liberty, including liberty of contract, could be protected by the courts. One is what Justice Holmes accused the majority of doing in *Lochner*; the other is what the majority actually did in that case and in other liberty-of-contract decisions. In other words, this section will describe what a true "laissez-faire constitutionalism" would have been, what the courts would have done in *Lochner* and other cases if they truly had read Herbert Spencer's Law of Equal Freedom into the Constitution—a model radically different from what the courts actually did in enforcing liberty of contract. What the courts did was simply follow a general presumption in favor of liberty, which could be rebutted by a showing of a valid exercise of the police power in one of several recognized categories that were exceptions to the general rule favoring liberty.

Chapter 3 surveys the Court's protection of liberty of contract in its heyday, discussing not only its familiar applications in protecting economic liberty, as in cases like *Lochner*, but also some less familiar applications with regard to other aspects of personal liberty, including the protection of privacy rights and the prohibition of racial classifications. This chapter shows that what the courts protect today as "the right to privacy" really is the last vestige of liberty-of-contract jurisprudence. It also discusses an almost-forgotten case from the early 20th century that illustrates an alternative approach to the problem of de jure racial discrimination, from a time when the "separate but equal" doctrine limited the application of the equal protection clause.

Finally, chapter 4 discusses the demise of liberty of contract by the late 1930s, when the New Deal Revolution transformed substantive due process, replacing the general presumption in favor of liberty with a new paradigm incorporating the modern double standard in rights protection. As this chapter argues, the Court's liberty-of-contract jurisprudence did not come to an end simply as a result of political pressures in 1937—Franklin Roosevelt's announced plan to "pack" the Supreme Court with six new members, which seemingly precipitated the "switch in time that saved nine," the justices' shift in constitutional interpretation. Rather, more fundamentally, liberty of contract failed because of its weak jurisprudential foundations: it was based on an ill-defined standard, a general rule riddled with exceptions, under which the vast majority of challenged government regulations were increasingly upheld by the courts. As shown here, the road from liberty of contract as it was actually enforced in the courts—which was vastly different from the "laissez-faire constitutionalism" stereotype—to the post-1937 minimal "rational basis" test, was a short road indeed.

This book has been several years in the making. Earlier versions of the manuscript were presented as talks given at the Social Philosophy and Policy Center at Bowling Green State University and at Case Western Reserve University School of Law (sponsored by Case Western's chapter of the Federalist Society) in April 1998; at the Federalist Society's annual faculty conference in Washington, D.C., in January 2000; and at the annual Summer Seminar of the Objectivist Center (now the Atlas Society), at the University of Pittsburgh–Johnstown, Johnstown, Pennsylvania, in July 2001. Portions of the book have been published in two law review articles: "The Myth of 'Laissez-Faire Constitutionalism': Liberty of Contract during the *'Lochner* Era,'" 36 *Hastings Constitutional Law Quarterly* 217 (2009), and "Substantive Due Process Rediscovered: The Rise and Fall of Liberty of Contract," 60 *Mercer Law Review* 563 (2009). Finally, the text of the book has been improved in innumerable ways by the helpful editorial comments of Roger Pilon, vice president for legal affairs at the Cato Institute and director of Cato's Center for Constitutional Studies.

1. Historical Foundations of Liberty of Contract

Roscoe Pound, one of the Progressive-Era scholars who criticized courts for protecting liberty of contract, did not accept the prevalent view that this practice arose from individual judges projecting their "personal, social and economic views into the law." He observed that "when a doctrine is announced with equal vigor and held with equal tenacity by courts of Pennsylvania and of Arkansas, of New York and of California, of Illinois and of West Virginia, of Massachusetts and of Missouri, we may not dispose of it so readily." He nevertheless asserted that liberty of contract was a "new" doctrine that appeared suddenly in late 19th-century jurisprudence, and he identified seven "causes" for the doctrine's appearance in American jurisprudence—among them, the prevalence of "an individualist conception of justice" and of "mechanical" legal reasoning in late 19th-century legal thought.[1]

Contrary to Pound's assertion, however, liberty of contract did not suddenly emerge, as a "new" doctrine, at the end of the 19th century. Rather, it originated in two lines of precedents well established in early American constitutional law. The first was the protection of economic liberty and property rights through substantive use of the U.S. Constitution's due process clauses or equivalent provisions in state constitutions. The second was the limitation of state police powers through the enforcement of certain constitutional rules, both written and unwritten. What was new in the late 19th century was judicial identification of these doctrines, taken together, as the right of "liberty of contract" and the protection of this right through the due process clause of the Fourteenth Amendment.

Substantive Due Process in Early American Law

Constitutional protection of individual liberty in all its aspects, including economic liberty and the protection of property rights, did not suddenly appear in American law in the late 19th century, the result of classic liberal, laissez-faire ideology. Rather, high regard for economic liberty and property as fundamental rights of the individual was well established in American constitutionalism quite early in the nation's history—indeed, even predating the Constitution itself. "Liberty was the most cherished right possessed by English-speaking people in the eighteenth century," observes one preeminent legal historian:[2]

> It was both an ideal for the guidance of governors and a standard with which to measure the constitutionality of government; both a cause of the American Revolution and a purpose for drafting the United States Constitution; both an inheritance from Great Britain and a reason republican common lawyers continued to study the law of England.

The concept of liberty thus was central to Anglo-American constitutional thought during the era of the American Revolution; indeed, it was central to early American law.

The Patriot leaders of the Revolution were influenced profoundly by English radical Whig opposition thought, which departed from mainstream English legal theory in its understanding of both liberty and constitutionalism.[3] Radical Whigs conceptualized liberty apart from the rule of law, seeing it as something more than merely freedom to do what the law permitted or even freedom from arbitrary government. Rather, believing that liberty was a natural right, they saw it as the freedom of individuals to do what they will, provided they do not violate the equal right of others. In their constitutional thought, radical Whig philosophers—like the framers of early American constitutions who implemented their ideas—understood two critically important foundational principles: first, that the essential function of government was to protect the rights of individuals (including their right to liberty); and second, that the essential function of a constitution was to limit or control government power, which both protected and threatened individual rights. Constitutionally speaking, what was truly radical about the American Revolution was that it made the protection of individual rights (including liberty in this broader sense as well as property rights) the test for government's legitimacy.[4]

As historian Gordon Wood has shown, the American Revolution was far more radical than commonly believed. Indeed, Wood maintains that it was "as radical as any revolution in history" as well as "the most radical and most far-reaching event in American history," one that altered not only the form of government—by eliminating monarchy and creating republics—but also Americans' conception of public or state power. "Most important," he adds, "it made the interests and prosperity of ordinary people—their pursuits of happiness—the goal of society and government."[5] Scholars, particularly legal historians who have focused on the constitutional arguments advanced by American Patriot leaders,[6] have overlooked the extent to which the Revolution transformed not only the form of American government but also Americans' view of government and the law. By rejecting the British monarchical system, the Founders also rejected the paternalism through which the British system operated in the realms of law and politics.[7] The rejection of paternalism was manifest in many developments in Revolutionary-era society, among them the rise of contract law[8] and even the growing popularity of laissez-faire economics, perhaps best illustrated by the Philadelphia merchants' opposition to price controls in 1777–78.[9] Moreover, Wood notes, "[t]he Revolution did not merely create a political and legal environment conducive to economic expansion; it also released powerful popular entrepreneurial and commercial energies that few realized existed and transformed the economic landscape of the country."[10]

The far-reaching social changes that came into being with the American Revolution also were accompanied by correspondingly significant changes in law and constitutionalism. Although early American law fell short of the ideal envisioned by late 19th-century classical liberals or by modern libertarians,[11] it nevertheless departed radically from the British paternalistic system by the degree to which it explicitly protected and promoted individual freedom. To some extent, the uniquely individualistic premises of the American legal system did not suddenly appear in 1776; as legal historians have shown, the so-called Americanization of the English common law was a long, evolutionary process that had begun well before the Revolution.[12] With independence, however, the American legal system—particularly the constitutional system—was free to depart dramatically from its English roots. "We have it in our power to begin the world over again," wrote Thomas Paine, succinctly describing the unprecedented opportunity Americans had after 1776 to frame new forms of government.[13]

When the Second Continental Congress adopted Thomas Jefferson's draft of the Declaration of Independence, it declared "life, liberty, and the pursuit of happiness" to be inherent and unalienable rights that government was created to secure. In drafting the Declaration, Jefferson sought, as he later described it, to express the "harmonizing sentiments" of American Whigs.[14] Those sentiments included the "self-evident" truth of the theory of natural rights[15] as expounded by English radical Whigs, Enlightenment philosophers, and legal theorists such as Jean Jacques Burlamaqui, the Swiss jurist whose treatise on natural law not only influenced Jefferson and his contemporaries but remained influential with Americans well into the 19th century.[16] A detailed exposition of the early American understanding of natural rights theory is beyond the scope of this book; however, in essence, one can summarize it by noting that rights such as life, liberty, and the pursuit of happiness are possessed by persons by their nature, or status as human beings, and that therefore these rights are "inalienable."[17] As Mark Hopkins, president of Williams College, observed in a lecture he gave in Boston in 1862, "Inalienable rights are those of which a man cannot divest himself by contract; which he may not, under any circumstances, lawfully demit; but he may forfeit them by crime, and be wrongfully deprived of them by others."[18]

Both "liberty" and "pursuit of happiness," as the terms were understood by the Founders, were rather broad concepts. Although some scholars have asserted that the Founders' conception of liberty was quite narrow, limited only to "freedom from physical restraint of the person,"[19] the concept as understood in early American political thought, on the contrary, was quite broad, encompassing economic liberty as well as other forms of liberty less tangible than mere freedom from physical restraint.

Cato's Letters, the great radical Whig tract of the 1720s that continued to be quoted in American newspapers well into the later 18th century, defined liberty comprehensively as "the Power which every Man has over his own Actions, and his Right to enjoy the Fruits of his Labour, Art, and Industry, as far as by it he hurts not the Society, or any Members of it, by taking from any Member, or by hindering him from enjoying what he himself enjoys." Liberty included the Right of every Man to pursue the natural, reasonable, and religious Dictates of his own Mind; to think what he will, and act as he thinks, provided not to the Prejudice of another; to spend his own Money himself, and lay out the Produce of his Labour his own Way; and to labour for his own Pleasure and Profit, and not for others who are idle, and would live and riot by pillaging and oppressing him, and those that are like him.[20]

More succinctly, "Liberty is, to live upon one's own Terms," the opposite state of "Slavery," which is "to live at the mere Mercy of another."[21]

While the authors of *Cato's Letters* acknowledged that this "natural and absolute Liberty" must be restrained by civil government, they emphasized that the restraint must be partial, or limited, consistent with the purpose for which government was established. "The entering into political Society, is so far from a Departure from this natural Right, that to preserve it, was the sole Reason why Men did so; and mutual Protection and Assistance is the only reasonable purpose of all reasonable Societies." If the power of government were to go beyond this legitimate purpose—that is to say, if the restraint put on natural liberty were to become unlimited—then tyranny would result. "Free Government is the protecting the People in their Liberties by stated Rules; Tyranny is a brutish Struggle for unlimited Liberty to one or a few, who would rob all others of their Liberty, and act by no Rule but lawless Lust." *Cato's Letters* also acknowledged the danger of majority tyranny, calling it "a mistaken Notion in Government" that the interest of the majority was alone to be consulted, "since in Society every Man has a Right to every Man's Assistance in the Enjoyment and Defence of his private Property; otherwise the greater Number may fell the lesser, and divide their Estates amongst themselves; and so, instead of a Society where all peaceable Men are protected, become a Conspiracy of the Many against the Minority."[22]

Burlamaqui's influential treatise on natural law similarly defined liberty quite broadly and emphasized that in civil society, positive law supplemented but did not supplant natural law and the rights held thereunder. Following an analysis reminiscent of the "state of nature" posited by English radical Whig philosopher John Locke,[23] Burlamaqui defined "natural liberty" as essentially synonymous

15

with individuals' freedom to do as they please provided they do not interfere with the equal freedom of others:

> Natural liberty is the right, which nature gives to all mankind, of disposing of their persons and property, after the manner they judge most convenient to their happiness, on condition of their acting within the limits of the law of nature, and of their not abusing it to the prejudice of their fellow men. To this right of liberty there is a reciprocal obligation corresponding, by which the law of nature binds all mankind to respect the liberty of other men, and not to disturb them in the use they make of it, so long as they do not abuse it.

He then compared natural liberty to "civil liberty." Beginning with the basic definition that civil liberty was "nothing more than natural liberty, so far restrained by human laws (and no further) as is necessary for the preserving of human rights, and the maintenance of peace and order in society," Burlamaqui noted that this state had two advantages over natural liberty: first, "the right of insisting that the magistrate shall confine himself within the limits of the power conferred upon him, and use it agreeably to the purposes for which he was entrusted with it"; and second, "the security which the people should reserve to themselves for the preservation of the right above named." From these corollary principles of limitations on government power and the people's right of self-defense against the government itself, Burlamaqui derived his final definition: "[C]ivil liberty is natural liberty, regulated by such laws as are necessary for the maintenance of justice, and attended with the right of insisting that the government shall make the proper use of its authority, and a security that this right shall be respected."[24]

Liberty so conceptualized encompassed the right to property. Indeed, liberty and property were so interconnected in early American political thought that they were almost impossible to separate.[25] Historian Edmund S. Morgan has observed, "For eighteenth-century Americans, property and liberty were one and inseparable, because property was the only foundation yet conceived for security of life and liberty: without security for his property, it was thought, no man could live or be free except at the mercy of another."[26] An essayist in a New York newspaper observed in 1735 that both the full enjoyment of liberty and full protection for property rights were essential in a well-ordered society: "As for liberty, it cannot be bought at too great a rate; life itself is well employed when 'tis hazarded for liberty. . . . As for property, it is so interwoven with liberty that whenever we perceive the latter weakened, the former cannot fail of being impaired." And as a modern legal historian has noted, "liberty in the eighteenth century was personal property"; indeed, "it was the concept of property that bestowed on liberty much of its substance as a constitutional entity. . . . [f]or, as everyone then appreciated, liberty existed through security of property and yet, as John Dickinson said, liberty itself was the *only security* of property."[27]

"Pursuit of happiness," as used in the Declaration of Independence and in many early state constitutions, also encompassed economic liberty and property rights; it included the right to acquire, possess, and dispose of property.[28] The bill of rights for the Virginia state constitution, written by George Mason and adopted on June 12, 1776, noted "all men are by nature equally free and independent, and have certain inherent rights. . . namely, the enjoyment of life and liberty, with *the means of acquiring and possessing property*, and pursuing and obtaining happiness and safety."[29] Virtually identical provisions identifying property rights as natural and inalienable appeared in the Pennsylvania constitution of 1776, the Massachusetts constitution of 1780, and the New Hampshire constitution of 1783,[30] as well as in many state constitutions adopted in the early 19th century.[31] Indeed, a leading scholar of the early state constitutions has concluded from these provisions that "the acquisition of property and the pursuit of happiness were so closely connected with each other in the minds of the founding generation that naming only one of the two sufficed to evoke both."[32]

Further evidence of the interrelatedness of liberty and property rights in early American thought can be found in James Madison's 1792 essay on property. The essay was written for the *National Gazette*, the Republican Party newspaper published by Philip Freneau in Philadelphia and launched with Madison's support. Madison was an occasional contributor to the paper, writing 19 unsigned essays, of which this essay is perhaps the most famous.[33]

According to Madison, the term "property" can be understood not only in the narrow sense, such as "a man's land, or merchandize, or money," but also in a broader sense, as "every thing to which a man may attach a value and have a right; and which leaves to every one else the like advantage." In this "larger and juster" sense,

> [One] has a property of peculiar value in his religious opinions, and in the profession and practice dictated by them. He has a property very dear to him in the safety and liberty of his person. He has equal property in the free use of his faculties and free choice of the objects on which to employ them.

In short, "as a man is said to have a right to his property, he may be equally said to have a property in his rights." Madison then followed Locke in maintaining that the essential function of government is to protect property in both the narrow and broad senses—to protect all the rights of individuals:

> Government is instituted to protect property of every sort; as well that which lies in the various rights of individuals, as that which the term particularly expresses. This being the end of government, that alone is a *just* government, which *impartially* secures to every man, whatever is his *own*.

If government exercises "an excess of power," then "property of no sort is duly respected," he added. "No man is safe in his opinions, his person, his faculty, or his possessions."[34]

Indeed, to Madison, the standard for measuring a good or just government was the degree to which it impartially protected property rights of all sorts. "That is not a just government, nor is property secure under it," where "a man's religious rights are violated by penalties, or fettered by tests, or taxed by a hierarchy," or where press gangs are in operation, arbitrarily seizing "one class of citizens for the service of the rest," and thereby violating "the property which a man has in his personal safety and personal liberty." Madison similarly regarded with contempt government restrictions on individuals' economic freedom, particularly their freedom to earn a living:[35]

> That is not a just government, nor is property secure under it, where arbitrary restrictions, exemptions, and monopolies deny to part of its citizens that free use of their faculties, and free choice of their occupations, which not only constitute their property in the general sense of the word; but are the means of acquiring property so called.

18

Nor did he favorably regard excessive or partial taxation.[36] In sum, Madison urged a public policy that protected equally and impartially property of all sorts, including not only freedom of expression and religious freedom but also economic freedom and property rights in the narrow sense of the word:

> If there be a government then which prides itself in maintaining the inviolability of property; which provides that none shall be taken *directly* even for public use without indemnification to the owner, and yet *directly* violates the property which individuals have in their opinions, their religion, their persons, and their faculties; nay more, which *indirectly* violates their property, in their actual possessions, in the labor that acquires their daily subsistence, and in the hallowed remnant of time which ought to relieve their fatigues and soothe their cares, . . . such a government is not a pattern for the United States.

He concluded, "If the United States mean to obtain or deserve the full praise due to wise and just governments, they will equally respect the rights of property, and the property in rights. . . ."[37]

Madison's allusion to the takings clause of the Fifth Amendment raises implicitly the question: where in the American constitutions, state or federal, were liberty and property rights generally—Americans' "rights of property" and their "property in rights"—protected against legislation and other government acts that abridged them? Certain aspects of these rights were protected by courts under particular constitutional provisions such as takings clauses or ex post facto clauses. At least two state courts—the supreme courts of Virginia and Indiana—directly applied the natural rights provision of their state constitutions in declaring unconstitutional laws that deprived citizens of their liberty or divested them of property rights.[38] The most important general protection of liberty and property rights, however, was found in another clause in the Fifth Amendment of the U.S. Constitution, the due process clause, and in its equivalent clauses found in the state constitutions.

The due process clauses of the federal and state constitutions have perhaps the longest pedigree of any American constitutional provision, for they can be traced directly back to the famous clause 39 of Magna Carta: "No freeman shall be captured or imprisoned or disseised or outlawed or exiled or in any way destroyed, nor will we go against him or send against him, except by the lawful judgment of his peers or by the law of the land."[39] The "law of the land" over time became synonymous with due process of law, and the early state constitutions typically contained law-of-the-land clauses in lieu of due process clauses. In the period before the U.S. Constitution was adopted, six states plus Vermont (which governed itself as an independent republic before being admitted to the Union in 1791) adopted bills of rights as parts of their constitutional documents; each of these bills of rights contained a law-of-the-land provision. In addition, two states inserted a law-of-the-land clause in the body of their constitutions rather than in a separate bill of rights.[40]

Contrary to the assertions of some modern scholars—that substantive due process did not originate until the middle of the 19th century, with the *Dred Scott* case[41]—American courts began applying the doctrine of substantive due process much earlier, not long after adoption of the Constitution itself. It should also be noted that only modern scholars have drawn the distinction between "procedural" and "substantive" due process. The phrase "substantive due process" is anachronistic: it has no known use before the early 1930s,[42] and it has been used since that time as a pejorative oxymoron by opponents of *Lochner*-era jurisprudence and, later, opponents of the Warren Court.[43] Indeed, it can be argued that the concept of "due process of law" logically entails both procedural and substantive elements and that the substantive element in turn logically derives from the rights—the rights to life, liberty, and property—that the constitutional provisions protect.[44] Moreover, one might further argue that the substantive component of due process was present from its very start, with the original "law of the land" clause of Magna Carta, for the grievances against King John included complaints that he had sent writs to his sheriffs ordering seizure of the lands and chattels belonging to his enemies and had granted rebel land to his own supporters. Hence, King John's promise not to "disseise," or dispossess, any free man or to "go against him. . ., except by. . . the law of the land" meant more than simply following the appropriate judicial proceedings: it was a promise not to arbitrarily imprison or seize property without valid legal cause to do so—a substantive as well as a procedural guarantee.[45]

It may be true, as a leading modern scholar of property rights has observed, that "[h]istorically the guarantee of due process was defined largely in procedural terms, requiring simply that customary legal procedures be followed before a person could be punished for criminal offenses."[46] Nevertheless, as that scholar adds, by the late 18th century, state courts began to view "law of the land" clauses in state constitutions as restrictions on legislation—in other words, as substantive protections for property rights.[47] Careful study of late 18th-century legal thought reveals much evidence that due process was understood to have substantive as well as procedural content.[48] Moreover, in a series of decisions from the 1790s to the 1850s, the highest courts of several states held that the "law of the land" clause in their state constitutions prohibited the legislature from passing laws that deprived citizens of their property.[49]

Two state court decisions in the antebellum period, both involving early liquor prohibition laws, are especially important. In *Herman v. State*, the Indiana Supreme Court in 1855 held that the state liquor prohibition law was invalid under the natural rights provision in the state constitution as an unconstitutional deprivation of liberty. In his opinion for the court, Judge Perkins declared that "the right of liberty and pursuing happiness secured by the constitution, embraces the right, in each *compos mentis* individual, of selecting what he will eat and drink, in short, his beverages, . . . and that the legislature cannot take away that right by direct enactment."[50] A year later, in *Wynehamer v. People*, the New York Court of Appeals held that a statute outlawing the sale of liquor was a deprivation of property—specifically, the liquor owned by tavern keepers when the law took effect—without due process of law. The court observed that "the legislature cannot totally annihilate commerce in any species of property, and so condemn the property itself to extinction." The decision not only was a striking instance of the substantive use of due process but also, as Professor Ely notes, was "the first time that a court determined that the concept of due process prevented the legislature from regulating the beneficial enjoyment of property in such a manner as to destroy its value."[51]

In the same year as the *Wynehamer* decision, the U.S. Supreme Court also adopted the view that the due process clause of the Fifth Amendment restricted Congress's powers. In *Murray's Lessee v. Hoboken Land and Improvement Company*, Justice Benjamin R. Curtis, writing for the Court, found that the clause was "a restraint on the legislative as well as on the executive and judicial powers of the government, and cannot be so construed as to leave congress free to make any process 'due process of law,' by its mere will."[52] This decision anticipated the Court's controversial ruling a year later, in the *Dred Scott* case, where Chief Justice Roger Taney interpreted the due process clause as a substantive limitation on the power of Congress to prohibit slavery in the territories. Specifically, Taney—writing on this issue for a Court majority comprising himself and five other justices—held that the 1820 Missouri Compromise law, which barred slavery from the northern part of the territory added to the United States by the Louisiana Purchase, "could hardly be dignified with the name of due process of law."[53]

Chief Justice Taney and the *Dred Scott* majority were not the first to see the Fifth Amendment due process clause as a substantive limit on Congress's power to legislate for the territories, however. A year before the *Dred Scott* decision, the platform of the newly created Republican Party understood the Fifth Amendment to require the opposite of what Taney interpreted the Constitution to require: focusing on the due process clause's protection of liberty, rather than property, Republicans understood it to impose a "duty" on Congress to *prohibit* slavery from the territories.[54] This position was not surprising, given that many Republicans were anti-slavery activists and that anti-slavery activists since the mid-1830s had been arguing that constitutional due process guarantees substantively protected the natural rights of life, liberty, and property of all persons.[55] Thus, it was not the Court's use of the Fifth Amendment's due process clause as a substantive limit on the power of Congress that made *Dred Scott* so controversial in the 19th century. Rather, it was Taney's particular application of substantive due process,[56] in what was arguably *obiter dictum* (that is, a holding not necessary to the Court's decision), to resolve a hotly contested political question.[57]

Following this line of precedents for substantive due process protection of property and economic liberty rights, state courts began recognizing liberty of contract in the years before the U.S. Supreme Court's recognition in *Allgeyer v. Louisiana*. The New York Court of Appeals, in two important decisions in the year 1885, interpreted the state constitution's due process clause to protect both property and liberty rights, in a broad sense.

In January 1885, in the *Jacobs* case, the court found unconstitutional a state law that prohibited the manufacture of cigars in tenement houses.[58] Anticipating the definition of "liberty" that the U.S.

Supreme Court would adopt in *Allgeyer* 12 years later, the New York court recognized:

> [O]ne may be deprived of his liberty and his constitutional rights thereto violated without the actual imprisonment or restraint of his person. Liberty, in its broad sense as understood in this country, means the right not only of freedom from actual servitude, imprisonment, or restraint, but the right of one to use his faculties in all lawful ways, to live and work where he will, to earn his livelihood in any lawful calling, and to pursue any lawful trade or avocation. All laws, therefore, which impair or trammel these rights, which limit one in his choice of a trade or profession, or confine him to work or live in a specified locality, or exclude him from his own house, or restrain his otherwise lawful movements (except as such laws may be passed in the exercise by the legislature of the police power. . .), are infringements upon his fundamental rights of liberty, which are under constitutional protection.[59]

The court rejected the argument that the law was a legitimate exercise of the police power, as a health measure, finding that it had "no relation whatever to the public health."[60] Rather, the court found that "[u]nder the guise of promoting the public health" the legislature had "arbitrarily interfere[d] with personal liberty and private property without due process of law."[61]

Six months later, in its June 1885 decision in *People v. Marx*, the New York Court of Appeals found unconstitutional a statute that prohibited the manufacture of oleomargarine, on the grounds that it deprived oleomargarine manufacturers of their economic freedom.[62] The court rejected the state's rationale for the statute as protecting consumers against fraudulent imitations of dairy butter and understood the statute instead as a "dangerous" measure protecting the dairy industry from competition—"an enactment which absolutely prohibits an important branch of industry for the sole reason that it competes with another, and may reduce the price of an article of food for the human race."[63] The court held that liberty, in the broad sense as it had defined it in *Jacobs*, was protected not only by the due process clause of the state constitution but also by its "law of the land" clause, as well as the Fourteenth Amendment of the U.S. Constitution.[64]

Ten years after these 1885 New York cases, in a decision that could be regarded as the first explicit protection of liberty of contract by an American court, the Illinois Supreme Court in *Ritchie v. People* held unconstitutional a statute providing that "no female shall be employed in any factory or workshop more than eight hours in any one day or forty-eight hours in any one week."[65] The court found that the statute exceeded the legitimate scope of the state's police power by abridging the freedom of both the employer and the employee "to contract with each other in reference to the hours of labor." The court based this "right to contract" on the due process clause of the Illinois Constitution, finding it to involve "both a liberty and property right": [66]

> Liberty includes the right to acquire property, and that means and includes the right to make and enforce contracts. . . . The right to use, buy, and sell property and contract in respect thereto is protected by the constitution. Labor is property, and the laborer has the same right to sell his labor, and to contract with reference thereto, as has any other property owner. In this country the legislature has no power to prevent persons who are *sui juris* from making their own contracts, nor can it interfere with the freedom of contract between the workman and the employer. The right to labor or employ labor, and make contracts in respect thereto upon such terms as may be agreed upon between the parties, is included in the constitutional guaranty above quoted [Section 2 of Article 2 of the state constitution, its due process clause].

Significantly, the court explicitly rejected sexual paternalism as a rationale for the statute, finding instead that women were "*sui juris*," or legally competent, and therefore "entitled to the same rights, under the constitution, to make contracts with reference to [their] labor, as are secured thereby to men." The Illinois court's recognition that the right to make and enforce contracts applied equally to women as to men is especially noteworthy, given that Illinois had been admitting women to the bar only since 1890. Now, in 1895, the court found that a woman held "the right to gain a livelihood by intelligence, honesty, and industry in the arts, the sciences, the professions, or other vocations" and that "her right to a choice of vocations cannot be said to be denied or abridged on account of sex."[67]

Other Limits on the Police Power in 19th-Century Constitutionalism

In early American constitutional law, courts checked the "police power," the general regulatory power of the states, by relying mainly on the substantive use of due process, or "law of the land," constitutional clauses. But they also used other provisions in both state constitutions and the U.S. Constitution, as well as certain unwritten constitutional limits on government power. And they recognized an important limitation on the police power inherent in the definition of the power itself. These various constitutional limitations all may have helped provide precedents for *Lochner*-era jurisprudence, as some modern revisionist scholars have argued. Nevertheless, liberty of contract was a right based on substantive due process and thus was distinct from the other constitutional limitations on the police power.

The cases discussed in the previous section—early precedents for the substantive use of the due process clauses or their equivalents—are especially significant given the generally broad scope that antebellum courts gave state legislatures in exercising the police power. Traditionally, the police power comprised the authority to protect public health, safety, and morals.[68] Sometimes courts also cited public "order" or the "general welfare" along with those three traditional categories.[69] As one modern commentator has observed, although it is by nature virtually incapable of enduring, comprehensive definition, the police power had its origins in the English common-law concept that one ought to use one's property in such a way as not to injure that of another: *sic utere tuo ut alienum non laedas*.[70] In his *Commentaries* on English law, Blackstone analogized its exercise in the state to the functioning of a well-ordered family, whose members "are bound to conform their general behaviour to the rules of propriety, good neighborhood, and good manners; and to be decent, industrious, and inoffensive in their respective stations."[71] Thomas M. Cooley, author of *Constitutional Limitations*, the most influential constitutional law treatise in the 19th century, similarly defined the police power as the "whole system of internal regulation" by which a state not only preserves public order but also establishes "for the intercourse of citizen with citizen those rules of good manners and good neighborhood which are calculated to prevent a conflict of rights, and to insure to each the uninterrupted enjoyment of his own so far as is reasonably consistent with a like enjoyment of the rights by others."[72]

Massachusetts Chief Justice Lemuel Shaw in 1851 gave perhaps the classic 19th-century view of the police power in one of his most often-cited decisions. In *Commonwealth v. Alger*, the Massachusetts Supreme Court upheld a statute limiting the length of wharves in Boston Harbor as a valid exercise of the legislature's power to

> make, ordain, and establish all manner of wholesome and reasonable laws, statutes, and ordinances, either with penalties or without, not repugnant to the constitution, as they shall judge fit to be for the good and welfare of the commonwealth and of the subjects of the same.

In a well-ordered society, Chief Justice Shaw observed, every holder of property, "however absolute and unqualified may be his title," holds it under the implied liability that the use of it may be so regulated "that it shall not be injurious to the equal enjoyment of others having an equal right to the enjoyment of their property, nor injurious to the rights of the community." He concluded that property rights were subject to "reasonable limitations" judged by the legislature to be necessary to "the common good and general welfare."[73] The supreme courts of two other New England states in the 1850s similarly described the police power as a general limitation on individuals' liberty or property rights.[74]

Notwithstanding the broad scope of the police power, however, courts and legal scholars in the 19th century recognized a number of limitations on its exercise, as the title of Cooley's treatise suggests. Ordinarily, courts were willing to declare invalid statutes that directly conflicted with positive constitutional prohibitions, including general protections of liberty and property rights under due process or "law of the land" provisions. Courts also cited other explicit limitations on state legislative powers, such as the Article I, Section 10, contract clause, in limiting the police power.

The provision of the U.S. Constitution prohibiting states from enacting any law "impairing the obligations of contracts"[75] was an important limit on state police power in the early 19th century. As one modern scholar has described it, the clause was "designed to protect the idea of individuals entering into agreements to order privately their arrangements."[76] Only three years after implementation of the Constitution, a federal circuit court found a Rhode Island debtor-relief measure to be invalid under the contract clause, in one of the first exercises of federal judicial review.[77] Under John Marshall's leadership as chief justice, the Supreme Court broadened the definition of contracts entitled to protection under the Constitution and thus made the contract clause "the most significant constitutional limitation on state power to regulate the economy" in the antebellum era.[78] In its landmark decision in *Fletcher v. Peck* in 1810, the Marshall Court found unconstitutional a Georgia law rescinding the Yazoo land grant made by a previous legislature amidst charges of bribery and corruption. In his opinion for the unanimous Court, Chief Justice Marshall held that the Georgia legislature "was restrained, *either by general principles which are common to our free institutions*, or by the particular provisions of the constitution of the United States"—namely, the contract clause, which he found applicable to "contracts of every description," including those made by the state.[79]

Marshall's reference to "general principles which are common to our free institutions," as an alternate basis for the holding in *Fletcher v. Peck*, illustrates another important category of limitations on the police power in 19th-century constitutional law: unwritten limitations, drawn either from natural rights theory or from general principles limiting all constitutional government. One important aspect of these limitations is the so-called vested rights doctrine for the protection of established property rights from legislative interference.[80] In a 1795 circuit court case, Justice William Paterson anticipated Marshall's reasoning in *Fletcher*, linking the contract clause with the doctrine of natural rights. Observing that "the right of acquiring and possessing property, and having it protected, is one of the natural, inherent and inalienable rights of man," Paterson added: "The preservation of property. . . is a primary object of the social compact." He then ruled that the repeal of a Pennsylvania statute confirming certain land grants impaired the obligation of contract.[81]

Three years later, Justice Samuel Chase in a separate opinion in *Calder v. Bull* expressed perhaps the most famous statement in support of unwritten constitutional limits in early American law when he observed: "There are certain vital principles in our free republican governments which will determine and overrule an apparent and flagrant abuse of legislative power." Among these, Chase maintained, was the principle that the legislature could not "violate the right of an antecedent lawful private contract; or the right of private property." Chase also cited some other examples of illegitimate legislative acts, including "a law that destroys, or impairs, the lawful contracts of citizens" and "a law that takes property from A. and gives it to B."[82]

It was not just the federal judiciary that used natural law or general constitutional principles in exercising judicial review in the late 18th and early 19th centuries. Many state court decisions—including several antedating the U.S. Constitution itself—based their holdings on both unwritten and written law. As noted in the previous section, at least two state supreme courts directly applied the natural rights provisions of their state constitutions in declaring unconstitutional laws depriving citizens of their liberty or divesting them of their property rights.[83]

Another important unwritten limitation on the police power was the requirement of equal treatment under the law. This requirement was frequently expressed by courts and commentators as the principle that laws must not single out specific groups or classes for special treatment unless the laws really related to the welfare of the community as a whole—in other words, unless they really advanced the traditional concerns of the police power in protecting public health, safety, or morality. Laws that failed to meet this test were seen as advancing purely "private" interests and thus were illegitimate, categorized variously as "unequal, partial, class, or special legislation."[84]

This prohibition of "class legislation," like the broader principle of equal treatment under the law from which it derived, can be traced back to John Locke, who in his *Second Treatise on Government* had linked equality with liberty in his discussion of natural rights. The state of nature that Locke posited was one in which individuals were "equal and independent." When Locke described individuals as equal with respect to their rights, he referred to "the *Equality* which all Men are in, in respect of Jurisdiction or Dominion one over another, . . . being that *equal Right* which every Man hath, *to his Natural Freedom*, without being subjected to the Will or Authority of any other Man."[85]

From Lockean theory, America's Founders derived the principle that "equality. . . ought to be the basis of every law," as James Madison put it in 1785 when he argued that this principle was violated when laws subject some to "peculiar burdens" or grant others "peculiar benefits."[86] During the Jacksonian period of the early 19th century, the emphasis that Jackson's Democratic Party placed on the equality principle—illustrated by Jacksonian Democrats' characteristic aversion to all forms of legally created "privilege"—was reflected in constitutional jurisprudence.[87] The Supreme Court under the leadership of Chief Justice Taney, a Jackson appointee, moved away from the Marshall Court's emphasis on vested rights and instead adopted a more flexible approach to police powers that emphasized instead equality under the law, or prohibition of class legislation.[88]

State constitutional law during the antebellum period also limited police powers by enforcing the prohibition on class legislation, typically through the due process or "law of the land" clauses of state constitutions,[89] or through specific constitutional provisions enforcing the equality principle. These included such provisions as "[N]o men or set of men are entitled to exclusive or separate emoluments or privileges from the community, but in consideration of public services"; "Government [is] instituted for the common benefits, protection, and security of the whole community, and not for the private interest or emolument of any one man, family, or class of men"; and "The general assembly shall not grant to any citizen or class of citizens privileges and immunities which upon the same terms, shall not equally belong to all citizens." One late 19th-century author explained that the inclusion of such provisions in new state constitutions adopted during the Jacksonian period reflected "a very general feeling of hostility to all local and special legislation" and a renewed commitment to general laws, "designed neither for one or more particular persons, nor to operate exclusively in any particular part or parts of the State."[90]

By the late 19th century, the prohibition of class legislation had become "a mainstay of constitutional jurisprudence," incorporated into state constitutions and enforced by the courts as a limitation on the police power.[91] Indeed, 19th-century jurists saw the police power, in its legitimate exercise, as limited to laws of general application that had a public purpose: "reasonable laws" were those that treated all equally or, if they did treat people differently, did so for justifiable reasons related to a legitimate public purpose; "unreasonable" laws were partial, treating people differently for unjustifiable reasons.[92] Thomas M. Cooley, in his influential treatise, *Constitutional*

Limitations, identified as a general principle of constitutional law the maxim that lawmakers "are to govern by promulgated, established laws, not to be varied in particular cases, but to have one rule for rich and poor, for the favorite at court and the countryman at plough." By this maxim, he added, "we may test the authority and binding force of legislative enactments."[93] Indeed, as chief justice of the Michigan Supreme Court, Cooley had applied this principle in declaring unconstitutional a special act of the Michigan legislature that in 1864 had authorized the town of Salem to pledge its credit in aid of the Detroit and Howell Railroad. In his opinion for the court, Judge Cooley wrote: "[T]he discrimination between different classes of occupations, and the favoring of one at the expense of the rest, whether that one be farming, or banking, or merchandising, or milling, or printing, or railroading is not legitimate legislation, and is a violation of that equality of right which is a maxim of state government. . . . [The business of the state is] to protect the industry of all, and to give all the benefit of equal laws," and not to subsidize any particular industry.[94]

The authors of some recent revisionist scholarship have interpreted *Lochner*-era jurisprudence mainly in terms of this prohibition on class legislation.[95] Chief among these revisionist scholars is political scientist Howard Gillman, who in his 1993 book *The Constitution Besieged: The Rise and Demise of Lochner Era Police Powers Jurisprudence* argues that *Lochner*-era jurisprudence "represented a serious, principled effort to maintain one of the central distinctions in nineteenth-century constitutional law—the distinction between valid economic regulation, on the one hand, and invalid 'class' legislation, on the other—during a period of unprecedented class conflict."[96] But Gillman's interpretation is flawed in at least two critical ways: first, it ignores the explicit rationale on which *Lochner* itself and other liberty-of-contract decisions were based; and second, it fails to consider many significant liberty-of-contract decisions that do not fit the class legislation model.

Gillman's first basic error is to overlook the rather obvious fact that *Lochner* itself and other liberty-of-contract decisions were based on substantive due process protection of liberty and property rights. Gillman interprets the two 1885 New York decisions, *In re Jacobs* and *People v. Marx*, as if the court were concerned solely with the unequal burdens that the laws in question imposed—and fails to mention that both decisions were based explicitly on substantive due process protection of economic liberty and property rights. Similarly, his discussion of the 1895 Illinois decision, *Ritchie v. People*, ignores the court's explicit protection of liberty of contract through a substantive use of the state constitution's due process clause and instead suggests that the "partial" character of the law in question—that the maximum-hours law applied only to women employed in factories—was the sole basis for its unconstitutionality.[97] And in discussing the *Lochner* decision, Gillman overlooks Justice Peckham's explicit grounding of the Court's decision in liberty of contract and instead focuses on the class legislation arguments presented in the brief submitted by Lochner's lawyers and on Justice Peckham's characterization of the maximum-hours law in question as "purely a labor law."[98]

The second basic flaw in Gillman's interpretation is that it overlooks many significant liberty-of-contract decisions because they do not fit the class legislation model. Among the key liberty-of-contract decisions that are not even mentioned in the Gillman book are some of the principal cases discussed in chapter 3 of this book: *Buchanan v. Warley* (1917), *Meyer v. Nebraska* (1923), and *Pierce v. Society of Sisters* (1925). These decisions illustrate important aspects of the Supreme Court's protection of liberty of contract but fail to fit the orthodox model, or caricature, of *Lochner*-era jurisprudence focused solely on economic liberty in the business and/or labor context. By confining his analysis to those cases that best fit the class legislation model—particularly to cases concerned with maximum-hours laws, minimum-wage laws, and other labor laws—Gillman helps perpetuate the overly narrow, and thus misleading, view of liberty-of-contract jurisprudence.[99]

To be sure, judicial protection of equal rights under law—especially as a prohibition on class legislation enforced through the due process, or "law of the land," clauses of state constitutions—was, in 19th-century constitutional law, closely related to judicial protection of liberty and property rights through the substantive application of those same clauses. A law deemed "arbitrary" because it conferred special benefits or imposed special burdens on one class of persons also deprived those whom it adversely affected of their liberty or property rights. Failure to be sufficiently general was not the sole grounds on which courts found laws to be "arbitrary" and thus unconstitutional, however. As

Cooley noted in his discussion of the phrase "the law of the land," even a general law could be voided as "arbitrary" if it restricted persons' "rights, privileges, or legal capacities in a manner before unknown to the law."[100] Thus, courts in the late 19th century often supplemented equal-rights analysis with due process analysis, or vice versa.

Perhaps a false dichotomy has been created by those modern revisionist scholars who debate *Lochner*-era jurisprudence as an either-or alternative between the prohibition on class legislation and substantive due process protection of liberty or property rights.[101] Nevertheless, Gillman's class legislation model applies best to 19th-century state court decisions; when applied to 20th-century U.S. Supreme Court decisions, it fails to take into account the Court's narrower application of the class legislation prohibition and tends to confuse cases decided on due process grounds with cases decided on equal protection grounds.[102] Hence, the prohibition of class legislation is best viewed as a limitation on the police power that was conceptually related to, but jurisprudentially distinct from, the courts' substantive use of due process clauses to protect what eventually came to be recognized as liberty of contract.

Finally, at least a few 19th-century courts recognized a broader, theoretical limitation on the police power that was implicit in the definition of its legitimate operation in terms of the *sic utere* maxim. If the purpose of the police power was, as Cooley described it, "to prevent a conflict of rights, and to insure to each the uninterrupted enjoyment of his own so far as is reasonably consistent with a like enjoyment of the rights by others," then it followed that a statute that did not deal with a true conflict in private rights but that simply abridged them, albeit for an asserted public purpose, might be found invalid as an illegitimate exercise of the police power. For example, as noted earlier, in the 1854 Vermont case of *Thorpe v. Rutland & Burlington Railroad Company*, the court upheld a statute requiring railroads to construct and maintain fences as cattle guards along their routes, finding the statute to be a valid application of the police power "in regard to those whose business is dangerous and destructive to other persons' property or business." Chief Justice Redfield contrasted the statute in question with a hypothetical statute requiring landowners to build all their fences of a given quality or height. Such a statute, he argued, would "no doubt be invalid, as an unwarrantable interference with matters of exclusively private concern."[103]

Antebellum America was not a laissez-faire society; government, especially at the state and local levels, passed many laws regulating various aspects of their citizens' lives—and particularly their economic activities—as several legal historians have observed.[104] Nevertheless, in the decades before the Civil War, courts rarely declared such regulations to be unconstitutional. Perhaps there were so few decisions like *Wynehamer* or like Justice Redfield's hypothetical case because, during this period, state legislatures generally exercised the police power within certain well-defined limits. The scope of the power was restricted to the traditional concerns of protecting public health, safety, and morals; in exercising it, the states imposed controls that were relatively modest and tailored to specific harmful activities that were truly matters of public concern.[105]

By the end of the 19th and the beginning of the 20th century, however, two critical developments would change American constitutional law as it pertains to limits on state police power. One was the rise of "social legislation" during the so-called Progressive Era, when state legislatures began regulating citizens' lives in unprecedented ways that went far beyond the traditional scope of the police power.[106] The other was the addition to the Constitution of an amendment, worded in very broad language, that authorized federal courts and Congress to impose significant limitations on the police power during the very time that the states were pushing its exercise beyond its traditional scope.

Federalizing Constitutional Limits: The Fourteenth Amendment

The three amendments added to the Constitution after the Civil War—the Thirteenth Amendment, abolishing slavery and involuntary servitude; the Fourteenth Amendment, limiting the powers of the states; and the Fifteenth Amendment, prohibiting denial of the right to vote on the basis on race—were the most important additions to the Constitution since the first 10 amendments, the Bill of Rights. And of these three postwar amendments, the most far-reaching in its importance was the Fourteenth, which in its first section defined national citizenship and then provided that

> [n]o State shall make or enforce any law which shall abridge the privileges or immunities of citizens of the United States; nor shall any State deprive any person of life, liberty, or prop-

> erty, without due process of law; nor deny to any person
> within its jurisdiction the equal protection of the laws.[107]

For the past half-century or more, since the publication of a seminal article by Charles Fairman questioning the Fourteenth Amendment's incorporation of the Bill of Rights against the states,[108] the interpretation of Section 1, including the question of its original meaning, has been a matter of continuing controversy among constitutional scholars.[109] Nevertheless, virtually all scholars who have researched the historical origins of the amendment have found that its privileges or immunities clause was intended to be the key substantive provision of Section 1.[110] Moreover, there is ample evidence that the framers of the amendment, at least, intended it to impose significant substantive limits on the police power of the states, including—but not limited to—all the specific rights protected by the federal Bill of Rights. These included economic liberty rights as well as property rights.

The Fourteenth Amendment was born out of the political conflict over Reconstruction policy between Democratic President Andrew Johnson and the Republican Congress. Congress had passed, over Johnson's veto, the Civil Rights Act of 1866 in response to the so-called Black Codes enacted by many Southern states, which deprived the newly freed slaves of many basic rights.[111] The 1866 act was intended to invalidate these state laws and thus to give black persons equality with white persons in regard to certain rights—including the right "to make and enforce contracts."[112] Although "there was widespread agreement in the first Reconstruction Congress regarding the substance of the act," there also was "considerable unease about its constitutionality."[113] President Johnson had vetoed the law on constitutional grounds, maintaining that Congress lacked the power to legislate with regard to "the internal police and economy of the respective States."[114] Accordingly, one of the clear purposes of the Fourteenth Amendment, as originally proposed by Representative John Bingham (R-Ohio),[115] was to "constitutionalize" the Civil Rights Act, by expressly giving Congress the power to enact laws that would secure citizens' "privileges and immunities" and guarantee "equal protection in the rights of life, liberty, and property."[116]

As ultimately adopted by Congress and ratified by the states, however, the amendment went beyond this original purpose. Two significant changes were made in the text of the proposed amendment during the debates in Congress in the spring of 1866.[117] First, the key substantive language of what became ultimately the first section of the amendment was transformed from a grant of power to Congress to a limitation on the power of the states. This transformation in the format of Section 1 is significant because it meant that the amendment did not depend on Congress for its enforcement but could also be enforced by the courts through their judicial review power. (The framers of the amendment were concerned that future Congresses, not controlled by Republicans, could change policy.)[118] The second significant change in the amendment was the addition of four other sections, with the fifth and final section empowering Congress to enforce the amendment's provisions "by appropriate legislation."

Although the final version of the amendment clearly went further than Bingham's original proposal—and its Section 1 went further than the 1866 act in the scope of individual rights that it protected against state abridgement[119]—the amendment's proponents, both in the debates in Congress and in state ratification debates, continually downplayed its effect on federalism, the balance of powers between the national government and the states.[120] Bingham, the principal author of the final language of Section 1, stated that the Fourteenth Amendment was designed to remedy a "want" in the Constitution: namely, the power in the people, by express authority of the Constitution, "to protect by national law the privileges and immunities of all the citizens of the Republic and the inborn rights of every person within its jurisdiction whenever the same shall be abridged or denied by the *unconstitutional* acts of any State."[121] Other proponents similarly maintained the amendment merely would correct the illegitimate actions of state governments.[122]

Nevertheless, the framers of the Fourteenth Amendment understood that its first section limited state police powers in significant ways. Senator Jacob Howard (R-Mich.), who managed the amendment for the joint committee in the Senate, maintained that "the great object" of Section 1 was "to restrain the powers of the States and to compel them at all times to respect" the Constitution's "great fundamental guarantees" of individual rights.[123] Like Bingham and the other proponents of the amendment, Howard identified those rights chiefly in terms of "the privileges or immunities of citizens of the United States." In his

May 23, 1866, speech presenting the proposed amendment to the Senate, Howard spoke chiefly of this clause, which he regarded as "very important." Like Bingham, Howard equated the rights that would be protected by this clause with the "privileges and immunities of citizens of the several states" protected in Article IV, Section 2, of the Constitution. He thus saw the proposed amendment's privileges or immunities clause as protecting the rights of citizens, while the second and third clauses of Section 1 protected all persons from deprivation of their rights to life, liberty, and property without due process of law or from denial of the equal protection of the laws. In the May 23 speech, Howard said little about the latter two clauses, other than that the equal protection clause "abolishes all class legislation in the States and does away with the injustice of subjecting one caste of persons to a code not applicable to another."[124]

The terms "privileges" and "immunities" were well known in 19th-century Anglo-American law. Blackstone had described the distinction this way: "immunities" were retained natural rights, or "that *residuum* of natural liberty, which is not required by the laws of society to be sacrificed to public convenience"; "privileges" were civil rights, or rights "which society hath engaged to provide, in lieu of the natural liberties so given up by individuals."[125]

Senator Howard accordingly identified the "privileges" and "immunities" protected by the amendment in very broad terms, as rights that "are not and cannot be fully defined in their entire extent and precise nature."[126] They included the rights protected by the privileges and immunities clause of Article IV as those rights had been identified by the courts—chiefly by Justice Bushrod Washington, who in his classic decision in *Corfield v. Coryell* had described them as rights "which are in their nature fundamental, which belong of right to citizens of all free Governments, and which have at all times been enjoyed by the citizens of the several States which compose this Union from the time of their becoming free, independent, and sovereign." While acknowledging that these rights would be "more tedious than difficult to enumerate," Justice Washington categorized them under the following "heads":

> [P]rotection by the Government, the enjoyment of life and liberty, with the right to acquire and possess property of every kind, and to pursue and obtain happiness and safety, subject nevertheless to such restraints as the Government

> may justly prescribe for the general good of the whole. The right of a citizen of one State to pass through or reside in any other State, for purposes of trade, agriculture, professional pursuits, or otherwise; to claim the benefit of the writ of *habeas corpus*; to institute and maintain actions of any kind in the courts of the State; to take, hold, and dispose of property, either real or personal, and an exemption from higher taxes or impositions than are paid by the other citizens of the State. . . .

These rights, together with "the elective franchise, as regulated and established by the laws or constitution of the State in which it is to be exercised," constitute "some of the particular privileges and immunities of citizens. . . deemed to be fundamental," noted Judge Washington.[127]

Senator Howard then added to Judge Washington's list of rights "the personal rights guaranteed and secured by the first eight amendments of the Constitution," which he then partially enumerated. Howard nevertheless excluded suffrage, noting pointedly that it was "not, in law, one of the privileges or immunities secured by the Constitution" but was rather "merely the creature of law," "the result of positive local law," and "not regarded as one of those fundamental rights lying at the basis of all society and without which a people cannot exist except as slaves, subject to a despotism." His understanding was consistent with the hierarchical view of rights that prevailed in 19th-century constitutionalism, which distinguished natural rights from rights protected under positive law and which further divided the latter into two categories, civil rights and political rights. Voting, like the right to hold office or serve on juries, was a privilege held only by certain classes of citizens; others—women, for example—were excluded. Summing up his understanding of the rights to be protected by Section 1, Senator Howard concluded that the proposed amendment sought to protect against infringement by the states "a mass of privileges, immunities, and rights, some of them secured by the second section of the fourth article of the Constitution, . . . some by the first eight amendments of the Constitution. . . ."[128]

Thus, like Bingham and other proponents of the amendment, Senator Howard identified the rights enumerated in the first eight of the Bill of Rights amendments as among the rights the Fourteenth

Amendment was meant to protect—thus supporting the view taken by modern scholars who interpret the Fourteenth Amendment as totally "incorporating" the federal Bill of Rights protections, making them applicable against the states.[129] And like the other proponents of the amendment, Senator Howard maintained it was needed because the Constitution, at least as it had been interpreted by the Supreme Court in the antebellum period, did not require the states to respect these rights. The "mass of privileges, immunities, and rights" protected by the amendment "do not operate in the slightest degree as a restraint or prohibition upon State legislation," Howard maintained. Both he and Bingham pointed to the U.S. Supreme Court's decision in *Barron v. Baltimore* (1833), which held that the Fifth Amendment's takings clause did not apply to the states. When offering his original proposal for the amendment, Bingham stated that it was needed "to enforce the bill of rights" and that *Barron* "makes plain the necessity of adopting this amendment."[130]

It is reasonably clear from the history of the Fourteenth Amendment that the civil rights it was intended to protect included economic liberty and property rights. Indeed, because some of the most important civil rights denied to black persons by the 1865 Southern codes were the rights to make contracts and own property, the Fourteenth Amendment could be justly characterized, as it has been by some modern scholars, as "economic by design."[131]

Although the earliest federal court decisions applied the Fourteenth Amendment consistent with this broad design,[132] the Supreme Court, in its infamous decision in the *Slaughterhouse Cases*, thwarted temporarily Congress's intent to impose substantive limitations on the police power of the states. The Court, in a split decision, upheld against a Fourteenth Amendment challenge a 1869 Louisiana law chartering the Crescent City Livestock Landing and Slaughterhouse Company, granting the company a 25-year monopoly on the slaughtering of cattle in the New Orleans area.[133] Justice Miller, speaking for the five-justice majority of the Court, ignored evidence of the Fourteenth Amendment's framers' intent that had been briefed to the Court[134] and instead relied on his own view of the "one pervading purpose" of the three post–Civil War amendments, which he maintained was to guarantee "the freedom of the slave race . . . and the protection of the newly-made freeman and citizen from the oppressions of those who had formerly exercised unlimited dominion over him."[135] Focusing narrowly on the language in Section 1's privileges or immunities clause—and ignoring its context[136]—Justice Miller held that the clause protected only those few rights that pertained to national citizenship. He then listed several of those privileges or immunities of national citizenship: the rights "to come to the seat of [national] government," or to have "free access to its seaports, . . . to the sub-treasuries, land offices, and courts of justice"; to "demand the care and protection of the Federal Government over [one's] life, liberty, and property when on the high seas and when in the jurisdiction of a foreign government"; to "use the navigable waters of the United States"; and "all rights secured to our citizens by treaties with foreign nations."[137] None of these rights, obviously, was jeopardized by the Louisiana monopoly.

In opposition to this narrow view of the privileges or immunities clause, however, Justices Field, Bradley, and Swayne (with whom Chief Justice Chase concurred) delivered vigorous dissents. Justice Field maintained that "the privileges and immunities designated are those *which of right belong to the citizens of all free governments*," among which he said was "[c]learly" included "the right to pursue a lawful employment in a lawful manner, without other restraint than such as equally affects all persons."[138] Field particularly exposed the logical inconsistency of the majority's opinion, noting that if the only rights protected by the Fourteenth Amendment were those few rights pertaining to national citizenship that Justice Miller identified, "it was a vain and idle enactment, which accomplished nothing, and most unnecessarily excited Congress and the people on its passage."[139] Justice Bradley similarly described the rights protected by the amendment as the "fundamental rights" of life, liberty, property, and the pursuit of happiness. Like Field, Bradley saw "the right of any citizen to follow whatever lawful employment he chooses" to be among those fundamental rights. "This right to choose one's calling is an essential part of that liberty which it is the object of government to protect; and a calling, once chosen, is a man's right and property." Like Field too, Bradley saw government grants of monopoly, such as that involved in the Louisiana charter to the Crescent City Company, as a palpable abridgement of this fundamental right, and of personal liberty generally.[140]

Significantly, many legal experts at the time agreed with the dissenters, considering the majority's interpretation of the amendment to be erroneous.[141] Fortunate for the future of the Fourteenth Amendment as an important limitation on the powers of the states, Justice Miller's opinion for the majority focused almost entirely on the privileges or immunities clause, allowing the Court in future periods to limit the reach of the *Slaughterhouse* decision and to give more expansive interpretations to the other clauses—the due process clause and the equal protection clause—of Section 1.[142]

The justices in the *Slaughterhouse* majority interpreted the Fourteenth Amendment so narrowly because they were concerned about the amendment's effect on federalism, as Justice Miller's opinion explicitly admitted. Too broad an interpretation of the amendment "would constitute this court a perpetual censor upon all legislation of the States, on the civil rights of their own citizens," he warned. To so "fetter and degrade the State governments" by subjecting them to the control of Congress or the federal courts would be to "radically" change "the whole theory of the relations of the State and Federal governments to each other and of both of these governments to the people." The dissenters did not share this fear, understanding that the very purpose of the amendment was to impose significant new limitations on the powers of the states, and to make those limitations enforceable through the federal courts' powers of judicial review.[143]

The *Slaughterhouse* majority's concern for the traditional antebellum balance of state and federal powers prompted the Court to continue interpreting the Fourteenth Amendment narrowly—and thus to refrain from limiting the autonomy of state legislatures in exercising police powers—up until the early 1890s.[144] For example, shortly after its decision in the *Slaughterhouse Cases*, the Court in *Bradwell v. Illinois* refused to interfere with a state's determination that women could not practice law.[145] A few years later, in *Munn v. Illinois*, the Court upheld one of the so-called Granger laws, enacted by midwestern state legislatures under pressure from farmers—in this case, an Illinois law setting a maximum on the rates charged by grain elevators in Chicago—on the theory that the "virtual monopoly" held by the facilities made them subject to the police power, as businesses "affected with a public interest."[146] Similarly, the Court rejected a brewer's challenge to a liquor prohibition law in *Mugler v. Kansas* (1888),[147] a grocer's challenge to a law prohibiting manufacture or sale of butter substitutes in *Powell v. Pennsylvania* (1888),[148] and a grain elevator's challenge to a New York maximum-rate law in *Budd v. New York* (1892).[149] In a series of cases, the Court also held, nearly unanimously, that the Fourteenth Amendment did not apply the federal Bill of Rights to the states.[150]

By the late 1890s, however, changes in the Court's membership helped pave the way for a more expansive interpretation of the amendment. As one scholar has observed, by 1892, six of the Court's justices had concluded that the privileges or immunities clause of the Fourteenth Amendment applied the Bill of Rights to the states; "[u]nfortunately, they did not sit and reach their conclusions at the same time."[151] Although the Court's evisceration of the privileges or immunities clause remained the unhappy legacy of its decision in the *Slaughterhouse Cases*, the new majority on the Court in the late 1890s was able to breathe life into the other clauses of Section 1. While failing to apply the equal protection clause as a broad prohibition against all class legislation, the justices took the clause beyond its *Slaughterhouse* limits[152] and applied it to invalidate even facially neutral laws that, when enforced, adversely affected certain classes of persons on account of race.[153] More importantly, with the 1895 appointment to the Court of Justice Rufus W. Peckham[154]—the justice who was to write the opinions for the Court in both *Allgeyer* and *Lochner*—the Court was ready to follow state court decisions of the 1880s and 1890s, using due process substantively to protect liberty of contract.

The Progressive movement historian Charles Warren maintained in 1926 that the Court was prompted to expand the "new liberty" under the Fourteenth Amendment's due process clause because of the efforts of "skilful counsel" who, thwarted by the Court's narrow interpretation of the privileges or immunities clause, instead attempted to use the due process clause's protection of "liberty" as "an especially convenient vehicle into which to pack all kinds of rights." Warren's thesis ignores the history of state courts' substantive use of due process to protect economic liberty and property rights throughout the 19th century, discussed in the first section of this chapter. It also ignores the views of congressional Republicans—the framers of the Fourteenth Amendment—who saw due process as a substantive restraint on legislation that deprived persons of essential liberty and property rights, as discussed above. Skilled legal counsel indeed may deserve part of the credit Warren gave them for the rise of liberty of contract by the late 1890s, but their use of the Fourteenth Amendment's due process clause as a "convenient vehicle" for protecting liberty rights really was made possible by the addition to the Court of justices like Peckham, who were willing to enforce the limits on state powers that the amendment's framers had intended.[155]

2. Philosophical Foundations of Liberty of Contract

In his famous *Lochner* dissent, Justice Holmes was both right and wrong. He was right in criticizing the majority of justices of the Court for being inconsistent in their protection of liberty of contract; as chapter 4 will discuss, *Lochner* was indeed logically inconsistent with a number of the Court's decisions upholding various laws that, in Holmes's words, "equally interfere" with liberty.[1] Nevertheless, Holmes was wrong to suggest that the majority used the Fourteenth Amendment to "enact Mr. Herbert Spencer's Social Statics." Contrary to Holmes's assertion, the majority in *Lochner*—and in the other key liberty-of-contract decisions both before and after *Lochner*—did not base its protection of liberty of contract on "an economic theory which a large part of the country does not entertain," still less on Herbert Spencer's Law of Equal Freedom, the "shibboleth," as Holmes put it, favoring "[t]he liberty of the citizen to do as he likes so long as he does not interfere with the liberty of others to do the same."[2]

When Holmes cited Herbert Spencer's *Social Statics*, he was referring to the best-known work written by the foremost English classical liberal, or laissez-faire, theorist of his time. As this reference to the work suggests, Spencer's writings were familiar to American intellectuals—but that does not mean they were widely influential. Indeed, classical liberal ideas were as controversial at the turn of the last century as they are today, not only in popular politics but also in legal culture. True laissez-faire constitutionalism challenged established principles of Anglo-American common law and 19th-century American constitutional law nearly as much as did the new sociological jurisprudence and legal realism advocated by so-called Progressive reformers in the early 20th century. True laissez-faire constitutionalists advocated a much narrower scope for the exercise of the police power—and hence a broader scope for liberty, including liberty of contract—than the courts allowed under the traditional police-power categories of public health, safety, and morals. Progressive reformers, on the other hand, advocated a much broader exercise of the police power, well beyond those traditional categories.

Rather than consistently protecting liberty through a true "laissez-faire constitutionalism," judicial protection of liberty of contract in the early 20th century adhered to traditional principles of 19th-century constitutional law—including a traditional understanding of the scope of state police power. In protecting liberty of contract as a right under the due process clauses of the Fifth and Fourteenth Amendments, the Court was merely applying a general presumption in favor of liberty that could be overridden by various exercises of the police power that the justices considered legitimate. This conservative constitutionalism can easily be confused with laissez-faire constitutionalism by modern scholars because both conservatives and laissez-faire theorists were opposed to the expansion of the police power advocated by "Progressive" reformers (and assumed to be reasonable by most modern scholars). The confusion arises from a failure to notice simply that conservative constitutionalists on the Court in that era were more willing to accept limits on liberty of contract, under the traditional police-power categories, than were true laissez-faire constitutionalists.

"A Society Based on Contract"

Legal historians have frequently characterized the 19th century as "the golden age of the law of contract" in American law. Lawrence Friedman has observed, for example, that contract law, as "the body of law that pertained to the growing market economy," had developed in Anglo-American law as the medieval period gave way to the early modern period. It "grew up in the era when the last vestiges of feudalism vanished, and a capitalist order flourished," and by the close of the 18th century, "the age of Adam Smith," it had "bec[o]me indispensable." The domain of contract law steadily expanded in the 19th century, Friedman adds, when it "greedily swallowed up other parts of the law."[3]

Yet contract law, in its modern form, was a relatively recent development. In the words of historian John Orth, it "began to take shape only in the eighteenth century, and the modern law of contract developed only in the nineteenth century." English common law had been based on property and lacked a robust notion of contract; contracts were regarded as "the handmaidens of property, a useful means of transferring title from one person to another." William Blackstone's *Commentaries on the Laws of England*, first published in the late 1760s, said little about contract, which it conceptualized as part of the "rights of persons" based on special relationships. Orth explains that it was at about the time that Blackstone's *Commentaries* were first published, in the middle of the 18th century, that "contract began to emerge from the shadow of property"; with the emergence of contract there arose in Anglo-American common law "a new way of thinking about legal relations, emphasizing intention rather than possession, voluntarism rather than vestedness."[4]

The emergence of contract law in both England and America in the latter half of the 18th century coincided with a profound shift in the role of law generally that was described famously by the great 19th-century English legal historian Sir Henry Maine: "The movement of progressive societies has hitherto been a movement *from Status to Contract*."[5] The transition from a status-based society to a contract-based society has a dual significance. First, with regard to the evolution of the rule of law, the transition meant a movement away from a regime of special rules that single out particular persons or groups toward general, abstract rules equally applicable to all. Recognizing this shift, Friedrich Hayek has suggested that Maine's distinction between contract and status may be "a little misleading." Status means that each individual occupies an assigned place in society; in law, it is reflected in legal rules which are "not fully general but single out particular persons or groups and confer upon them special rights and duties." The true contrast to such a legal regime, Hayek argues, is a system of "general and equal laws, of the rules which are the same for all, or, we might say, of the rule of *leges* in the original meaning of the Latin word for laws—*leges*, that is, as opposed to the *privi-leges*."[6]

The second significant consequence of the transition from status to contract concerned the evolving concept of individual rights. The transition meant an expanded understanding of persons' right to liberty. In status-based society, one's status determined what "liberties" or "privileges" one held, under the law. In contrast, under the regime of contract, each person who is sui juris, that is, legally competent to make a contract, becomes what the literal translation of the Latin phrase means, "of one's own right," or a law unto oneself. Thus, in the modern era, contract becomes, as Hayek aptly characterizes it, "the most important of the instruments that the law supplies to the individual to shape his own position." Legal historian J. Willard Hurst similarly emphasized individualism when he described the 19th-century American legal order as one that sought to "protect and promote the release of individual creative energy to the greatest extent compatible with the broad sharing of opportunity for such expression."[7]

Not only scholars but late 19th-century American lawyers and judges frequently described contemporary American society as one based on contract, in contrast to medieval society, based on status. They also appreciated the significance of this shift for what it meant for individual liberty. For example, the attorneys challenging a New York rate-fixing law in 1892 argued that the American constitutional tradition rejected "medieval darkness, which permitted every detail of one's life to be regulated," and instead embraced the "modern" doctrine of "freedom of action."[8] And when the New York Court of Appeals in its 1885 *Jacobs* decision struck down the law prohibiting cigar manufacturing, it expressed the fear that upholding the law would reverse the progress society had made from the paternalism of the past:

> Such legislation may invade one class of rights today and another tomorrow, and if it can be sanctioned under the Constitution, while far removed in time we will not be far away in practical statesmanship from those ages when government prefects supervised the building of houses, the rearing of cattle, the sowing of seed and the reaping of grain, and governmental ordinances regulated the movements and labor of artisans, the rate of wages, the price of food, the diet and clothing of the people, and a large range of other affairs long since in all civilized lands regarded as outside of government functions.[9]

Classical liberal, or "laissez-faire," theorists in the late 19th century went even further, using the concept of contract—and the policy of individualism that it implied—as virtually synonymous with progress. To them, what made America "modern" was its use of contract, in this broad sense. William Graham Sumner, perhaps the best known of the

American theorists of laissez faire,[10] in his classic work, *What Social Classes Owe to Each Other*, identified the transition this way:

> In the Middle Ages men were united by custom and pre-
> scription into associations, ranks, guilds, and communities
> of various kinds. These ties endured as long as life lasted.
> Consequently society was dependent, throughout all its de-
> tails, on status, and the tie, or bond, was sentimental. In our
> modern state, and in the United States more than anywhere
> else, the social structure is based on contract, and status is of
> the least importance.[11]

Sumner further described contract relationships as based, not on "sentiment," but rather on "rational—even rationalistic" considerations; such modern relationships are "not permanent" but endure "only so long as the reason for [them] endures." What resulted was individualism:

> A society based on contract is a society of free and independ-
> ent men, who form ties without favor or obligation, and
> co-operate without cringing or intrigue. A society based on
> contract, therefore, gives the utmost room and chance for in-
> dividual development, and for all the self-reliance and dig-
> nity of a free man.[12]

Sumner's notion of "a society based on contract" was somewhat reminiscent of American society as it had been described in the early 1830s by Alexis de Tocqueville, the young French aristocrat who in his classic book, *Democracy in America*, had used the recently coined term "individualism" to identify the unique phenomenon he discerned during his travels in America. Individualism, wrote Tocqueville, "disposes each citizen to isolate himself from the mass of his fellows and withdraw into the circle of family and friends"; individualists "owe no man anything and hardly expect anything from anybody"; they "imagine that their whole destiny is in their own hands." By way of contrast, Tocqueville reverently described the importance of family connections in aristocratic societies. He then decried the individualism prevalent in democratic societies as "based on misguided judgment" in which "[e]ach man is forever thrown back on himself alone" and thus "shut up in the solitude of his own heart."[13]

Sumner was not appalled by individualism. Instead, he embraced it as the chief organizing principle of society. The son of a poor English immigrant, he had high regard for such middle-class virtues as productivity and prudence; he also appreciated the opportunities for individuals to rise or fall according to their own merit in the post–Industrial Revolution market society about which he wrote.[14]

A free society, as Sumner understood it, was one in which each individual is "sovereign," both free and equal, owing no political or legal duties toward others except "respect, courtesy, and good will."[15] In the final chapter of the book, entitled "Wherefore We Should Love One Another"—a title that belies the stereotype of laissez-faire writers as "rugged individualists" or "Social Darwinists"—Sumner identified a *moral* duty of benevolence. Because of their "common participation in human frailty and folly," persons do owe "aid and sympathy" to one other, he explained. Nevertheless, emphasizing the political or *legal* duty of respect for the rights of others, he concluded the book by stating that "we all owe to each other good-will, mutual respect, and mutual guarantees of liberty and security. Beyond this nothing can be affirmed as a duty of one group to another in a free state."[16]

The duty of respect—and especially respect for others' equal rights—was particularly important to Sumner:

> Rights should be equal, because they pertain to chances, and all ought to have equal chances so far as chances are provided or limited by the action of society. . . . We each owe it to the other to guarantee mutually the chance to earn, to possess, to learn, to marry, etc., etc., against any interference which would prevent the exercise of those rights by a person who wishes to prosecute and enjoy them in peace for the pursuit of happiness. If we generalize this, it means that All-of-us ought to guarantee rights to each of us.

This was Sumner's full answer to the question he raised in the book's introduction: "What ought Some-of-us do for Others-of-us? or, What do social classes owe to each other?" His short answer there was that "the State" owes nothing to anybody "except peace, order, and the guarantee of rights." In arguing that rights pertain to "chances," he emphasized that "[r]ights do not pertain to *results*"; they pertain "to the *pursuit* of happiness, not to the possession of happiness," and they will produce "unequal results," and justly so, because results should be "proportioned to the merits of individuals."[17]

"Civil liberty" in a free society meant that *"each man is guaranteed the use of all his own powers exclusively for his own welfare."* Moreover, "[a]ll institutions are to be tested by the degree to which they guarantee liberty."[18] Equally important to Sumner was self-responsibility, for he also stressed that everyone has "one big duty" in society, "to take care of his or her own self," as well as his family, if he has dependents.[19] From this vision of a free society, Sumner arrived at "the old doctrine—*Laissez-faire*," which he translated into "blunt English" as "Mind your own business."[20]

The philosophy called "laissez faire"[21] followed from a body of thought known as liberalism and today called "classical liberalism," to distinguish it from the term "liberalism" as used in modern American political thought.[22] Classical liberalism, or libertarianism, has been described by one of its leading 20th-century exponents, Ludwig von Mises, as "the great political and intellectual movement that substituted free enterprise and the market economy for the precapitalistic methods of production; constitutional representative government for the absolutism of kings or oligarchies; and freedom of all individuals from slavery, serfdom, and other forms of bondage."[23] A modern libertarian scholar, David Boaz, has identified libertarianism as a centuries-old political tradition that emphasizes individual liberty and limited government and holds, among its key concepts, individualism and the supremacy of individual rights. "Individualism," as understood by libertarians, means viewing the individual as the basic unit of social analysis, regarding each person as an end in himself.[24]

Liberty, under this tradition, means freedom from physical compulsion. As libertarians see it, only through the initiation of force—or fraud, which is an indirect form of force—can individuals be deprived of their liberty. Thus, libertarians see as the basic social rule the "no-harm principle": that no one ought to use force or fraud to harm another, to the detriment of another's life, liberty, or property.[25]

In Anglo-American political thought, libertarianism originated with the 17th-century English radical Whig political writers, the most famous of whom was John Locke.[26] Eighteenth-century radical Whig writers on both sides of the Atlantic expanded on Lockean ideas.[27] For example, the authors of *Cato's Letters*—those political essays originally published in the 1720s that continued to influence

America's Founders during the Revolutionary period—restricted the legitimate power of government to the protection of "natural liberty." This libertarian Whig tradition had a continuing influence on early American political thought well into the 19th century—for example, on radical Jeffersonian Republicans and on the so-called Locofoco wing of the Jacksonian Democratic Party.[28]

The 19th-century classical liberal tradition took to their logical conclusions the English radical Whig ideas about maximizing individual liberty and minimizing the role of government. Consider the broad notion of liberty adopted by the authors of *Cato's Letters*, discussed in chapter 1: "the Power which every Man has over his own Actions, and his Right to enjoy the Fruits of his Labour, Art, and Industry, as far as by it he hurts not the Society, or any Members of it, by taking from any Member, or by hindering him from enjoying what he himself enjoys." That concept of liberty was developed fully and applied consistently by 19th-century classical liberals as the principle that everyone ought to be free to do as he pleases, so long as he does not harm others or interfere with others' equal freedom. The most famous expression of this principle was Herbert Spencer's "Law of Equal Freedom": "*Every man has freedom to do all that he wills, provided he infringes not the equal freedom of any other man.*"[29] Similarly, *Cato's* notion that the role of the magistrate was confined to the preservation of "this natural Right" became, to 19th-century classical liberals, an absolute limitation on the legitimate scope of government power. John Stuart Mill espoused this principle in his popular tract *On Liberty*, first published in 1859, which maintained that government should be limited to the role of protecting individuals from harming one another:

> The sole end for which mankind are warranted, individually or collectively, in interfering with the liberty of action of any of their number, is self-protection. . . . [T]he only purpose for which power can be rightfully exercised over any member of a civilized community, against his will, is to prevent harm to others. His own good, either physical or moral, is not a sufficient warrant. . . .

"Over himself, over his own body and mind, the individual is sovereign," Mill concluded.[30]

Like modern libertarians, 19th-century classical liberals differed in the philosophical foundations of their laissez-faire ideology: some grounded it in pragmatic, utilitarian justifications while others grounded it in a moral philosophy that saw individualism as an end in itself.[31] Nevertheless, however they grounded their ideology, they reached the same fundamental conclusion regarding the role of government. "As the liberal sees it," noted Ludwig von Mises, "the task of the state consists solely and exclusively in guaranteeing the protection of life, health, liberty, and private property against violent attacks."[32] Libertarians believe that the legitimate functions of government are confined, at most, to those powers necessary to protect individuals from harming one another in their persons or their property. [33] Thus, "the only actions that should be forbidden by law are those that involve the initiation of force against those who have not themselves used force—actions like murder, rape, robbery, kidnapping, and fraud."[34] When government goes beyond this minimal role of protecting persons or property against harm by others and instead seeks to protect persons from harming themselves—when government invades the realm of individual sovereignty described by John Stuart Mill—it loses its legitimacy and becomes an invader rather than a protector of rights. Hence, laissez-faire theorists, whether 19th-century classical liberals or modern libertarians, have opposed all forms of "legal paternalism" as illegitimate uses of the coercive power of the law.[35]

Like today's libertarians, the classical liberals of the early 20th century also were radicals, not conservatives. To fully implement their vision of a free society, advocates of laissez faire called for major changes in the law, including many traditional principles of the Anglo-American common-law system.[36] Although many modern scholars—particularly nonlibertarians—mistakenly identify Anglo-American common law, as it had evolved by the 19th century, with classical liberalism,[37] the two traditions are distinct, based on fundamentally different premises and with fundamentally different applications to the leading legal and public policy questions of the early 20th century.[38]

Sumner's book, *What Social Classes Owe to Each Other*, illustrates how laissez-faire theorists' opposition to all forms of legal paternalism prompted them to criticize not only the new uses for the police power proposed by Progressive-Era reformers but also many of the traditional uses of the police power championed by conservatives of the time. Sumner devoted much of the book to his thesis that all "schemes" for government intervention advocated by "social reformers," presumably to aid certain persons or classes, really violate the rights of the "Forgotten Man," the prudent, responsible, taxpaying citizen.

Sumner stated his thesis in the first chapter of the book and elaborated on it in the 9th and 10th chapters, which focused on "a certain man who is never thought of," the "Forgotten Man." All the "schemes and projects" for "the organized intervention of society through the State" may be reduced to a simple formula, Sumner argued: "A and B decide what C shall do for D." A and B are the "social reformers," who are unmindful of the single great duty that all individuals owe one another in society—Sumner's version of the Golden Rule—"Mind your own business." Instead, they mind other people's business by advocating use of the coercive power of government to come to the aid of D, the "poor man," who is Sumner's model for all persons who are "negligent, shiftless, inefficient, silly, and imprudent." The one whose interest is overlooked in such schemes is C, the "industrious and prudent," whom Sumner calls the Forgotten Man.[39] As described by Sumner, the Forgotten Man is "worthy, industrious, independent, and self-supporting"; "he minds his own business and makes no complaint," and yet he is the one "threatened by every extension of the paternal theory of government" because "[i]t is he who must work and pay." "The real victim" of legal paternalism "is the Forgotten Man": "the man who has watched his own investments, made his own machinery safe, attended to his own plumbing, and educated his own children, and who, just when he wants to enjoy the fruits of his care, is told that it is his duty to go and take care of some of his negligent neighbors, or, if he does not go, to pay an inspector to go."[40]

Sumner particularly condemned two types of paternalistic "schemes" that were popular in his time. The first were liquor prohibition laws, which were advocated by a coalition of Progressive social reformers and conservative Victorian-era moralists.[41] The second was the protective tariff, which was advocated by business interests and was a key plank in the political platform of the Republican Party and its predecessor, the Whig Party, throughout the 19th century.[42]

Sumner used liquor prohibition as the chief example in his argument that "[t]he fallacy of all prohibitory, sumptuary, and moral legislation is the same":

> A and B determine to be teetotalers, which is often a wise determination, and sometimes a necessary one. . . . But A and B put their heads together to get a law passed which shall force C to be a teetotaler for the sake of D [the "poor man"— in this case, the alcoholic], who is in danger of drinking too much. . . . Who is C? He is the man who wants alcoholic liquors for any honest purpose whatsoever, who would use his liberty without abusing it, who would occasion no public question, and trouble nobody at all. He is the Forgotten Man again. . . .

Sumner also cited liquor prohibition laws as the chief example illustrating his argument about anti-vice legislation generally, that "[a]lmost all legislative effort to prevent vice is really protective of vice, because all such legislation saves the vicious man from the penalty of his vice."[43]

So-called protective tariffs were high taxes imposed by Congress on imported manufactured goods—a trade regulation supposed to foster domestic economic development by shielding U.S. manufacturers from foreign competition. Sumner condemned such tariffs as the worst form of "jobbery," which he defined as "any scheme which aims to gain, not by the legitimate fruits of industry and enterprise, but by extorting from somebody a part of his product under guise of some pretended industrial undertaking." He called jobbery "the greatest social evil" of his time, and he considered it "the vice of plutocracy," which was corrupting the democratic and republican form of government in the United States.[44] In the case of the protective tariff, the Forgotten Man was the consumer who must pay more for the goods he imported; the "poor man" who was the supposed beneficiary of this form of "corporate welfare" (as it would be called today) was the business that benefited from the indirect government subsidy that the tariff on his competitors' goods provided.

Both liquor prohibition laws and the protective tariff, it should be noted, comfortably fit within the traditional scope of the exercise of government regulatory powers. Courts generally upheld liquor prohibition laws as valid exercises of the police power to protect public health or morals, as the U.S. Supreme Court's decision in

Mugler v. Kansas (1887) illustrates.[45] The authority of Congress to impose protective tariffs, under either its taxing power or its regulatory power over foreign commerce, was never successfully challenged in court, although antebellum Southerners—most famously, the "nullifiers" of South Carolina—strenuously objected to protective tariffs as an abuse of congressional power.[46]

Sumner also criticized government regulations of the labor market, regardless of whether such laws were traditional exercises of the police power to protect health or morals or were the new forms of "protective" legislation advocated by Progressive reformers. Among the laws addressed by Sumner were those providing for government inspection of workplaces, "[t]he safety of workmen from machinery, the ventilation and sanitary arrangements required by factories, the special precautions of certain processes," as well as Sunday-closing laws, laws limiting the hours of labor of women and children, and laws setting "limits of age for employed children."[47] Maintaining that "free men in a free state" ought to "protect themselves," Sumner opposed paternal legislation even for the protection of women and children, arguing that free laborers "ought to protect their own women and children," either individually or through collective bargaining, rather than rely on government to do so.[48]

Sumner advocated total freedom of contract in labor: employers and employees should freely bargain over wages, hours, and working conditions, making contracts "on the best terms which they can agree upon." He saw labor contracts, or contracts between "employer and employed," as essentially no different from other forms of contracts—those between "buyers and sellers, renters and hirers, borrowers and lenders"—and preferred that government not interfere in any contracts, leaving their terms to the parties' negotiations and the natural laws of supply and demand.[49] He recognized workers' freedom to strike as a legitimate last resort in the bargaining process,[50] and he regarded trade unions as "right and useful, and perhaps, necessary"[51]—and so took a far more benign view of labor unions than did the courts of his time, which tended to regard unions as unlawful combinations in restraint of trade, under Anglo-American common-law precedents.[52]

Diametrically opposed to the ideas of laissez-faire theorists like Sumner were the public policy ideas championed by activists in the so-called Progressive movement, the reform movement that arose in the late 19th century and became increasingly influential in the early decades of the 20th century.[53] The movement was a diverse coalition of persons who sought to increase government regulation of economic and social life. A pithy definition of a Progressive reformer was offered by the free-thinking early 20th-century journalist H. L. Mencken: "one who is in favor of more taxes instead of less, more bureaus and jobholders, more paternalism and meddling, more regulation of private affairs and less liberty."[54] Although considered a new movement advocating reforms in the law, Progressivism was itself based on the paternalistic and collectivist threads that ran deeply through the Anglo-American common-law tradition.

Like the Fabian socialists, their counterparts in Britain, who harkened back to the "Tory paternalism" of the 18th century,[55] American Progressives championed various "protective" labor laws (particularly regarding women, children, and other supposedly vulnerable classes of workers),[56] liquor prohibition and other forms of paternal morals legislation, and in general a category of laws called "social legislation" by modern scholars. As noted in the introduction, "social legislation" is a modern term of art—not used by the Supreme Court before 1940—that originated in 19th-century Germany and referred to measures "intended for the relief and elevation of the less favored classes of the community." Not only were these laws unprecedented, in that they did not fall within the traditional scope of the police power to protect public health, safety, and morality, but these laws also would be considered unconstitutional under 19th-century prohibitions of "partial" or "class" legislation, for by promoting the special interests of certain economic classes, they perfectly fit the traditional definition of such invalid class laws.[57]

Not surprisingly, both traditionalist conservatives and laissez-faire reformers viewed the "reform" agenda of the Progressives as a reactionary return to a form of government paternalism, turning back the clock from a society based on contract to one again based on status. Christopher Tiedeman, the laissez-faire constitutionalist whose views are discussed in the next section, warned in his book *The Unwritten Constitution* (1890), that

> the old superstition that government has the power to banish evil from the earth, if it could only be induced to declare the supposed causes illegal, has been revived. . . . The State is

> called on to protect the weak against the shrewdness of the
> stronger, to determine what wages a workman shall receive
> for his labor, and how many hours he shall labor. Many trades
> and occupations are being prohibited, because some are dam-
> aged incidentally by their prosecution, and many ordinary
> pursuits are made government monopolies. The demands of
> the Socialists and Communists vary in degree and in detail,
> but the most extreme of them insist upon the assumption by
> government of the paternal character altogether, abolishing all
> private property in land, and making the State the sole posses-
> sor of the working capital of the nation.

Tiedeman's warning about the advent of "the absolutism of a democratic majority" was echoed by John F. Dillon, president of the
then-conservative American Bar Association, in his address at the
ABA's 1892 convention. "[W]hat is now to be feared and guarded
against is the despotism of the many—of the majority," Dillon
observed, calling on the legal profession "to defend, protect and
preserve our legal institutions unimpaired," in the face of "popular demands" threatening private property, through "unjust or discriminatory legislation in the exercise of the power of taxation, or
of eminent domain, or of that elastic power known as the police
power."[58]

Because the idea of pervasive government regulation of
economic and social life seems to hark back to medieval, prein-
dustrial public policy, many modern libertarians regard the term
"Progressive" as a misnomer. A truly "progressive" policy, from
the libertarian perspective, would fully implement the 19th-cen-
tury classical liberal vision of free-market capitalism with minimal government intrusions.[59] That policy, as William Graham
Sumner's work suggests, was nearly as far removed from the
traditional understanding of the police power to regulate public health, safety, order, and morality as was the newer, virtually
unlimited scope of the police power advocated by Progressive
reformers. Thus, it could be argued that in early 20th-century
American debates over law and public policy, both laissez faire
and Progressivism were competing "counter-currents" of opinion (to borrow a term used by the great British constitutional-law
writer, Albert Venn Dicey), both challenging the status quo, the
traditional understanding of the police power.[60]

Judicial Review and Two Paradigms of Liberty

Perhaps the greatest misunderstanding or myth concerning judicial protection of liberty of contract in the early 20th century was that it resulted from an illegitimate "activist" jurisprudence in which judges, rather than following objective standards of constitutional law, were following their own subjective views. As discussed in the introduction, much recent revisionist scholarship of the *Lochner*-era —by both scholars sympathetic to and scholars hostile to liberty of contract—has challenged this myth. Even some Progressive-Era scholars, who sought to rewrite constitutional history to advance their political agenda, did not really believe the orthodox criticism that *Lochner*-era judges were "activists."[61]

In modern debates over constitutional interpretation, the "judicial activist" label has become virtually "an all-purpose term of opprobrium," used by both the left and the right as an epithet to criticize court decisions with which they disagree.[62] Notwithstanding the variety of definitions of "activism" that scholars have advanced—most of them regarding activism as bad, or even pernicious, but with a few seeing it in a more positive light [63]—it is possible to define the term, at least when used pejoratively to describe illegitimate judicial behavior, in a conceptually meaningful way. The term originated during the late 1940s, at a time when the justices on the Supreme Court, although all New Deal "liberals," nevertheless were divided over issues of constitutional interpretation.[64] As originally used then, and as resurrected in recent decades by conservative critics of the Warren Court,[65] the term "judicial activism" refers to the practice of judges deciding cases according to their own subjective policy preferences or desired results rather than according to the law.[66] Judge Laurence Silberman has used the term in this sense when he defined it as "policymaking in the guise of interpreting and applying law."[67] This is the sense in which "activism" is most frequently deplored in political dialogue today, as judges who "legislate from the bench."[68] It also is the sense in which judicial protection of liberty of contract during the *Lochner* era was criticized by proponents of the orthodox Holmesian view—by scholars who coined the term "Lochnerizing" as a pejorative synonymous with improper judicial activism.

Properly speaking, then, an "activist judge" is one who decides the outcome of a given case or controversy by applying something other than the law—his own values, his conception of "evolving social values," his sense of a "just" result, and so forth.[69] The basic vice of judicial activism, as understood in this sense, is that it violates the fundamental American constitutional principle of separation of powers, for it is an abuse of the courts' legitimate judicial power; it is an attempt to usurp the lawmaking, or legislative, power that our constitutions (both state and federal) vest in the legislative branch of government. To avoid this problem, American courts themselves have devised the so-called political questions doctrine, as part of the self-limiting principle known as nonjusticiability, which holds that courts should refrain from deciding subject matter inappropriate for judicial consideration.[70] When a court disregards this doctrine, it tends to use policy arguments—the kinds of arguments more appropriately made in a legislative chamber rather than in a courtroom—to support its decision.[71]

Activist jurisprudence is result oriented, focused on reaching the particular result, or outcome, that a judge desires in a particular case. What makes a given decision "activist," however, is not the result it reaches so much as the reasoning the judge gives in support of his or her decision. Although most decisions that are criticized as "activist" are ones in which the courts strike down laws as unconstitutional, courts may be just as activist, properly speaking, when they improperly uphold laws against constitutional challenge. Whether or not a decision is "activist," again, depends not on its outcome but on the reasons on which a court bases its decision—whether it is based objectively on the applicable law or subjectively on some other non-legal consideration. Thus, a court abuses its judicial review power, by being "activist," when it decides questions of constitutionality on impermissible grounds, regardless of whether it ultimately finds the law in question either constitutional or unconstitutional. Some of the most egregious examples of judicial activism, in the proper sense of the term, are cases where the courts have upheld laws they should have found unconstitutional.[72]

Judicial protection of liberty of contract, as actually done by the Supreme Court in the early 20th century, was not "activist" under this definition. Nor was it in any real sense "laissez-faire constitutionalism," protecting liberty in the broad sense advocated by classical liberal, or libertarian, philosophers. Rather, in protecting liberty of contract, the Supreme Court followed a more moderate approach that recognized traditional uses of the state's police power. To show this, the remainder of this section will examine two different approaches, or paradigms, for judicial protection of liberty. The first is the more radical, and possibly more activist,[73] pure laissez-faire approach that the Court would have followed if it truly had done what Justice Holmes accused the majority of doing in *Lochner*, that is, of constitutionalizing the Law of Equal Freedom as articulated in Herbert Spencer's *Social Statics*. The second is the more restrained, moderately libertarian approach that the Court actually followed in protecting liberty of contract, which was nothing more than the application of a general presumption in favor of liberty. That presumption could be rebutted by a showing that the challenged government action fit within one of the recognized "exceptions," as a valid exercise of the police power. Implicit in these two contrasting approaches for protecting liberty are two contrasting views of the police power itself: the first, defining it strictly in terms of a libertarian "no-harm" principle (by strict application of the *sic utere* formulation); the second, defining it in terms of the traditional categories of protecting public health, safety, order, and morality.

The Radical Paradigm: True "Laissez-Faire Constitutionalism"

What would it have meant for the Supreme Court and other courts during the *Lochner* era to have interpreted the Fourteenth Amendment as if it had "enact[ed] Mr. Herbert Spencer's Social Statics," as Justice Holmes accused the majority of doing in *Lochner*? In other words, what would have been the results of a true laissez-faire constitutionalism, one that protected liberty as absolutely as Holmes implied with his paraphrasing of Spencer's Law of Equal Freedom as "[t]he liberty of the citizen to do as he likes so long as he does not interfere with the liberty of others to do the same"?

In his *Lochner* dissent, Holmes himself suggested an answer—one that exposed the falsity of his own claim. He listed several laws upheld by the Court as valid exercises of the police power that to him seemed inconsistent with Spencer's "shibboleth," as he characterized the Law of the Equal Freedom. These included Sunday-closing laws, usury laws, the prohibition of lotteries, "school laws" (probably meant as a reference to compulsory-attendance laws), the Post Office, and the Massachusetts vaccination law upheld by the Court earlier that year in *Jacobson v. Massachusetts*.[74] That virtually all of those laws would be regarded as illegitimate paternal legislation by laissez-faire theorists (whether late 19th-century classical liberals or modern-day libertarians) and that the Court did uphold them as valid exercises of the police power may suggest either that the Court was inconsistent in its protection of liberty, as Holmes was implying, or rather that the Court was not following a laissez-faire approach at all. For example, in *Jacobson* the Court upheld the Massachusetts compulsory vaccination law because the majority saw it as having a "real or substantial relation to the protection of the public health and public safety" against infectious diseases such as smallpox. In this case, the liberty of the individual, including control over one's own body, yielded to what the majority saw as "reasonable regulations" required to protect the safety of the general public.[75]

One need not rely on speculation, however, to construct a radical paradigm for the judicial protection of liberty as laissez-faire theorists would advocate. Something close to such a paradigm may be found in the legal literature of the time.

The leading advocate of incorporating the laissez-faire philosophy into constitutional law—that is, of a true laissez-faire constitutionalism—was Christopher G. Tiedeman.[76] Tiedeman was one of the foremost American legal scholars at the turn of the last century. A respected law teacher and treatise writer, he was the author of a treatise on the limitations of the police power that commentators have long regarded as the preeminent work of laissez-faire constitutionalism.[77] Although Tiedeman shared with conservatives of his age a general aversion to what he called "the radical experimentation of social reformers,"[78] he surely went much further than most of his contemporaries in denouncing all forms of legal paternalism. In this respect, Tiedeman outshone the other leading treatise writer of the late 19th century, Thomas M. Cooley, who was less consistent and far less radical in his constitutional defense of liberty.[79] Tiedeman, in short, was to constitutional law what William Graham Sumner was to political theory generally: a fairly pure exponent of the laissez-faire philosophy.

As Tiedeman understood the police power, it was limited by various constitutional provisions as well as by unwritten higher-law principles.[80] By far the most important limitation Tiedeman would place on state power, however, was tied neither to the text of the Constitution nor to unwritten higher law; rather, it was a limitation that inhered in the very definition of the police power. The government's police power "as understood in the constitutional law of the United States," he wrote, "is simply the power of the government to establish provisions for the enforcement of the common as well as civil law maxim, *sic utere tuo ut alienum non laedas*"[81]—"so use your own so as not to harm that of another." In Anglo-American common law, especially in the law of nuisance, the word *tuo* (your own) was generally understood to refer to property, particularly to real property, or land. As used by Tiedeman, however, the word applied not only to property but also to liberty: it obliged everyone to use one's "own"—to use one's own property, to exercise one's own liberty—so as not to harm that (the property or the liberty) of another. The legitimate exercise of the police power thus was limited to enforcing the *sic utere* principle:

> Any law which goes beyond that principle, which undertakes to abolish rights, the exercise of which does not involve an infringement of the rights of others, or to limit the exercise of rights beyond what is necessary to provide for the public welfare and the general security, cannot be included in the police power of the government.[82]

Because Tiedeman also defined liberty in terms of the *sic utere* principle, his formulation meant that individuals should be free to act, provided they do not harm others or interfere with others' like freedom—in short, legal protection for Herbert Spencer's Law of Equal Freedom.[83]

Throughout both editions of his treatise on the police power,[84] Tiedeman drew a basic distinction between legitimate regulations— that is, regulations that affected only trespasses or other matter of legitimate government concerns under Tiedeman's formulation— and regulations that went beyond the proper scope of the police power.[85] He sought not merely to summarize the state of the law as it had developed by his time but, in addition, to show what the law should be, given his general formulation of the police power. Thus, for example, Tiedeman condemned as unconstitutional not only laws regulating the hours or wages of workers[86] but also usury laws,[87] the protective tariff,[88] anti-miscegenation laws,[89] and even laws regulating morality through the prohibition of such vices as gambling or the use of narcotic drugs.[90]

Tiedeman's view regarding morals legislation, or laws regulating "vice," was especially interesting. He distinguished vice from crime, defining "vice" as "an inordinate, and hence immoral, gratification of one's passions and desires," which primarily damages one's self. So defined, vice was not a trespass on the rights of others and therefore not a criminal act, subject legitimately to police regulation. Crimes involved direct "trespasses upon rights," not the "secondary or consequential damage to others" that might result from individuals' indulgence in their own vices. Accordingly, Tiedeman maintained that vices, as actions harmful only to oneself, did not fall within the legitimate scope of the police power:

> The object of the police power is the prevention of crime, the protection of rights against the assault of others. The police power of the government cannot be brought into operation for the purpose of exacting obedience to the rules of morality, and banishing vice and sin from the world. . . . The municipal law has only to do with trespasses. It cannot be called into play in order to save one from the evil consequences of his own vices, for the violation of a right by the action of another must exist or be threatened, in order to justify the interference of law.

Thus, for example, "[i]t cannot be made a legal wrong for one to become intoxicated in the privacy of his own room," because the person who becomes drunk in private "has committed no wrong, *i.e.,* he has violated no right, and hence he cannot be punished" under Tiedeman's formulation.[91] He acknowledged that his distinction between vice and crime "ha[d] not been endorsed by the courts," but he continued to insist upon it "because the adverse decisions have not convinced me that the distinction is unsound."[92]

As far as Tiedeman's laissez-faire constitutionalism went, it nevertheless fell short of protecting liberty rights as broadly as modern libertarian theory—or a complete and consistent adherence to Spencer's Law of Equal Freedom—would imply. Not even Tiedeman would restrict altogether the state's power to enforce rules of morality; for although he advocated decriminalization of vices per se, he nevertheless would allow government to criminalize trade in a vice. No one can claim the right to make a trade in vice, Tiedeman maintained: "a business may always be prohibited, whose object is to furnish means for the indulgence of a vicious propensity or desire."

Thus, according to him, although fornication and gambling ought not to be punishable offenses, the state could prohibit the keeping of houses of prostitution, the keeping of gambling houses, or the sale of lottery tickets. Tiedeman did not explain his position but simply asserted, "A business that panders to vice may and should be strenuously prohibited, if possible."[93] Tiedeman's distinction seems untenable: If personal indulgence in a vice involves (by definition) no trespass on the rights of others, how can government legitimately use its police power (as formulated by Tiedeman) to prohibit trade in the vice—in other words, business relationships that merely facilitate acts that do not harm others? In drawing this peculiar distinction, Tiedeman certainly fell short of modern libertarian arguments for the decriminalization of "victimless crimes."

Moreover, notwithstanding his generally broad view of liberty of contract in the employment context—which generally left matters such as hours and wages subject to bargaining between the parties, free of government regulation[94]—Tiedeman did concede to the government the ability legitimately to regulate the labor contract in order to protect workers' health and safety,[95] as well as to protect against fraud.

Under a true laissez-faire constitutionalism, the general right to liberty is absolute and can be limited only by legitimate government actions protecting persons from harmful trespasses on their rights; in other words, only by enforcement of the no-harm principle. Thus, not only the laws cited by Justice Holmes in his *Lochner* dissent but also most laws that fell within the traditional scope of the police power—the protection of public health, safety, order, and morals— would be held to be unconstitutional deprivations of liberty.

The Moderate Paradigm: A Presumption in Favor of Liberty

Liberty of contract as actually protected by the courts in the early 20th century did not fit the radical paradigm for the protection of liberty rights that a true laissez-faire constitutionalism would imply. Rather, it followed from a paradigm that was more moderate in at least two basic respects. First, rather than protecting in all its aspects a general and absolute right to liberty (limited only by the definitional constraints imposed on liberty itself by the no-harm principle or Spencer's Law of Equal Freedom), the courts protected liberty in a particular context—the freedom to make contracts. Second, the courts protected that freedom under a standard that permitted the government to limit it through various exercises of the police power, within its traditional scope. That standard, in effect, created at most a general presumption in favor of liberty that could be rebutted by a showing that the law being challenged was a legitimate police-power regulation.

The scope of the right protected by liberty of contract was given its classic definition by Justice Peckham in *Allgeyer v. Louisiana*, the 1897 case that was the Supreme Court's first decision explicitly protecting the right. In his opinion for the Court, Peckham described the liberty protected by the Fourteenth Amendment's due process clause:

> The liberty mentioned in that amendment means not only the right of the citizen to be free from the mere physical restraint of his person, as by incarceration, but the term is deemed to embrace the right of the citizen to be free in the enjoyment of all his faculties; to be free to use them in all lawful ways; to live and work where he will; to earn his livelihood by any lawful calling; to pursue any livelihood or avocation, and for that purpose to enter into all contracts which may be proper, necessary and essential to his carrying out to a successful conclusion the purposes above mentioned.

Although quite broad, this liberty right was not unlimited; it was a particular aspect of an individual's general right to liberty, constrained by law—the freedom to use one's own faculties "in all lawful ways," to earn a livelihood "by any lawful calling." Moreover, it pertained to those lawful exercises of one's freedom that could be realized through legally enforceable contracts that were "proper, necessary and essential" to one's purpose.[96] The emphasis on contract meant that this liberty right was necessarily subject to certain legal constraints, as Peckham recognized.[97] As the Illinois Supreme Court similarly had recognized in one of the earliest liberty-of-contract decisions, *Ritchie v. People*, "the right to contract may be subject to limitations growing out of the duties which the individual owes to society, to the public, or the government."[98]

Liberty of contract was not absolute. Justice George Sutherland explicitly acknowledged this in his opinion for the Court in *Adkins v. Children's Hospital*, one of the most important liberty-of-contract decisions, second only in fame and historical significance to *Lochner* itself.[99] "There is, of course, no such thing as absolute freedom of contract," Justice Sutherland wrote, noting that it was "subject to a great variety of restraints." Nevertheless, he immediately added, "freedom of contract is. . . the general rule and restraint the exception; and the exercise of legislative authority to abridge it can be justified only by the existence of exceptional circumstances."[100]

In thus protecting the right by a "general rule forbidding legislative interference with freedom of contract,"[101] the Court in effect was applying what some modern scholars have advocated as a general presumption in favor of liberty.[102] It was a presumption that could be overcome, however, by a court's finding that the law in question—the law being challenged as an abridgement of the right to liberty of contract—was a legitimate exercise of one of the many recognized functions of the police power. Courts during the *Lochner* era generally did not accept the government's rationale for a challenged law at face value. Rather, they followed what Justice Harlan had identified in *Mugler v. Kansas* as the "solemn duty" of the courts, in exercising judicial review, "to look at the substance of things"—that is, to critically examine whether "a statute purporting to have been enacted to protect the public health, the public morals, or the public safety" had "a real or substantial relation to those objects" or instead was "a palpable invasion of rights secured by the fundamental law."[103]

The test applied by the courts in protecting liberty of contract was stated by Justice Peckham in his opinion for the Court in *Lochner*. The basic inquiry was, "Is this a fair, reasonable, and appropriate exercise of the police power of the State, or is it an unreasonable, unnecessary and arbitrary interference with the right of the individual to his personal liberty or to enter into those contracts in relation to labor which may seem to him appropriate or necessary for the support of himself and his family?"[104] To answer this question, Peckham added, courts must apply a means-ends test:

> The mere assertion that the subject relates though but in a remote degree to the public health [or some other legitimate exercise of the police power] does not necessarily render the enactment valid. The act must have a more direct relation, as a means to an end, and the end must be appropriate and legitimate, before an act can be held to be valid which interferes with the general right of an individual to be free in his person and in his power to contract in relation to his own labor.[105]

Modern scholars are correct when they describe the test applied in *Lochner* and other liberty-of-contract cases as one that distinguished valid, or "reasonable," police-power exercises from invalid, or "arbitrary," exercises of government power. However, some modern scholars—including Howard Gillman in his book *The Constitution Besieged*—err in assuming that the distinction between "reasonable" and "arbitrary," as applied by the courts, referred to the prohibition of "class legislation" under 19th-century constitutional law.[106] Rather, the distinction referred to the traditional scope of the police power as a protection of public health, safety, order, and morality: "reasonable" laws fit within one or more of these traditional categories, while "arbitrary" laws did not.[107] The test applied by the old Court has been aptly characterized by one modern scholar as a "moderate" means-ends analysis[108]—that is, a fairly rigorous rational basis review that can be distinguished from both of the tests used by the modern Court in substantive due process cases.[109]

Thus, both in the scope of the liberty interests that it guaranteed and in the standard applied by the Court in reviewing challenged legislation, the Court's protection of liberty of contract in the early 20th century fell short of Christopher Tiedeman's more stridently libertarian jurisprudence, with its protection of all aspects of liberty and its strict adherence to the *sic utere* maxim as an absolute definitional limitation on the legitimate scope of the police power. Perhaps the most telling difference between the moderate paradigm actually followed by the Court in its protection of liberty of contract and the radical paradigm of a true laissez-faire constitutionalism is the difference in the two paradigms' treatment of "morals" legislation, such as bans on lotteries and other forms of gambling, Sunday-closing laws, and the regulation or prohibition of alcohol. The Court during the *Lochner* era consistently upheld such laws as valid exercises of the police power under its traditional scope (which included protection of morality as well as public health).[110] A true laissez-faire constitutionalism would have regarded all such forms of legal paternalism as abuses of government power and abridgement of fundamental liberties.

Contrary to the orthodox, Holmesian view, the Court was not engaged in judicial activism when it protected liberty of contract as a fundamental right during the 40-year period prior to 1937. Rather, the Court was simply enforcing the law of the Constitution, specifically the right to liberty as protected substantively under the Fifth Amendment's or the Fourteenth Amendment's due process clause. Under the moderate paradigm for the protection of liberty that the Court followed, the scope of the right was limited by laws that legitimately fit within one of the traditional exercises of the police power, for the protection of public health, safety, order, or morals. The Court did not follow the more radical paradigm suggested by Christopher G. Tiedeman's treatises on the police power, which would have strictly limited the scope of the police power to enforcement of the *sic utere* doctrine. Only in Justice Holmes's imagination was the Court "enact[ing] Mr. Herbert Spencer's *Social Statics*," for neither in *Lochner* nor in any of its other liberty-of-contract decisions did the Court follow any sort of laissez-faire ideology.

3. Liberty of Contract in Its Heyday: The Many Facets of Liberty

Another flaw in the orthodox view of liberty of contract is its myopic conception of the scope of the right. Liberty of contract, as protected by the courts in the early 20th century, protected more than just economic freedom in the context of the labor market. In addition, it protected noneconomic aspects of liberty, a point most scholars ignore today because it does not fit the caricature of liberty-of-contract jurisprudence as "laissez-faire constitutionalism" that orthodox Holmesians put forward.

The scope of liberty of contract, as described originally by Justice Peckham in his opinion for the Court in its 1897 *Allgeyer* decision, was quite broad indeed: it encompassed not only freedom from "mere physical restraint" but also the right of a person "to be free in the enjoyment of all his faculties; to be free to use them in all lawful ways; to live and work where he will; to earn his livelihood by any lawful calling; to pursue any livelihood or avocation"; and of course, as the name of the right implies, freedom to enter into "all contracts which may be proper, necessary and essential" to carrying out those purposes.[1] Considering especially the status of contract in late 19th-century American law, the freedom to enter into contracts for the purposes mentioned by the Court in *Allgeyer* was tantamount to the legal expression—through society's protection of contracts under positive law—of the natural rights mentioned in the Declaration of Independence, of liberty and of the pursuit of happiness. It is little wonder, then, that when he anticipated liberty of contract in his dissent in the *Slaughterhouse Cases*, Justice Field spoke of such things as "the right to pursue a lawful employment in a lawful manner," "equality of rights in the lawful pursuits of life," and "the right of free labor" as interchangeable concepts, all realizing in law "the natural and inalienable rights which belong to all citizens" in a free society.[2]

The types of economic freedom illustrated by *Allgeyer* and the *Slaughterhouse Cases*—the freedom to enter into a business contract for the sale and purchase of insurance and the freedom to engage in a business such as livestock slaughtering—plus other types of economic freedom, such as the freedom of both sides in a labor contract to bargain over hours and wages, are the more obvious aspects of liberty of contract. As broadly described in *Allgeyer*, however, the right may include other aspects of freedom that could be seen as noneconomic, or "personal," freedom, including what is today regarded as the constitutional right to privacy. Just as liberty generally may be seen as a fundamental right with an infinite number of aspects, one of those aspects, liberty of contract, may itself be seen as a single basic right with many aspects or facets.

The Right to Economic Liberty

Most famously, liberty of contract, as protected by the Supreme Court during the so-called *Lochner* era, encompassed economic liberty: the freedom of people to enter into business contracts and to bargain over the terms of those contracts, free of government interference. This basic right of economic liberty had three important aspects: first, freedom of labor (including the freedom of both employers and employees to bargain over hours, wages, and other terms of their labor contracts); second, freedom to compete (including the freedom to pursue a lawful trade or occupation and to compete with others already in the market); and third, freedom of dealing (including the right of refusal to deal—or, in other words, the freedom to discriminate). This section examines those three aspects of economic liberty.

Freedom of Labor

The best-known aspect of the Supreme Court's protection of liberty of contract as a fundamental right, under the due process clauses of the Fifth and Fourteenth Amendments, was its use to declare unconstitutional such regulations of business as minimum-wage or maximum-hours legislation.[3] Indeed, the traditional account of liberty of contract so closely identified the right with freedom of labor that other important aspects of economic liberty, as protected by the courts, have been ignored or misunderstood by scholars from the Progressive-Era to the present day.[4] Perhaps this was so because in the early 20th century, in the eyes of both conservatives and laissez-faire commentators, it was labor legislation that posed the most important threat to economic liberty. For example, Christopher Tiedeman noted that "[i]n no phase of human relations is there a more widespread manifestation of legislative determination to interfere with and to restrict the constitutional liberty of contract, than in the contract for labor between employer and employee."[5] It was also labor legislation, particularly in the form of wage and hour specifications and other so-called protective regulations, that represented perhaps the most significant and unprecedented expansions of the police power beyond its traditional scope.[6] Even when limited to its application against labor laws, however, liberty of contract has been widely misunderstood by scholars.

Superficially—and as generally understood under the orthodox caricature of laissez-faire constitutionalism—the right involved the freedom of businessmen from "unreasonable" regulatory legislation. But it was not only the liberty, or property, of employers that the courts protected; they also protected the liberty, or property, interests of employees. This aspect of the right involved, to use Justice Peckham's classic *Allgeyer* formulation, "the right of the citizen to be free in the enjoyment of all his faculties; to be free to use them in all lawful ways; . . . to earn his livelihood by any lawful calling; . . . and for that purpose to enter into all contracts which may be proper, necessary and essential" to these purposes.[7] When the Illinois Supreme Court, in one of the earliest liberty-of-contract decisions, invalidated a maximum-hours law that applied to women working in factories, it did so because the law denied female employees "the same rights, under the constitution, to make contracts with reference to [their] labor, as are secured thereby to men."[8]

By its decision in *Lochner v. New York*, therefore, the Court recognized the right of both employers and employees to bargain over the terms of labor contracts—specifically with regard to the hours of work—free of interference from the state. The maximum-hours regulation at issue in *Lochner* was just one provision of the New York Bakeshop Act of 1895, a bakery reform law that was modeled on England's Bakehouse Regulation Act of 1863. Most of the New York law's provisions were sanitary regulations—specifying such things as drainage and ventilation, the type of flooring, the height of ceilings, and the whitewashing of walls in bakery buildings—similar to those in the English law; those provisions were not challenged in the case. The provision that was challenged, the maximum-hours provision in Section 1 of the act, prohibited employees in "biscuit, bread, or cake" bakeries from working "more than sixty hours in any one week, or more than ten hours in any one day."[9]

The historical background of the case—behind both the law and the constitutional challenge to the law—involved a conflict between unionized and nonunionized bakeries in the state of New York. More precisely, it was a conflict between unionized bakeries staffed by bakers of German descent who came to dominate the bakers' union and their smaller, nonunionized competitors who employed workers from what one modern scholar has called "a hodgepodge of ethnic groups," particularly Italian, French, and Jewish immigrants. The 10-hour law was strongly supported by the German unionized bakeries whose union contracts contained a similar provision limiting the hours of their workers. On the other hand, the smaller, nonunionized bakeries, like Joseph Lochner's in Utica, New York, opposed the law because they frequently provided their bakers with sleeping quarters, enabling them to spend long hours on the job, and they could not afford to hire more workers.[10]

Although scholars disagree about the extent to which the act truly was a special-interest law designed to undermine the competitiveness of smaller, nonunionized bakeries,[11] virtually all scholars who have written about the factual background of *Lochner* agree that it was a test case challenging the hours provision of the Bakeshop Act, brought by the New York Association of Master Bakers, the bitter enemy of the 10-hour law. Ironically, Henry Weismann, the man who as a leader of the bakers' union had "made" the 10-hour law, was the same man, as a lawyer representing Lochner before the Supreme Court, who helped have it "unmade," as a *New York Times* feature article of April 19, 1905, put it. Weismann was a German immigrant who came to the United States as a young adult. After he moved to New York in 1890, he became the bakers' union unofficial leader and spokesman for the campaign for the 10-hour law. In 1897, he resigned from the union leadership and soon opened a bakery of his own while studying law and passing the New York bar exam. He became active in the New York Association of Master Bakers, which opposed the 10-hour law, and later wrote that as a master baker, he underwent "an intellectual revolution" and "saw where the law which I had succeeded in having passed was unjust to the employers." Together with prominent Brooklyn attorney Frank Harvey Field, Weismann was chosen by the master bakers' association to represent Lochner before the Supreme Court.[12]

Justice Rufus Peckham wrote the opinion for the Court's five-justice majority.[13] His opinion turned on the question of whether the maximum-hours provision in the Bakeshop Act was "a fair, reasonable, and appropriate exercise of the police power" or "an unreasonable, unnecessary and arbitrary interference" with the parties' liberty of contract. In holding the latter, Peckham examined the state's claim that this provision in the Bakeshop Act was a health law. Here he applied the moderate means-ends test that characterized the Court's liberty-of-contract jurisprudence, a standard that required the challenged law to have a "direct relation, as a means," to an end that was "appropriate and legitimate"—that is, was one of the traditional ends of the police power such as protecting the health of the public or, possibly, of employees.[14]

In concluding that "the limit of the police power has been reached and passed in this case," Peckham found, with ample justification, that there was "no reasonable foundation for holding this [hours provision] to be necessary or appropriate as a health law to safeguard the public health or the health of the individuals who are following the trade of a baker." It was not a protection of the public health, for "[c]lean and wholesome bread does not depend upon whether the baker works but ten hours per day or only sixty hours per week." Nor was the hours provision necessary to protect the health of bakers. Bakers are "in no sense wards of the State," Peckham noted; "There is no contention that bakers as a class are not equal in intelligence and capacity to men in other trades or manual occupations, or that they are not able to assert their rights and care for themselves without the protecting arm of the State, interfering with their independence of judgment and action."[15] Moreover, baking was an ordinary trade, one that was not especially unhealthful, as the available scientific evidence suggested.[16] Peckham then presented an argument *ad absurdum*: If "the mere fact of the possible existence of some small amount of unhealthiness" in any given occupation would justify exercise of the police power to protect employees' health—if, for example, the government should argue that it was "to the interest of the State that its population should be strong and robust"—then "[n]o trade, no occupation, no mode of earning one's living, could escape this all-pervading power." "Not only the hours of employe[e]s, but the hours of employers, could be regulated, and doctors, lawyers, scientists, all professional men, as well as athletes and artisans, could be forbidden to fatigue their brains and bodies by prolonged hours of exercise, lest the fighting strength of the State be impaired," Peckham warned.[17]

In reaching the conclusion that the hours provision of the Bakeshop Act was not a valid health law, Justice Peckham and the majority found it was a "labor law" that did not fall within the established limits of the police power. Thus, it failed to overcome the general presumption in favor of liberty of contract and, therefore, was "an illegal interference with the rights of individuals, both employers and employees, to make contracts regarding labor upon such terms as they think best, or which they may agree upon with the other parties to such contracts." Peckham briefly alluded to the fact that the law, "while passed under what is claimed to be the police power for the purpose of protecting the public health or welfare," was rather, "in reality, passed from other motives," although he did not specifically identify those motives. He wrote only that it seemed "the real object and purpose were simply to regulate the hours of labor between the master and his employees (all being men, sui juris), in a private business, not dangerous in any degree to morals or in any real and substantial degree, to the health of the employees."[18]

Arguably, the participation of Weismann—a former supporter of the law, now assisting counsel for Lochner—might have called the justices' attention to the circumstances surrounding enactment of the hours provision. Those circumstances, particularly the strong support by the bakers' union and owners of unionized bakeries, showed that the hours provision was illicit class legislation—a key argument in Lochner's brief that, significantly, played no explicit part in the majority's decision.[19]

In his dissent, Justice Holmes mischaracterized the majority opinion when he suggested it was using the Fourteenth Amendment to "enact Mr. Herbert Spencer's *Social Statics*."[20] Peckham's opinion for the Court was not based, either explicitly or implicitly, on this famous book by the great 19th-century English classical liberal philosopher, or on any other laissez-faire work, and still less on any particular "economic theory." Rather, Peckham relied on well-established principles of constitutional law, including the moderate means-ends analysis the Court had adopted as its standard of review in substantive due process cases.[21] Holmes's pithy dissent apparently failed to understand not only the majority's opinion but also those fundamental principles of early 20th-century constitutional law. Interestingly, Holmes did not reject substantive due process review per se, but he did maintain—following a majoritarian theory contrary to the Court's then-standard jurisprudence—that judicial protection of liberty was "perverted" when it was applied "to prevent the natural outcome of a dominant opinion," unless everyone could agree that the challenged statute "would infringe fundamental principles as they have been understood by the traditions of our people and our law."[22] Peckham's opinion for the Court showed, in fact, that the general presumption in favor of liberty that the Court followed should be applied in this case because the challenged law failed to fit within the traditional scope of the police power. In other words, Peckham's opinion showed that the hours provision in the Bakeshop Act did indeed "infringe fundamental principles" as traditionally understood in American law.

In contrast to Holmes's shoddy scholarship, the principal dissenting opinion in *Lochner*—authored by Justice John Marshall Harlan, joined by two other justices—followed the same moderate means-ends analysis used by the majority but reached a different conclusion, based on a more liberal reading of the state's power to enact health laws. According to Harlan, the Court should invalidate a purported health or safety law only if it had "no real or substantial relation to those objects, or is, beyond all question, a plain, palpable invasion of rights secured by the fundamental law."[23] Although Harlan's dissent accepted the legitimacy of liberty of contract as a constitutional right, it reduced the importance of the right, in effect, by implicitly reversing the Court's general presumption in favor of liberty. In fact, Harlan anticipated the Court's modern substantive due process jurisprudence with its general rule of deference to the legislature. "If there be doubt as to the validity of the statute, that doubt must therefore be resolved in favor of its validity," Harlan concluded.[24]

Although *Lochner* protected the freedom of both employers and employees to bargain over the hours of work, that freedom was qualified by two important decisions, one preceding *Lochner* and the other following it within a few years, both involving hours legislation affecting special classes of workers.

Lochner can be seen as consistent with the Court's earlier decision concerning a maximum-hours law, *Holden v. Hardy*, because that case did not concern an ordinary trade or occupation. At issue was a Utah law that limited the employment of workmen in underground mines, as well as in smelting and other operations for the reduction or refining of ores or metals, to eight hours per day, except in cases of emergency. In his opinion for the seven-justice majority that upheld the law as a valid exercise of the police power, Justice Henry Billings Brown emphasized the extraordinary risks to the safety and health (if not lives) of the workers engaged in such occupations and hence rationalized the law as a valid health law providing "special protection" to those workmen "peculiarly exposed to these dangers." Justice Brown wrote, "[T]he fact that both parties are of full age and competent to contract does not necessarily deprive the State of the power to interfere where the parties do not stand upon an equality, or where the public health demands that one party to the contract shall be protected against himself."[25]

In his opinion in *Lochner*, Justice Peckham easily distinguished *Holden v. Hardy* on these facts. The precedent meant, however, that according to the Court's understanding of the police power, valid health laws could extend beyond the protection of general public health to the protection of particular classes of workers, albeit those in extraordinarily dangerous occupations. Another important feature of the Court's liberty-of-contract jurisprudence illustrated by *Holden* was the Court's unwillingness to consider the supposed inequality of bargaining power between employers and employees as a justification for government intervention. Although Justice Brown briefly mentioned that inequality, his opinion for the Court focused on the workers' safety per se, rather than their ability to look after it themselves. As legal historian Charles McCurdy has observed, "the bulk of Brown's opinion emphasized the state legislature's competence to protect the mutual interest of workers in well-rested, alert associates during shifts of dangerous underground labor."[26]

The next major decision involving a maximum-hours law, issued just a few years after *Lochner*, is not as easy to square with the *Lochner* holding. *Muller v. Oregon* concerned a state law limiting the hours of women employed in factories to 10 hours a day.[27] The statute at issue in *Muller* was a new type of law passed in response to new social conditions, the entry of women into occupations traditionally held by men. Such "protective" laws, as some modern scholars have observed, really did not protect women but instead limited their economic opportunities by pricing their labor out of the market.[28] In *Muller*, however, the Court seemed oblivious to the economic reality behind the law and instead accepted unquestioningly the sexist and paternalistic arguments offered by the state in justification of the law—through the famous "Brandeis Brief," authored by Louis D. Brandeis, attorney for the National Consumers' League and future justice of the Supreme Court.[29]

In his opinion for the Court explaining its decision to uphold the Oregon law, Justice Brewer emphasized that "woman's physical structure, and the functions she performs in consequence thereof, justify special legislation restricting or qualifying the conditions under which she should be permitted to toil." The very kind of argument that he and the other justices in the *Lochner* majority rejected as absurd—that the state has a legitimate police-power interest in protecting the physical health of its male population generally, "lest the fighting strength of the State be impaired"—Justice Brewer and the majority in *Muller* accepted unquestioningly: "as healthy mothers are essential for vigorous offspring, the physical well-being of woman becomes an object of public interest and care in order to preserve the strength and vigor of the race."[30] The U.S. Supreme Court was not alone among courts in failing to treat women as fully equal citizens entitled to the same freedom of contract as men. Many other courts joined in accepting such paternalistic arguments to justify maximum-hours legislation for women— even the Illinois Supreme Court, which in 1910 overturned that court's pioneering liberty-of-contract decision, *Ritchie v. People*, that 15 years earlier had recognized women as sui juris and legally equal to men.[31]

Although *Lochner* is more famous, perhaps the best example of the Court's use of substantive due process to protect economic liberty is its 1923 decision in *Adkins v. Children's Hospital*.[32] *Adkins* deserves recognition as the paradigm liberty-of-contract case in many respects, not the least of which is the Court's clear articulation of the standard of review it applied in determining whether challenged laws were valid exercises of the police power or unconstitutional infringements of liberty of contract.

At issue in *Adkins* was a federal law, enacted by Congress pursuant to its power to legislate for the District of Columbia, fixing minimum wages for women and children employed in the District. The law created a three-member board that was authorized "to investigate and ascertain the wages of women and minors in the different occupations in which they are employed" and then to determine, for each type of occupation, the wage level the board considered "unreasonably low" for minors or "inadequate to supply the necessary cost of living" for women workers, "to maintain them in good health and to protect their morals." The law was challenged by the Children's Hospital, which employed "a large number of women in various capacities," some of whom worked for wages below the minimum fixed by the board.[33]

In a second case joined to the hospital's challenge, Ms. Willie Lyons, a 21-year-old elevator operator employed by the Congress Hall Hotel, also challenged the law. Ms. Lyons had been employed at a salary of $35 per month and two meals a day. She maintained "that the work was light and healthful, the hours short, with surroundings clean and moral, and that she was anxious to continue it for the compensation she was receiving." She lost her job, however, after the board had determined that a woman in her occupation could not be employed for less than $71.50 per month, twice what she had been paid. Although "it would have been glad to retain her," the hotel hired a man in her stead. Ms. Lyons further averred that the wages she had received from the hotel "were the best she was able to obtain for any work she was capable of performing" and that she could not secure any other position at which she could make a living "with as good physical and moral surroundings, and earn as good wages." Thus, as Hadley Arkes has poignantly summarized the facts of the case, the D.C. law, "in its liberal tenderness, in its concern to protect women, had brought about a situation in which women were being replaced, in their jobs, by men."[34] That consequence of the law may not have been unforeseen, for the law "protecting" women had been enacted by Congress in the final months of World War I, just as many of the men who had fought in the war were returning to the civilian job market.

The Court's opinion was written by Justice George Sutherland, whom many scholars consider the most distinguished of the "Four Horsemen"—the four conservative justices on the Court who would be labeled with that epithet in the 1930s because of their perceived opposition to the New Deal.[35] A majority of five justices held that the D.C. law was an "unconstitutional interference with the freedom of contract included within the guarantees of the due process clause of the Fifth Amendment."[36]

After stating the facts of the case, Sutherland began his opinion by eloquently reaffirming the Court's power to invalidate unconstitutional laws. He did so by restating the classic justification for judicial review, which can be traced back to Alexander Hamilton's *Federalist* essay No. 78. The Constitution, "by its own terms, is the supreme law of the land, emanating from the people, the repository of ultimate sovereignty under our form of government," while a congressional statute is merely "the act of an agency of this sovereign authority." Thus, when a law passed by Congress conflicts with the Constitution, it must fall, "for that which is not supreme must yield to that which is," Sutherland declared. Moreover, "[f]rom the authority to ascertain and determine the law in a given case, there necessarily results, in case of conflict, the duty to declare and enforce the rule of the supreme law" against an unconstitutional statute. To exercise judicial review, by declaring a law in conflict with the Constitution to be invalid, or "of no effect and binding on no one," was "simply a necessary concomitant of the power to hear and dispose of a case or controversy properly before the court," he concluded.[37]

Liberty of contract was a well-established constitutional right, Sutherland noted: "That the right to contract about one's affairs is a part of the liberty of the individual protected by [the due process] clause is settled by the decisions of this court and is no longer open to question." He added that "[w]ithin this liberty are contracts of employment of labor" and that "[i]n making such contracts, generally speaking, the parties have an equal right to obtain from each other the best terms they can as a result of private bargaining." Although Sutherland conceded there was "no such thing as absolute freedom of contract"—that it was "subject to a great variety of restraints"—he also observed that "freedom of contract is, nevertheless, the general rule and restraint the exception, and the exercise of legislative authority to abridge it can be justified only by the existence of exceptional circumstances."[38] Thus, Sutherland made clear the standard the Court was following in liberty-of-contract cases: a general presumption in favor of liberty, which could be rebutted by a showing that the challenged law fit within one of the recognized "exceptions" to the general rule—that is, one of those categories for which the Court had upheld restrictions on freedom to contract as valid exercises of the police power.

After reviewing those exceptions, Sutherland found that the D.C. law fixing minimum wages for women fit none of them:

> It is not a law dealing with any business charged with a pub-lic interest or with public work, or to meet and tide over a temporary emergency. It has nothing to do with the charac-ter, methods or periods of wage payments. It does not pre-scribe hours of labor or conditions under which labor is to be done. It is not for the protection of persons under legal disability or for the prevention of fraud.[39]

Rather, he concluded, the D.C. law was "simply and exclusively a price-fixing law, confined to adult women. . ., who are legally as capable of contracting for themselves as men." The law "forbids two parties having lawful capacity—under penalties as to the employer—to freely contract with one another in respect of the price for which one shall render service to the other in a purely private employment where both are willing, perhaps anxious, to agree, even though the consequence may be to oblige one to surrender a desirable engage-ment and the other to dispense with the services of a desirable employee."[40] The law, in other words, unjustifiably deprived both the employer and the employee of their constitutionally protected freedom of contract.

Although Justice Sutherland's opinion showed that the D.C. law fit none of the recognized categories of exceptions to the general rule of contractual freedom, two of those categories—laws prescribing hours of labor and laws protecting certain classes of persons—posed difficulties because of the Court's previous decision in *Muller v. Oregon*. Sutherland, who as a U.S. senator had been a champion of women's rights,[41] acknowledged that "[i]n view of the great—not to say revolutionary—changes" that had taken place since *Muller* " in the contractual, political and civil status of women, culminating in the Nineteenth Amendment," it was "not unreasonable" to maintain that legally cognizable differences between men and women "have now come almost, if not quite, to the vanishing point."[42] Although the Court did not overturn *Muller*—and indeed, Sutherland noted, "the physical differences" between the sexes "must be recognized in appropriate cases, and legislation fixing hours or conditions of work may properly take them into account"—Sutherland limited the *Muller* precedent to those specific types of laws, as valid exercises of the police power to protect health. Drawing a distinction between laws regulating the hours of labor and laws fixing wages,[43] Sutherland concluded, "we cannot accept the doctrine that women of mature age, *sui juris*, require or may be subjected to restrictions upon their liberty of contract which could not lawfully be imposed in the case of men under similar circumstances."[44]

Sutherland's opinion for the Court also included an extensive analysis of minimum-wage legislation, particularly as exemplified by the federal law at issue in *Adkins*, showing how such laws not only failed to meet the means-ends test but also violated basic requirements of due process. The statute empowered the District of Columbia board to fix wages under a standard that was "so vague as to be impossible of practical application with any reasonable degree of accuracy":

> What is sufficient to supply the necessary cost of living for a woman worker and maintain her in good health and protect her morals is obviously not a precise or unvarying sum—not even approximately so. The amount will depend upon a variety of circumstances: The individual temperament, habits of thrift, care, ability to buy necessaries intelligently, and whether the woman live[s] alone or with her family. . . . The relation between earnings and morals is not capable of standardization. It cannot be shown that well-paid women safeguard their morals more carefully than those who are poorly paid. Morality rests upon other considerations than wages, and there is, certainly, no such prevalent connection between the two as to justify a broad attempt to adjust the latter with reference to the former. As a means of safeguarding morals the attempted classification, in our opinion, is without reasonable basis.[45]

Moreover, the law took into account "the necessities of only one party to the contract"; it ignored "the necessities of the employer by compelling him to pay not less than a certain sum, not only whether the employee is capable of earning it, but irrespective of the ability of his business to sustain the burden."[46] Finally, "[t]he feature of this statute which, perhaps more than any other, puts upon it the stamp of invalidity," Sutherland noted, "is that it exacts from the employer an arbitrary payment for a purpose and upon a basis having no causal connection with his business, or the contract or the work the employee engages to do." The value of the employee's work, the number of hours that constitute a day's work, the type of place where the work is done, and the other circumstances of the employment—none of these factors is taken into account by the board when it fixes a wage based on what it presumes to be the needs of just one party to the contract, needs that have nothing to do with the employment itself. Thus, the statute completely ignores "[t]he moral requirement implicit in every contract of employment," that the amount to be paid and the service to be rendered "shall bear to each other some relation of just equivalence." Such a law, Sutherland justifiably concluded, "is so clearly the product of a naked, arbitrary exercise of power that it cannot be allowed to stand under the Constitution of the United States."[47]

As the modern scholar (and Sutherland biographer) Hadley Arkes has emphasized, the reasoning of Justice Sutherland in his opinion for the Court in *Adkins* was not based on any economic theories, whether of laissez faire or some other school of thought. Rather, it was "drawn from the same canons of reasoning that he employed when he considered restrictions on the press or the protection of defendants in a trial," or any other "attempt, through the law, to restrict the freedom of individuals, in any of its dimensions." Arkes adds, "For Sutherland, it was part of that same discipline of reasoning that constituted the discipline of 'constitutional' restraints on the exercise of authority"—in other words, it followed the "craft of judging" applied in American constitutional law.[48]

In 1923, in *Charles Wolff Packing Company v. Court of Industrial Relations*, the Court held another kind of wage-fixing law to be an unconstitutional deprivation of liberty of contract—a Kansas statute declaring the fuel, clothing, and food preparation industries to be businesses "affected with a public interest" and empowering a three-judge industrial court to fix wages within those industries. In a unanimous decision, including Holmes and Brandeis, the Court concluded that the state's attempt to fix wages in businesses like the Wolff Packing Company deprived the company of its "property and liberty of contract without due process of law."[49] Chief Justice Taft's opinion for the Court followed the standard of review articulated in *Adkins*—recognizing that "the right of the employer on the one hand, and of the employee on the other, to contract about his affairs" was part of the liberty protected by the Fourteenth Amendment's due process clause and that such contractual freedom was the "general rule," which could be abridged only by "exceptional circumstances."[50]

The exception at issue in the case was the "business affected with a public interest" doctrine. Acknowledging that the category had expanded well beyond its common-law origins since the Court first recognized it in *Munn v. Illinois*, Chief Justice Taft nevertheless maintained that "the circumstances which clothe a particular kind of business with a public interest. . . must be such as to create a peculiarly close relation between the public and those engaged in it," and "an affirmative obligation on [the business's] part to be reasonable in dealing with the public."[51] He divided such businesses into three categories. The first were those carried on "under the authority of a public grant of privileges which. . . [impose] the affirmative duty of rendering a public service demanded by any member of the public," such as railroads, other common carriers, and public utilities. The second were "[c]ertain occupations, regarded as exceptional," to which the public interest was still attached, surviving "from earliest times," the period when "arbitrary laws by Parliament or colonial Legislatures" had regulated all trades and callings; these included businesses such as inns or hotels, cabs, and gristmills. The third and final category included businesses that, "though not public at their inception," had become subject to government regulation because of some "peculiar relation to the public. . . superimposed upon them," by which it can be said that the owner of the business, "by devoting his business to the public use, in effect grants the public an interest in that use and subjects himself to public regulation." Such were the grain elevators at issue both in *Munn* and in the Court's subsequent late 19th-century decision, *Budd v. New York.*[52]

The "mere declaration by a Legislature that a business is affected with a public interest is not conclusive of the question," Taft observed. "It has never been supposed, since the adoption of the Constitution, that the business of the butcher, or the baker, the tailor, the wood chopper, the mining operator, or the miner was clothed with such a public interest that the price of his product or his wages could be fixed by state regulation." Similarly, the businesses subjected to the control of the Kansas industrial court are not within these categories; "[t]here is no monopoly in the preparation of foods," for prices are determined by "competition throughout the country at large."[53] Thus, when the industrial court fixes wages in order to resolve disputes between employers and workers, it deprives both parties of their liberty of contract rights: the employer "is bound. . . to pay the wages fixed, and while the worker is not required to work, at the wages fixed, he is forbidden, on penalty of fine or imprisonment, to strike against them and thus is compelled to give up that means of putting himself on an equality with his employer, which action in concert with his fellows gives him."[54]

At first glance, the Court's recognition in *Wolff Packing* of employees' rights to join a union or to go on strike, as part of their contractual freedom, might call into question two other decisions by the Court during the *Lochner* era that appear to contradict that freedom. In *Adair v. United States* and *Coppage v. Kansas*, the Court struck down laws outlawing so-called yellow-dog contracts under which employees agreed not to join a union or remain a union member while in the employer's employ.[55] Notwithstanding modern commentators' views that those two decisions were erroneous, reflecting the anti-union bias that was prevalent at the time,[56] *Adair* and *Coppage* can be explained by the Court's emphasis on equality of liberty-of-contract rights as between employers and employees. The two cases illustrate another important aspect of economic freedom protected by the Court's liberty-of-contract jurisprudence, the right of refusal to deal, discussed later in this section.

Freedom to Compete

Another aspect of economic liberty protected by the due process clause is the freedom of entry into lawful trades or occupations. This aspect of liberty of contract may be traced directly to the fundamental right identified by Justice Field in his dissent in the *Slaughterhouse Cases*, "the right to pursue a lawful employment in a lawful manner." But it had a far older history, as discussed in the 17th-century writings of Sir Edward Coke and as found in precedents in English law going back to the Magna Carta. The fundamental right to earn a living was recognized by Blackstone, who observed, "At common law, every man might use what trade he pleased." Indeed, long before the Supreme Court protected liberty of contract through the Fourteenth Amendment, American courts had protected the common-law right of an individual to pursue a gainful occupation against various efforts by the government to encroach on that right.[57]

An important part of this fundamental right was the right to enter a market—in other words, the freedom to compete. Because the Court did not follow a true laissez-faire constitutionalism, it did not protect this freedom absolutely. Indeed, during the *Lochner* era, the Court sustained a wide variety of laws restricting entry into a lawful profession, business, trade, or calling—typically, occupational licensing laws that were justified as protections of public health or safety or as protections against fraud.[58] In several significant decisions, however, the Court found that laws restricting entry into particular markets were invalid as "arbitrary" exercises of the police power that abridged the freedom to compete. The Court protected this right in *Allgeyer*, its first decision explicitly protecting liberty of contract, when it held that the law at issue—a Louisiana law banning insurance sales by companies not licensed to do business in Louisiana—interfered with the freedom of both the Allgeyer Company (the Louisiana firm convicted of violating the statute) and a New York marine insurance company (not licensed in Louisiana) to enter into a contract with each other.[59]

As a modern scholar has noted, freedom to compete "certainly is thwarted by laws that profess to protect the public by completely banning a particular business, trade, industry, or line of commerce."[60] In 1917, the Court considered one such prohibition in *Adams v. Tanner*, where it invalidated a Washington State law that prevented employment agencies from collecting fees for their services.[61] Considering the measure, practically speaking, as a prohibition of employment agencies, the Court found it unconstitutional as an arbitrary restriction of the right to engage in a useful business.[62]

In two well-known decisions from the late 1920s and early 1930s, the Court invalidated other forms of entry restriction. In its 1928 decision in *Louis K. Liggett Company v. Baldridge*, the Court struck down a Pennsylvania law essentially requiring that every pharmacy or drugstore be wholly owned by a licensed pharmacist or pharmacists. In his opinion for the seven-justice majority, Justice Sutherland rejected the state's rationale for the law—that it protected public health—and instead found that it was an effort by in-state pharmacists to block competition from chain stores.[63] Four years later, in *New State Ice Company v. Liebmann*, Justice Sutherland again wrote the opinion for a six-to-two Court majority invalidating an Oklahoma statute restricting entry into the ice business. The Depression-era law, purporting to help alleviate the problem of "cut-throat competition" among small businesses in the state, declared the manufacture, sale, and distribution of ice to be a "public business"—that is, a business "charged with a public use"—and restricted the business to firms that had been licensed by a government commission empowered to determine the number of firms sufficient within a given territory to meet the public's need for ice. The challenge to the law arose after an existing business sued to block entry by a new unlicensed competitor, Liebmann. After first concluding that the ice business was not affected with a public interest—that it was, rather, "an ordinary business," "essentially private in its nature"[64]—Sutherland explained why the challenged law did not fall within the proper scope of the police power and instead unreasonably restricted the freedom to compete:

> Stated succinctly, a private corporation here seeks to prevent a competitor from entering the business of making and selling ice. It claims to be endowed with state authority to achieve this exclusion. There is no question now before us of any regulation by the state to protect the consuming public either with respect to conditions of manufacture and distribution or to insure purity of product or to prevent extortion. The control here asserted does not protect against monopoly, but tends to foster it. The aim is not to encourage competition, but to prevent it; not to regulate the business, but to preclude persons from engaging in it. There is no difference in principle between this case and the attempt of the dairyman under state authority to prevent another from keeping cows and selling milk on the ground that there are enough dairymen in the business; or to prevent a shoemaker from making or selling shoes because shoemakers already in that occupation can make and sell all the shoes that are needed.[65]

In response to Justice Brandeis's dissent defending the Oklahoma statute as a legislative experiment,[66] Sutherland maintained, "There are certain essentials of liberty with which the state is not entitled to dispense in the interest of experiments." No "theory of experimentation in censorship" could justify interference with freedom of the press; "[t]he opportunity to apply one's labor and skill in an ordinary occupation. . . is no less entitled to protection," he concluded.[67]

Freedom of Dealing

Finally, yet another part of the economic liberty protected by the due process clause was the common-law right of refusal to deal. Thomas M. Cooley, in his 19th-century treatise on tort law, described the right in this way:

> It is a part of every man's civil rights that he be left at liberty to refuse business relations with any person whomsoever, whether the refusal rests upon reason, or is the result of whim, caprice, prejudice, or malice. With his reasons neither the public nor third persons have any legal concern. It is also his right to have business relations with any one with whom he can make contracts, and if he is wrongfully deprived of this right by others, he is entitled to redress.[68]

In early 20th-century American law, the right of refusal to deal was subject to few restrictions outside of antitrust legislation. Further restrictions, in the form of unfair trade practices legislation and, ironically, "civil rights" legislation (such as anti-discrimination statutes), had not yet curtailed this broad common-law right.[69]

The Court's decisions striking down prohibitions of "yellow-dog" contracts in *Adair v. United States* and *Coppage v. Kansas*, briefly discussed earlier in this section, can best be understood in this context. The statute at issue in *Adair* made it a federal crime for a railroad or other common carrier engaged in interstate transportation, or any of its officers or agents, to require any employee or any person seeking employment, as a condition of such employment, to enter into any agreement not to become or remain a member of any labor organization. It also made it criminal for such employers to threaten any employee with loss of employment or to discriminate against any employee because of his membership in a labor organization.[70] Writing the opinion for the six-justice majority of the Court holding the federal statute to be unconstitutional,[71] Justice John Marshall Harlan emphasized that employers had no less liberty of contract than did employees, and that this liberty included the freedom of either party to set conditions:

> [I]t is not within the functions of government—at least in the absence of contract between the parties—to compel any person in the course of his business and against his will to accept or retain the personal services of another, or to compel any person, against his will, to perform personal services for another. The right of a person to sell his labor upon such terms as he deems proper is, in its essence, the same as the right of the purchaser of labor to prescribe the conditions upon which he will accept such labor from the person offering to sell it. So the right of the employé to quit the service of the employer, for whatever reason, is the same as the right of the employer, for whatever reason, to dispense with the services of such employé.

"In all such particulars," Harlan stressed, "the employer and the employé have equality of right, and any legislation that disturbs that equality is an arbitrary interference with the liberty of contract which no government can legally justify in a free land."[72]

The right of refusal to deal was, in effect, the right to discriminate, on whatever grounds a party to a contract chose—whether rational or, as Cooley had written, as a result of "whim, caprice, prejudice, or malice." It was, in other words, the right to do that which modern anti-discrimination laws, such as the Civil Rights Act of 1964, forbid. As one modern libertarian legal scholar has put it, "if any anti-discrimination laws could have been passed" before 1937, "they would have fallen. . . to the same challenges that doomed the forbidden labor statutes."[73] Similarly, this aspect of liberty of contract would have doomed labor laws like the National Labor Relations Act of 1935, which "subordinates the worker's right of contract to the majority vote of his colleagues," as one modern commentator aptly describes it.[74]

Origins of the Right to Privacy

Given that the orthodox view has closely and repeatedly associated the Supreme Court's liberty-of-contract jurisprudence with cases like *Lochner*, modern students of constitutional law often do not realize that liberty of contract reached well beyond the realm of labor or business regulation. Among its frequently overlooked aspects was the right now known as the right to privacy.

Despite the popular assumption that the Court's protection of privacy as a fundamental right began with its 1965 decision in *Griswold v. Connecticut*,[75] some scholars have recognized that, long before the *Griswold* Court attempted to derive privacy rights from the "penumbras" that emanated from particular Bill of Rights guarantees,[76] the *Lochner*-era Court had protected what today is regarded as an important aspect of privacy, so-called parental rights. As one scholar has observed, "[t]he right to privacy achieved constitutional status in two cases of the *Lochner* era, the only substantive due process decisions that survived the 1937 revolution."[77] The two cases referred to were the so-called school cases from the 1920s, *Meyer v. Nebraska* and *Pierce v. Society of Sisters*.[78] Although these two cases are still frequently cited today as the earliest precedents for the right of privacy—and particularly for protecting the freedom of parents to determine the upbringing and education of their children—the modern reconceptualization of *Meyer* and *Pierce* as "privacy" cases distorts their true nature as liberty-of-contract decisions.

Meyer concerned one of the United States' first "English-only" laws, a statute passed by the Nebraska legislature that prohibited teaching children who had not yet passed the eighth grade in any language other than English. It was enacted following World War I, during a time when anti-German prejudice was at its height in America, and targeted Nebraska's large German-speaking immigrant population.[79] The plaintiff in error, Meyer, was a teacher in a parochial school who had been convicted of violating the statute by teaching the subject of reading in the German language to a 10-year-old boy. Writing the opinion for a near-unanimous Court,[80] Justice James C. McReynolds—ironically, the justice who has the reputation of being the *Lochner*-era Court's worst "reactionary"[81]—described the liberty guaranteed by the Fourteenth Amendment in broad terms:

> Without doubt, it denotes not merely freedom from bodily restraint but also the right of the individual to contract, to engage in any of the common occupations of life, to acquire useful knowledge, to marry, establish a home and bring up children, to worship God according to the dictates of his own conscience, and generally to enjoy those privileges long recognized at common law as essential to the orderly pursuit of happiness by free men.

He then held that both Mr. Meyer's "right. . . to teach" the German language and "the right of parents to engage him so to instruct their children" were within the liberty protected by the amendment and were abridged by the statute.[82]

In reaching this conclusion, Justice McReynolds rejected the argument that the Nebraska statute was a valid police regulation, finding "no adequate foundation for the suggestion that the purpose was to protect the child's health by limiting his mental activities." Indeed, he added, "[i]t is well known that proficiency in a foreign language seldom comes to one not instructed at an early age, and experience shows that this is not injurious to the health, morals, or understanding of the ordinary child." McReynolds also found that the Nebraska law was an unconstitutional attempt "materially to interfere with the calling of modern language teachers," as well as with the "opportunities of pupils to acquire knowledge" and "the power of parents to control the education of their own."[83]

The law at issue in *Pierce* was also the product of bigotry. The Compulsory Education Act passed by the Oregon legislature in 1922 required all children between the ages of 8 and 16 to attend public schools; enacted at the insistence of the Ku Klux Klan, the law aimed to eliminate private and parochial schools in the state.[84] The owners of two schools—the Society of Sisters, a Roman Catholic charitable group, and Hill Military Academy, a private, for-profit boys military school—brought suit to enjoin enforcement of the law.[85] Affirming the lower court's grant of a preliminary injunction, the Court, in another opinion written by Justice McReynolds, followed "the doctrine of *Meyer v. Nebraska*" in holding that the Oregon law "unreasonably interferes with the liberty of parents and guardians to direct the upbringing and education of children under their control." McReynolds then added a stridently libertarian statement that is often quoted in modern case law as a broad explanation of parents' rights to control their children's education:

> The fundamental theory of liberty upon which all governments in this Union repose excludes any general power of the state to standardize its children by forcing them to accept instruction from public teachers only. The child is not the mere creature of the state; those who nurture him and direct his destiny have the right, coupled with the high duty, to recognize and prepare him for additional obligations.[86]

What is often omitted from modern summaries of the decision, however, is McReynolds's explanation for the Court's holding affirming the injunction that had been sought by the schools, barring enforcement of the law. The plaintiffs, the Society of Sisters and Hill Military Academy, were "threatened with destruction through the unwarranted compulsion which [the state of Oregon was] exercising over present and prospective patrons of their schools," the Court found. Thus, the injunction was properly issued to prevent irreparable injury and to protect the plaintiffs against "arbitrary, unreasonable and unlawful interference with their patrons and the consequent destruction of their business and property."[87]

The post-1937 reconceptualization of *Meyer* and *Pierce* as privacy cases, or cases concerning only parents' rights, misrepresents the full scope of the liberty that the Court protected in those two decisions from the 1920s. That right to liberty did not only include the right of parents to control the education and upbringing of their children; it also included, and primarily so in light of the real parties in interest in the cases, the right of teachers to pursue their occupation and the right of private schools to engage in business, which were equally important aspects of liberty. Indeed, it could be argued, the only way effectively to protect the parents' rights to control their children's education would be to protect the educators' freedom to enter into contracts with the parents. Thus, the foundation that *Meyer* and *Pierce* still provide today for the modern constitutional right to privacy is, in reality, the last remaining vestige of the Court's pre-1937 liberty-of-contract jurisprudence.

Other Forgotten Aspects of the Right

Finally, thanks to the orthodox view's caricature of liberty of contract as a narrow form of economic liberty, still other aspects of the right have been overlooked by constitutional scholars and historians, including its use to combat de jure racism, or racism established by law, such as compulsory racial segregation laws.

The Supreme Court's 1917 decision in *Buchanan v. Warley*[88] illustrates a noteworthy forgotten episode in the history of the Court's protection of liberty of contract—one that is forgotten, or overlooked, because it does not accord with the caricature of *Lochner*-era jurisprudence presented by most legal historians and constitutional scholars.[89] In *Buchanan*, the Court used the due process clause of the Fourteenth Amendment to declare unconstitutional a Louisville, Kentucky, ordinance mandating racial segregation in housing. The ordinance in question was titled

> An ordinance to prevent conflict and ill-feeling between the white and colored races in the city of Louisville, and to preserve the public peace and promote the general welfare by making reasonable provisions requiring, as far as practicable, the use of separate blocks for residences, places of abode and places of assembly by white and colored people respectively.

As summarized by Justice William R. Day in his opinion for the Court, the ordinance prohibited persons of color from moving into or occupying "any house upon any block upon which a greater number of houses are occupied as residences, places of abode, or places of public assembly by white people than are occupied. . . by colored people." In short, as Justice Day succinctly characterized the ordinance: "This interdiction is based wholly upon color; simply that and nothing more. In effect, premises situated as are those in question in the so-called white block are effectively debarred from sale to persons of color, because if sold they cannot be occupied by the purchaser nor by him sold to another of the same color."[90]

At the time, the equal protection clause of the Fourteenth Amendment did not prohibit such de jure segregation. That was because the controlling case law was the Court's infamous 1896 decision in *Plessy v. Ferguson* in which it had upheld a Louisiana law requiring separate railway carriages for white and black persons as a "reasonable regulation" not in violation of the clause. As summarized by Justice Day, segregation per se did not violate the equal protection clause, under the principle of *Plessy v. Ferguson*, because "[racial] classification of accommodation was permitted upon the basis of equality for both races"—in other words, because segregation laws applied equally to both black and white persons.[91]

In his opinion for the unanimous Court,[92] however, Justice Day further noted that the equal protection clause was not the only provision of the Fourteenth Amendment that limited the police power of the states: "We think this attempt to prevent the alienation of the property in question to a person of color was not a legitimate exercise of the police power of the State, and is in direct violation of the fundamental law enacted in the Fourteenth Amendment of the Constitution preventing state interference with property rights except by due process of law." "Property is more than the mere thing which a person owns," he declared; "it includes the right to acquire, use, and dispose of it"—which also entailed (although he did not explicitly say so) the freedom to enter into contracts for that purpose.[93]

In thus affirming the due process clause's protection of individual rights, Justice Day also explicitly rejected all the police-power rationales that Kentucky had argued in support of state-enforced segregation, including the state's overtly racist justification that the segregation law promoted the "maintenance of the purity of the races."[94] In rejecting these arguments, the Court declined to broaden the scope of police power beyond its traditional bounds, holding that none of the state's justifications for the segregation law legitimately trumped the basic individual right at issue in the case: "the civil right of a white man to dispose of his property if he saw fit to do so to a person of color and of a colored person to make such disposition to a white person."[95]

The reaction to the *Buchanan* decision was quite interesting, revealing much about the leading conflicts in early 20th-century American jurisprudence. Moorfield Storey, the cofounder and president of the National Association for the Advancement of Colored People who argued the case before the Court,[96] was overjoyed, as were other civil-rights advocates and the African-American media. Storey wrote to *Nation* editor and NAACP cofounder Oswald Garrison Villard that *Buchanan* was "the most important decision that has been made since the *Dred Scott* case, and happily this time it is the right way."[97] By contrast, law review commentators were generally displeased with the *Buchanan* decision—with some writers in prominent law journals overtly hostile to the Court's overturning of a segregation law, which they thought was amply justified by Progressivism and sociological jurisprudence. For example, a student comment in the *Yale Law Journal* attacked the Court for subordinating "the interests of the public in race segregation" to the private interests of "landowners whose power of alienation segregation would restrict." A Michigan law student similarly complained that the Court had ignored "all this direct and emphatic expression of opinion that the ordinance was reasonably necessary and conducive to public welfare." And the author of a 1934 article in the *Michigan Law Review* criticized *Buchanan* for the Court's failure to give "some conscious appraisal of the social desirability of segregation by legal device."[98]

Although one might expect modern scholars to applaud at least the result of the decision and to regard it as a landmark victory for individual rights, *Buchanan v. Warley* has been largely ignored in modern American constitutional law scholarship. Remarkably, constitutional law casebooks and constitutional history textbooks fail to mention the case at all, even when discussing the history of segregation laws or of the Supreme Court's interpretation of the Fourteenth Amendment during the period between *Plessy v. Ferguson* and the Court's rejection of *Plessy* (as applied to public schools) in its landmark 1954 decision in *Brown v. Board of Education*. One might easily assume that a Supreme Court decision declaring segregation laws unconstitutional from the World War I era—a period of the Court's history not generally known for its protection of civil liberties—would be regarded as a landmark decision. But because the Court struck down the Louisville, Kentucky, ordinance on substantive due process grounds, rather than equal protection grounds, most modern constitutional scholars and legal historians ignore the *Buchanan* decision. The reason, as suggested above, is that it does not fit their stereotype of *Lochner*-era substantive due process jurisprudence.

As some modern scholars have suggested, a full appreciation for the significance of *Buchanan* sheds new light on both *Lochner*-era jurisprudence and the increasingly influential Progressive movement that was challenging it in the early 20th century. *Buchanan* caused the end of explicit de jure residential segregation in the United States.[99] Despite the limited effect of its direct holding,[100] it may be credited with helping save the country, or at least the South, from instituting South African–style apartheid, as legal scholar David Bernstein has argued.[101]

More broadly, *Buchanan* suggests a different approach that the Supreme Court might have taken with regard to the problem of racism in America—one that perhaps more closely approximated the "color-blind Constitution" model proposed by the first Justice Harlan in his famous dissent in *Plessy v. Ferguson*. In that dissenting opinion, Harlan maintained that "[o]ur Constitution is color-blind, and neither knows nor tolerates classes among citizens. . . . The law regards man as man, and takes no account of his surroundings or of his color when his civil rights as guaranteed by the supreme law of the land are involved."[102] As noted earlier, the Court's protection of liberty of contract guaranteed an individual's right of refusal to deal and, therefore, in a sense, the right of individuals to discriminate. Had the Court not repudiated its liberty-of-contract jurisprudence in 1937, civil-rights legislation today would have been of a fundamentally different character, without labor laws and anti-discrimination laws in education and employment—laws that put the government into the position of classifying persons by race and, in the eyes of critics of such laws, engaging in "reverse discrimination." With the courts broadly protecting an individual's freedom of contract under the Constitution's due process clauses, individualism and free choice would have replaced collective action and government coercion in dealing with problems of racism and other forms of bigotry.

Along with other nonstereotypical liberty-of-contract decisions, such as *Meyer* and *Pierce*, the *Buchanan* decision shows that the Court's protection of individual liberty and property rights, through a substantive application of the due process clauses, "often safeguarded the interests of vulnerable and powerless segments of society," as legal historian James W. Ely Jr. has aptly summarized the jurisprudence.[103] While so-called Progressive reformers were advocating not only segregation laws and laws that would "protect" women out of their jobs but also a wide variety of new forms of legal restrictions on both economic and personal freedoms—all in the name of protecting "public welfare" and all justified by new sociological theories of jurisprudence—conservative judges during the *Lochner* era were able to halt, at least partially and temporarily, the Progressives' dangerous expansion of the police power by enforcing traditional limitations on government power and guarantees of liberty and property rights.[104]

4. The Demise of Liberty of Contract

The mythology that historians and constitutional scholars have created to support the orthodox view of *Lochner*-era jurisprudence also includes the story most frequently told to explain the demise of liberty of contract. That story, at the heart of the "laissez-faire constitutionalism" caricature, is that the right "activist" judges supposedly invented in 1897 was killed 40 years later by a different group of judges, who atoned for their predecessors' jurisprudential sins by accepting social "reality"—the reality, that is, of the 20th-century regulatory state.[1]

What doomed liberty of contract, however, was not the judicial acceptance of "reality," as legal realists argued. Rather, it failed because of jurisprudential weaknesses in the doctrine itself, as applied by the courts. And the judges who overturned *Lochner*-era jurisprudence were not following what scholars have called "neutral principles" of constitutional adjudication.[2] In fact, they were ignoring principles—the principles of the Constitution. They were judicial activists who abdicated their twin duties of enforcing constitutional limits on government power and protecting the fundamental rights of individuals—all in order to advance the New Deal policy agenda.

Cracks in the Foundation: The Failure of *Lochner*-Era Jurisprudence

The coalescence of several factors explains why the Supreme Court's protection of liberty of contract as a fundamental constitutional right was so short-lived. Three factors were most important: first, the changing membership of the Court; second, the standard of review used by the justices to protect liberty of contract; and third, significant changes in the law, both in constitutional law principles and in theories of jurisprudence, during the first few decades of the 20th century. Each of these factors deserves attention.

The Changing Composition of the Court

The first factor is the composition of the Supreme Court itself. Noting how changes in the membership of the Court affected its substantive due process review of legislation, some scholars have suggested that the so-called *Lochner* era really consisted of three different eras.[3] In each era, a different group of justices gave liberty of contract differing degrees of protection, both in scope and in consistency.

The first period began with the *Allgeyer* decision and ended in about 1911; in this period, the Court was dominated by what David Bernstein has called "moderate Lochnerians." During this period, the two most libertarian justices of the entire era, Rufus Peckham, and David Brewer, sat on the Court, but as Bernstein points out, "with the notable exception of *Lochner* itself, they rarely cobbled together a majority for their views." Both were off the Court by 1911, as were the moderately libertarian Justices Brown, Fuller, and Harlan.[4]

During the second period, lasting approximately from 1911 to 1923, the Court, while not explicitly repudiating *Lochner*, generally refused to expand liberty of contract by applying it to new contexts, and at times seemed to limit the doctrine. Over this period, "*Lochner* skeptics," relatively speaking, appointed by Presidents Theodore Roosevelt, Taft, and Wilson, helped comprise a new majority that was disinclined to use the Fourteenth Amendment to strike down state legislation while frequently asserting a doctrine of presumed constitutionality of laws.[5]

Finally, from 1923 (the year of the *Adkins* decision) until the mid-1930s, the Court was dominated by justices who revived liberty of contract by expanding the doctrine and limiting the power of government in both economic and noneconomic contexts. "By the early 1920s," Bernstein notes, "Harding appointees Taft, Sutherland, Sanford, and Butler, joined by conservative Taft and Wilson appointees Van Devanter and McReynolds, and *Lochner* holdover McKenna, took control of the Court." Bernstein continues, "The 'Four Horsemen'—McReynolds, Sutherland, Van Devanter, and Butler—dominated the Court through the early 1930s, joined by other Justices, especially Taft and Sanford." Although favorably inclined toward liberty of contract, the Four Horsemen nevertheless accepted a broader scope for the police power than did Peckham and Brewer. Indeed, legal scholar Barry Cushman, citing dozens of cases, has concluded that they "upheld a simply enormous array of state police power regulations."[6] It was this majority of justices, dominated by the Four Horsemen, that struck down federal New Deal legislation in the early 1930s, so infuriating President Franklin Roosevelt that in early 1937, he proposed his infamous "Court-packing" plan as a way of achieving a new, pro–New Deal majority on the Court. Despite its reputation, however, the pre-1937 Court's majority was fragile, frequently deciding key cases by a five-to-four vote.

The changing composition of the Supreme Court is especially important when considered in light of the justices' dubious commitment to constitutional protection of individual liberty in the early 20th century. From the time of Progressive-Era historian Charles Warren to the present day, many scholars have observed, with ample empirical support, that the Court's protection of liberty of contract was a relatively minor part of its early 20th-century constitutional jurisprudence, and that the Court upheld many more state laws challenged under the Fourteenth Amendment than it struck down.[7] One modern scholar who has done a quantitative analysis of *Lochner*-era decisions, focused on the Court's substantive due process review of social and economic regulations during the 1897-1937 period, has concluded that liberty-of-contract decisions "were simply one category of substantive due process decision—and not the numerically most significant category either."[8] Thus, a full account of the story of the demise of liberty of contract as a fundamental right must take into account the doctrine's relatively minor role in the Court's body of decisions in the early 20th century.

A General Rule Riddled with Exceptions

A second, equally important factor explaining the eventual demise of *Lochner*-era substantive due process jurisprudence was the type of protection that the Court gave to liberty of contract. This was the moderate paradigm for the protection of liberty, with its moderately stringent means-ends analysis, discussed in chapter 2. Because liberty of contract in practice, as actually protected by the Supreme Court, was nothing more than a general presumption in favor of liberty, it was a right that was apparently riddled with exceptions.

In his opinion for the Court in *Adkins v. Children's Hospital*, Justice Sutherland observed, "There is, of course, no such thing as absolute freedom of contract. It is subject to a great variety of restraints." He added that "freedom of contract is, nevertheless, the general rule and restraint the exception," and that laws abridging this freedom "can be justified only by the existence of exceptional circumstances." Prior to his analysis of the District of Columbia minimum-wage law involved in that case, he identified several categories of what he called "exceptions to the general rule forbidding legislative interference with freedom of contract." Sutherland's list of such broad categories showed just how far-reaching those "exceptions" were.[9]

One of those categories—which proved to be especially troublesome for Sutherland in *Adkins*, as discussed in chapter 3—was that of statutes fixing the hours of labor. Both before and after *Lochner*, with its decisions in *Holden v. Hardy* (1898) and *Muller v. Oregon* (1908), the Court had upheld maximum-hours laws that restricted the freedom of contract of particular classes of workers—namely, workers in extraordinarily dangerous occupations and women workers—as valid exercises of the police power to protect health, even though these laws involved the health of those particular classes of workers rather than the health of the general public. The line that the Court apparently had drawn in *Lochner*, preserving liberty-of-contract rights for male workers in ordinary trades, appears to have virtually vanished in the Court's decision in a 1917 case, *Bunting v. Oregon*, a decision that many commentators have seen as effectively overruling *Lochner*.[10]

Bunting concerned an Oregon statute that prohibited the employment of anyone, except watchmen or employees engaged in emergency repairs, in a mill, factory, or manufacturing establishment for more than 10 hours a day, with a provision permitting work up to 13 hours a day if the employer paid time-and-a-half for the extra hours. In a short opinion by Justice McKenna, the Court upheld the law as a valid health regulation.[11] Looking ahead, *Bunting* signaled that a majority of the justices, during the period between the two world wars, were unwilling to question any exercises of the police power that seemed to protect workers' health—even if legislation effectively barred certain classes of persons from particular occupations. Just one year after *Adkins*, for example, the Court upheld a law banning night work for women under the rationale that women have weaker constitutions than men.[12]

Police-power regulations protecting health or safety constituted a broad category of exceptions to the general rule of liberty of contract, or personal freedom generally, that extended far beyond the cases upholding hours laws listed by Sutherland in his *Adkins* opinion. It was under the rationale of protecting public health that the Court had upheld a Massachusetts law compelling citizens to be vaccinated against smallpox.[13] Moreover, another important line of cases concerning workers' health, safety, and welfare—cases often overlooked in standard treatments of the *Lochner* era—upheld workers' compensation laws and other measures regulating employee recovery for on-the-job injuries.[14]

Two other broad categories of exceptions to the general rule of freedom of contract cited by Justice Sutherland in *Adkins* concerned "statutes relating to contracts for the performance of public work" and "statutes prescribing the character, methods, and time for payment of wages."[15] In the first line of cases, the Court based its rulings on "the right of the government to prescribe the conditions upon which it will permit work of a public character to be done for it."[16] In the second, the Court viewed the regulations as being aimed at preventing fraud or other abuses rather than at the substance of the deal.[17] The fraud rationale that enabled such cases to pass muster meant that the Court was upholding some forms of "social legislation"—laws aimed at protecting workers—without having to recognize inequality of bargaining strength as "a legitimate justification for legislative interposition between employer and employee," as one legal historian has put it.[18]

The final, and perhaps most important, category of exceptions listed by Justice Sutherland in *Adkins* was that of businesses "affected with a public interest." As discussed in chapter 3, the Court in its 1923 *Wolff Packing* decision had tried to articulate a clear standard to determine whether a business truly was affected with a public interest and therefore was subject to government regulation, even of the price terms of its contracts. Applying the standard, the Court in a series of opinions written by Justice Sutherland in the late 1920s struck down laws fixing maximum prices for services or commodities sold to the public, holding that the businesses involved in those cases were not affected with a public interest.[19] Justice Stone dissented in two of the cases, finding justification for price regulations in some sort of market failure.[20]

Although the Court would continue to enforce limits defining businesses "affected with a public interest"—striking down the market entry restrictions in its 1932 *New State Ice* decision, with Sutherland again writing the Court's opinion—changes in the membership of the Court helped pave the way for abandonment of the doctrine altogether.[21] In *Nebbia v. New York*, a bare majority of five justices upheld a Depression-era New York statute that created a state Milk Control Board with authority to fix minimum prices for the retail sale of milk. One of the Court's newer justices, Owen Roberts, wrote the opinion for the majority, declaring that "there is no closed class or category of businesses affected with a public interest." Virtually any business could be "subject to control for the public good," and "upon proper occasion and by appropriate measures the state may regulate a business in any of its aspects, including the prices to be charged for the products or commodities it sells," Roberts declared.[22] Moreover, Roberts's opinion for the Court seemed to announce a new standard of review in substantive due process cases, at least those involving government regulation of business—a standard that seemed to turn on its head the general presumption in favor of liberty:

> So far as the requirement of due process is concerned, and in the absence of other constitutional restriction, a state is free to adopt whatever economic policy may reasonably be deemed to promote public welfare, and to enforce that policy by legislation adapted to its purpose. The courts are without authority either to declare such policy, or, when it is declared by the legislature, to override it. . . . The Constitution does not secure to anyone liberty to conduct his business in such fashion as to inflict injury upon the public at large, or upon any substantial group of people. Price control, like any other form of regulation, is unconstitutional only if arbitrary, discriminatory, or demonstrably irrelevant to the policy the legislature is free to adopt, and hence an unnecessary and unwarranted interference with individual liberty.[23]

Thus, with the *Nebbia* decision in the mid-1930s, the "public interest" category proved to be the proverbial exception that swallowed up the rule.

One additional broad category of cases, not cited in Sutherland's *Adkins* opinion, also deserves mention. These are decisions that involved exercises of police power that, as seen by the Court, fit within the traditional exercises of the police power, including the protection of public morality. As noted in chapter 2, one of the critically important ways in which the Court's protection of liberty of contract can be distinguished from a true laissez-faire constitutionalism is its general tolerance for paternalistic legislation, particularly where morals are concerned. Thus, as one modern scholar has summed it up, "liberty of contract was consistently limited by the invocation of common law doctrines that restricted individual freedom for the perceived social good," with the Court upholding such "morals" laws as bans on lotteries and other forms of gambling, Sunday-closing laws, and laws regulating and even prohibiting alcohol consumption.[24]

With liberty of contract resting on such shaky jurisprudential grounds, it perhaps should not be surprising that the Court ceased protecting it as a fundamental right by the late 1930s. Near the end of his *Adkins* opinion, Justice Sutherland again stressed that "[t]he liberty of the individual to do as he pleases, even in innocent matters, is not absolute." He added that liberty "must frequently yield to the common good, and the line beyond which the power of interference may not be pressed is neither definite nor unalterable but may be made to move within limits not well-defined, and with changing need and circumstance."[25] The so-called New Deal Revolution marked the Court's redrawing of that line in response to changed political, as well as jurisprudential, circumstances.

Legal Realism and the Expanding Scope of the Police Power

Finally, another important factor explaining the failure of *Lochner*-era jurisprudence involved broader changes in the law itself. Two significant developments in constitutional law and jurisprudence in the early 20th century also help explain the eventual—and, perhaps, the inevitable—demise of liberty of contract: the expanding scope of the police power and the rise of "legal realism."

Contemporaneous with the Supreme Court's inconsistent protection of liberty of contract during the first part of the *Lochner* era, a fundamental shift took place in the way the American legal culture defined the police power. The traditional definition, expressed in terms of the *sic utere* formulation and the fairly well-defined categories of protecting public health, safety, and morality, had begun to be replaced with a far looser, less well-delineated conception. Just a few years after publication of the second edition of Christopher Tiedeman's treatise, and a year after Tiedeman's death, an influential new work on the police power, written by Ernst Freund, was published.

Freund defined the police power as "the power of promoting the public welfare by restraining and regulating the use of liberty and property."[26] Freund viewed the *sic utere* maxim as merely one segment of the police power, those "self-evident limitations upon liberty and property in the interest of peace, safety, health, order and morals. . . punishable at common law as nuisances." But, added Freund, "no community confines its care of the public welfare to the enforcement of the principles of the common law":

> The state. . . exercises its compulsory powers for the prevention and anticipation of wrong by narrowing common law rights through conventional restraints and positive regulations which are not confined to the prohibition of wrongful acts. It is this latter kind of state control which constitutes the essence of the police power. The maxim of this power is that every individual must submit to such restraints in the exercise of his liberty or of his rights of property as may be required to remove or reduce the danger of the abuse of these rights on the part of those who are unskillful, careless, or unscrupulous.[27]

Thus, unlike Tiedeman, who confined the legitimate scope of the police power to the enforcement of the *sic utere* principle, Freund stressed that "the essence of the police power" was not confined to the prohibition of wrongful acts. For Freund, the police power must be "elastic," or "capable of development"; it was not "a fixed quantity" but the expression of social, economic, and political conditions."[28] Not surprisingly, Progressive reformers who championed social legislation in the early 20th century embraced Freund's new, elastic conception of the police power, with its amorphous "public welfare" rationale.[29]

A second critically important change in American legal culture was also taking place in the early 20th century: the shift from "formalism" to "realism" in the law.[30] The rise of legal realism was made possible by the acceptance of sociological theories of jurisprudence by a new generation of legal scholars, including such Progressive reformers as Roscoe Pound and Louis Brandeis.

Pound, one of the early leaders in the realist movement, was a student of the German sociological school of jurisprudence; his early writings criticized 19th-century jurisprudence as being too "mechanical" and extolled the new sociological theories of the law as "pragmatic."[31]

With the rise of legal realism and sociological jurisprudence, the old jurisprudence of natural law and natural rights, which had informed America's founding generation and the original principles of liberty and property rights they had safeguarded in the Constitution, had become obsolete. Only the oldest generation of lawyers and judges in the early 20th century—men like Justice George Sutherland—had been exposed to theories of natural law and rights in their study for the bar.[32] Their eventual passing marked the death of natural rights jurisprudence in American law; the newer generations of lawyers and judges would all be legal realists. Objective principles in the law would be replaced by legal subjectivism in jurisprudence.

A New Paradigm: The "New Deal Revolution" of 1937

For more than 70 years, scholars have recognized the significance of what they call the "New Deal Revolution" of 1937. Indeed, it has become commonplace for historians and constitutional scholars to describe 1937 as the year marking a constitutional "revolution" and to explain the Supreme Court's apparently sudden reversal that year as a reaction to President Roosevelt's infamous plan to "pack" the Court— the famous "switch in time that saved nine."[33] Although most constitutional historians now recognize that the 1937 "revolution" was not prompted by political pressure—for the critical shift in particular justices' votes had occurred before Roosevelt's Court-packing plan was announced—they nevertheless continue to use the popular "switch in time" expression to describe the shift that occurred in 1937.

To explain that "switch," scholars generally have recognized three distinct voting blocks on the Supreme Court in the early 1930s: the conservative "Four Horsemen" (Justices George Sutherland, James C. McReynolds, Willis Van Devanter, and Pierce Butler), who are generally described as anti–New Deal (hence, the derogatory name given them by pro–New Deal journalists); the three "liberal," or pro–New Deal, justices (Louis D. Brandeis, Benjamin Cardozo, and Harlan F. Stone); and the two moderate, or "swing" vote, justices

(Chief Justice Charles Evan Hughes and Justice Owen Roberts). It was in 1937 that the latter two members of the Court, who previously had often joined the Four Horsemen, permanently switched their votes, siding instead with the three liberal justices, creating a new five-justice majority on the Court.[34] Some scholars, in dispelling the "switch in time that saved nine" myth, have emphasized that the critical shift in the views of the swing voters, Justice Roberts and Chief Justice Hughes, really occurred prior to 1937, well before President Roosevelt had announced his Court-packing plan.[35] Indeed, as we shall see, it may be argued persuasively that the death knell of the Court's liberty-of-contract jurisprudence was sounded three years before 1937, with the two significant decisions of 1934, *Nebbia* and *Blaisdell*. Nevertheless, it remains common for scholars to regard 1937 as the critical watershed year for the Court's jurisprudential change, especially because it was in 1937 and 1938 that the Court articulated the constitutional theory that would guide its decisions thereafter.

The shift that occurred, apparently so suddenly and dramatically in the spring of 1937, came in a series of five-to-four decisions in which both Chief Justice Hughes and Justice Roberts joined the majority upholding New Deal legislation.[36] The shift was actually twofold. First, with regard to the scope of federal power, the Court abandoned its previous holdings limiting Congress's powers, in effect eviscerating the Tenth Amendment as a fundamental rule of interpretation. Before 1937, the Court had cited the Tenth Amendment and the rule it confirmed—that the federal government had limited powers, enumerated in the Constitution—in order to reserve either powers to the states or rights to individuals. In 1937 and the years following, however, the Court allowed Congress to assume virtually limitless powers, especially under the commerce clause and the so-called spending power.[37] Second, with regard to limitations on both state and federal legislative powers through the substantive use of the due process clauses, the Court in the landmark case *West Coast Hotel v. Parrish*[38] abandoned its protection of liberty of contract as a fundamental right. And a year later, in *Carolene Products v. United States*,[39] the Court adopted the minimal "rational basis" test for economic legislation,[40] a test that in the eyes of many commentators established a "double standard" in modern constitutional law, affording less protection for property rights and economic liberty than for other, noneconomic rights.[41]

Although obviously it is only the second aspect of the New Deal Revolution that is directly relevant here, both aspects are interrelated and illustrate the fundamental nature of the Court's shift. Under the guise of judicial restraint, the majority of the justices on the Court—reflecting their own policy preferences favoring the New Deal—discarded long-established constitutional precedents in order to uphold the validity of the modern regulatory and welfare state. Chief Justice Hughes's opinion for the Court in *West Coast Hotel*, for example, was based on assumptions about the "evils of the 'sweating system'" and policy arguments in favor of minimum-wage laws. Hughes, a former Progressive Republican governor of New York, wrote:

> The exploitation of a class of workers who are in an unequal position with respect to bargaining power and are thus relatively defenseless against the denial of a living wage. . . casts a direct burden for their support on the community. What these workers lose in wages the taxpayers are called upon to pay. . . . The community is not bound to provide what is in effect a subsidy for unconscionable employers.

As legal scholar Richard Epstein has shown, the passage is replete not only with dubious policy arguments but with unsound economic theories.[42] In contrast to Hughes, Justice Sutherland in his dissenting opinion criticized the majority for amending the Constitution "in the guise of interpretation," arguing that the meaning of the Constitution "does not change with the ebb and flow of economic events."[43]

Contrary to the orthodox story about *Lochner*-era jurisprudence, it seems that the dissenting justices, the Four Horsemen who had supported the Court's protection of liberty of contract, were adhering to "neutral principles"—that is, established, objective principles of constitutional law. It was the new majority, comprised of the Court's "liberal" justices, now joined by the moderate swing votes of Hughes and Roberts, who seemed to be the judicial activists. Indeed, notwithstanding the prevalent view that judicial restraint is neutral,[44] it is not the outcome of a case—whether the court strikes down a law as unconstitutional or upholds it against a constitutional challenge—that determines whether the decision reflects judicial activism. As discussed in chapter 2, judges can be just as "activist" when they defer to the legislature and uphold a law as when they declare it to be unconstitutional. What makes a decision activist is the reasoning used by the judge in support of the decision.

Hughes's reasoning in support of the Washington minimum-wage statute at issue in *West Coast Hotel* was based on policy arguments. It better fit the stereotype alleged by Holmes's dissent in *Lochner*—a case decided on an "economic theory," he said—than did *Lochner*, *Adkins*, or any of the Court's other liberty-of-contract decisions. Thus, rather than criticizing the old Court for protecting liberty of contract based on "Mr. Herbert Spencer's *Social Statics*," it would be fairer to criticize the 1937 Court for abandoning liberty of contract based on, say, "Mr. Ernst Freund's *Standards of American Legislation*" or one of the economics texts of Henry W. Farnam, for it was the reasoning of such advocates of social legislation and government regulation of business as Freund and Farnam that the liberal justices of the 1930s seemed to be following.[45] Indeed, one might further argue that the notion of the modern, post-1937 Court's "neutrality" in constitutional adjudication concerning economic matters is a myth—that the jurisprudential position taken by modern liberal constitutionalists is definitely not neutral but rather is based on a social or economic theory that favors government regulation of the competitive process, despite the Constitution's clear limits on government control over such matters.[46]

Although most scholars recognize 1937 as the critical year for both sides of the Court's "New Deal Revolution," the shift did not suddenly happen in 1937. Earlier signs of the change in the Court's commerce clause jurisprudence, for example, can be traced back to very early in the 20th century,[47] if not before. The Court's virtually open-ended view of Congress's commerce power after 1937 was anticipated by a series of decisions broadening the scope of congressional powers, going back before the turn of the century to the Court's earliest decisions enforcing the Interstate Commerce Act of 1887 and the Sherman Antitrust Act of 1890.

Regarding more specifically the Court's jurisprudence protecting liberty of contract, it seems that the critical year marking a turning point toward the Court's eventual evisceration of the right was 1934, when the Court decided *Nebbia v. New York*. As noted in the previous section, Justice Roberts's opinion for the Court announced a new standard for substantive due process review of legislation regulating business. Under that new standard, according to Roberts, "the state is free to adopt whatever economic policy may reasonably be deemed to promote public welfare, and to enforce that policy by legislation adapted to its purpose."[48] That standard, in its practical application, seems nearly identical to the minimal "rational basis" test the Court announced in its *Carolene Products* decision a few years later—prompting some scholars to suggest that it was *Nebbia*, rather than *West Coast Hotel*, that marked the end of the Court's old substantive due process jurisprudence.[49]

Another significant decision from the 1930s suggests a critical shift by the Court in the years before 1937. In the same year *Nebbia* was decided, the Court in *Home Building & Loan Association v. Blaisdell* also upheld, by the same five-justice majority, a Minnesota statute allowing debtors greater time and flexibility in meeting their mortgage obligations. The Court's dismissal of the Article I, Section 10, contract clause challenge to the Minnesota law revealed the willingness of the majority of the justices to disregard constitutional limitations—even those explicitly in the text of the Constitution—in order to allow government experimentation to meet changed economic circumstances.[50] Had it not been for a famous series of decisions striking down major federal New Deal legislation in 1935 and 1936, the *Nebbia* and *Home Building & Loan* decisions of 1934 might have been regarded by scholars as the watershed marking the "New Deal Revolution."[51]

The fragile five-to-four majorities in favor of government regulation in 1937 became more sizable majorities as the "Four Horsemen," one by one, left the Court and were replaced by pro–New Deal appointees. President Franklin D. Roosevelt thus was able to "pack" the Court with justices favorable to his policies, not by his infamous 1937 proposal that Congress add six new seats to the Court but by the normal process of attrition as older justices retired or died, creating vacancies on the Court's nine seats. By the time the United States entered World War II, all but one of the Court's nine justices were Roosevelt appointees.[52] By the end of World War II, the justices on what some scholars call the "Roosevelt Court" had regularly come to ignore the clear language of certain clauses of the Constitution—among them, the Tenth Amendment and the due process clauses of the Fifth and Fourteenth Amendments insofar as they protected economic liberty and property rights—and, in effect, had read them out of document.[53]

The new jurisprudential order was decisively marked by the Court's ruling in *United States v. Carolene Products*, upholding the federal Filled Milk Act of 1923. The act prohibited the interstate shipment of skimmed milk compounded with any fat or oil other than milk fat. As legal scholar Geoffrey Miller has argued, it was "an utterly unprincipled example of special interest legislation" that mainly targeted skimmed milk laced with coconut oil, which was cheaper than canned milk containing milk fat. The major force behind the act was a segment of the dairy industry. One of *Carolene Products'* legacies, Miller notes, was "the unrivaled primacy of interest groups in American politics of the last half-century."[54]

In the due process portion of his opinion for the Court, Justice Stone announced the Court's new standard of review for such regulatory legislation:

> [T]he existence of facts supporting the legislative judgment is to be presumed, for regulatory legislation affecting ordinary commercial transactions is not to be pronounced unconstitutional unless in the light of the facts made known or generally assumed it is of such a character as to preclude the assumption that it rests upon some rational basis within the knowledge and experience of the legislators.[55]

This meant that substantive due process review of such legislation would follow what is generally now called the "rational basis test"-sometimes the "minimal rational basis test," to emphasis the weakness of its scrutiny. Notice that the test, in effect, seems to function as a presumption in favor of the constitutionality of such legislation. In other words, it reverses the Court's old, *Lochner*-era presumption in favor of liberty, replacing it with a presumption in favor of government action or regulation, or a presumption against liberty. Contrary to the orthodox view, which identifies formalism with judicial protection of liberty of contract and which sees Holmes, Brandeis, and their jurisprudential descendants as the enemies of formalism, the *Carolene Products* rational basis test, with its presumption of constitutionality, is "the very definition of formalism," as legal scholar Timothy Sandefur has noted. "So long as the government's action bears some connection to a minimally rational economic policy, the Court refuses to look further, to the real motive or real effect of the policy."[56]

110

To dispel the impression that all legislation would enjoy this presumption of constitutionality, Stone immediately added his famous footnote 4, in which he stated that a stricter standard of scrutiny might be applied when the challenged law violated a specific provision of the Constitution, such as one of the Bill of Rights guarantees; or when it restricted political participation in such matters as voting, speech, political organization, or peaceable assembly; or when it discriminated against particular religious, national, or racial minorities.[57] The footnote, which was technically dictum because it was not essential to the Court's holding, thus became the origin of the double standard in the Court's modern substantive due process jurisprudence.

That double standard means that the Court not only gives less constitutional protection to economic liberty and property rights—the rights formerly protected by its *Lochner*-era liberty-of-contract jurisprudence—than it gives to other rights, the modern Court's so-called preferred freedoms. It means also that, even regarding the latter, the Court has applied differing standards of review. Despite what the first category of cases mentioned in Stone's footnote suggests, the Court has not even given uniform protection to the rights explicitly protected by Bill of Rights amendments. Beginning with Justice Cardozo's opinion for the Court in *Palko v. Connecticut*—another 1937 decision—the Court has followed the doctrine of "selective incorporation," applying some, but not all, of the rights guaranteed in the Bill of Rights against the states through the Fourteenth Amendment's due process clause.[58]

The Court's double standard is evident in several aspects of modern American constitutional law. One is the way the Court and most constitutional scholars have drawn an artificial distinction between "economic" liberty and "personal" freedoms, with the rational basis test rarely protecting the former while the more rigorous "strict scrutiny" standard more effectively protects the latter. Justice Robert Jackson, one of FDR's new appointees to the Court, applied the higher standard in *West Virginia State Board of Education v. Barnette*, the famous World War II–era civil liberties case in which the Court invalidated a state law compelling schoolchildren to salute the U.S. flag. The Court held that the law violated First Amendment rights, applied to the states through the Fourteenth Amendment. In rationalizing the Court's decision, Justice Jackson had to explain not only why the Court was reversing its decision upholding a flag-salute law just a few years earlier in *Minersville School District v. Gobitis*, 310 U.S. 586 (1940) but also why the Court was applying a different due process test than the one it had applied in cases upholding laws regulating business. The justice emphasized that while legislatures need only a "rational basis" for adopting laws that restrict economic freedom, they could not restrict First Amendment freedoms "on such slender grounds." With regard to rights such as freedom of speech and press, or religious freedom, Jackson added:

> We must transplant these rights to a soil in which the laissez-faire concept or principle of non-interference has withered at least as to economic affairs, and social advancements are increasingly sought through closer integration of society and through expanded and strengthened government controls. These changed conditions often deprive precedents of reliability and cast us more than we would choose upon our own judgment.

Thus, Jackson not only conceded the existence of a double standard but also frankly admitted that the justices were following their own subjective values in giving a higher level of protection to First Amendment rights.[59]

Perhaps the most telling illustration of the double standard has been the failed attempt to reconcile *West Coast Hotel v. Parrish* with the Court's modern protection of the right to privacy. In treating privacy as one of the "preferred freedoms"—that is, as a right protected by the higher, strict scrutiny standard of review suggested in the *Carolene Products* footnote—the Court (or at least a majority of its justices) has treated privacy as though it were a right enumerated in the Constitution. As an unenumerated right, however, privacy fails to fall within one of the categories of cases announced in the footnote as justifying a higher level of scrutiny than the mere rational basis standard the Court announced in *West Coast Hotel* as the general rule in due process cases—an inconsistency in modern liberal constitutionalism that many conservative critics have recognized.[60] To critics of the modern Court's substantive due process jurisprudence, the Court's protection today of the right to privacy seems jurisprudentially indistinguishable from its protection of liberty of contract in the early 20th century. Not surprisingly, therefore, in many key privacy decisions, the Court's more liberal justices have sought to distinguish their holdings from those of their predecessors in the *Lochner* era. These attempts to distinguish modern liberal constitutionalism from the old Court's pre-1937 substantive due process jurisprudence have not been convincing.

For example, in the first modern decision explicitly protecting a right to privacy, *Griswold v. Connecticut* in 1965, Justice William O. Douglas's opinion for the Court based the right in "penumbras" emanating from particular rights enumerated in the Bill of Rights guarantees. He thus sought to give the unenumerated right to privacy a jurisprudential foundation in enumerated rights. In so doing, he was trying to distinguish this narrower protection of privacy, through substantive due process, from the Court's use of substantive due process to protect liberty more generally during the *Lochner* era—a time, Douglas maintained, when the Court sat "as a super-legislature to determine the wisdom, need, and propriety of laws that touch economic problems, business affairs, or social conditions."[61] Douglas's effort, however, proved less than persuasive to many of the Court's critics, as it had all the hallmarks of a political decision—to protect "personal" rights while leaving economic rights unprotected.

In the Court's 1992 decision in *Planned Parenthood v. Casey*—sustaining the basic holding of *Roe v. Wade* that the right to privacy encompassed a pregnant woman's decision to obtain an abortion, at least in the early stages of pregnancy—a plurality opinion by Justices Sandra Day O'Connor, Anthony Kennedy, and David Souter sought to explain why the Court should stand by its earlier decision in *Roe*, despite the great criticism it had generated in the two decades since *Roe* had been decided. The three justices cited *stare decisis*, the legal principle that courts should generally follow the precedents set by their earlier decisions, unless certain conditions are met that would justify overturning those precedents. One of those conditions was a change in facts, or in the understanding of facts, from those that justified earlier decisions, and the plurality opinion cited "the line of cases identified with *Lochner v. New York*" as a leading example. The justices maintained that the *Lochner* Court's protection of liberty of contract "rested on fundamentally false factual assumptions about the capacity of a relatively unregulated market to satisfy minimal levels of human welfare"[62]—a disputable interpretation of history and economics, as this book has shown.

Despite such efforts by the justices themselves to distinguish their protection of privacy rights from early 20th-century substantive due process decisions, the jurisprudential foundations of the right to privacy are virtually identical to—and thus potentially susceptible to the same demise as—the Court's pre-1937 protection of liberty of contract. As chapter 3 shows in discussing the Court's decisions in the two 1920s school cases, *Meyer v. Nebraska* and *Pierce v. Society of Sisters*, the modern right to privacy really is nothing but the last remaining vestige of the old Court's protection of liberty of contract, founded on the post-1937 survival and reconceptualization of the *Meyer* and *Pierce* decisions. Both the right to privacy and liberty of contract involve substantive due process protection of an unenumerated right, one aspect of the general right to liberty. Moreover, as between the two rights—one focused on the economic freedom of contracting parties to set the terms of their contracts, the other focused on the supposed noneconomic, "personal" freedom of consenting adults to engage in certain sexual practices free from interference by the state—it is liberty of contract, not the right to privacy (at least as defined in modern liberal constitutionalism), that arguably has a more secure foundation in constitutional law. It certainly has a more secure foundation in "fundamental principles as they have been understood by the traditions of our people and our law," the due process standard articulated by Justice Holmes in his *Lochner* dissent.

5. Conclusion: Distinguishing History from Legend or Propaganda

The orthodox view of the Supreme Court's protection of liberty of contract during the *Lochner* era—the view that identifies it as "laissez-faire constitutionalism"—is a myth, or perhaps more accurately, a folktale, the equivalent in constitutional law of a modern urban legend.[1] The folktale was invented by early 20th-century Progressive movement scholars[2] and has been perpetuated by modern-day apologists for the 20th-century welfare/regulatory state. In each of its key parts, that folktale not only is wrong but often turns the truth entirely on its head.

First and foremost, in protecting liberty of contract as a fundamental right, the Court during the *Lochner* era was not applying a laissez-faire political or economic philosophy—"enacting Mr. Herbert Spencer's *Social Statics*," as Justice Holmes accused the majority of doing in *Lochner*, rather than following a "laissez-faire constitutionalism"—which would have resulted in the overturning of literally hundreds of laws that the Court upheld as valid exercises of the police power—the Court reviewed challenged laws under a moderate means-ends test, which in effect created a general but fairly rebuttable presumption in favor of liberty. Thus, in protecting liberty of contract, the Court recognized the validity of the police power in its traditional scope, as a protection of public health, safety, and morals. Virtually every law that the Court invalidated as abridging liberty of contract was a new kind of "social legislation," unprecedented and inconsistent with the traditional scope of police powers. The Court, in short, based its liberty-of-contract jurisprudence on well-established principles of American constitutional law: the use of the due process clauses, substantively, to protect property and liberty rights, by enforcing certain recognized limits on the states' police power, limits that had become federalized with the addition of the Fourteenth Amendment to the Constitution.

The indisputable fact that the Court based its protection of liberty of contract on substantive due process refutes another myth that has been created by some modern revisionist scholars.[3] That new myth associates the Court's *Lochner*-era jurisprudence with judicial enforcement of the prohibition on "class legislation" in 19th-century American constitutional law. Many modern scholars who dislike the Court's substantive due process jurisprudence during the *Lochner* era have tried to distinguish it from the kind of substantive due process jurisprudence they like—the Court's modern liberal constitutionalism, including even the *Carolene Products* double standard—by denying that the Court was relying on a substantive use of the due process clauses in its *Lochner*-era decisions. But even a cursory reading of the Court's decisions protecting liberty of contract shows clearly that the Court did indeed use substantive due process. What happened to the old prohibition on class legislation—an unwritten rule of 19th-century constitutional law, which the U.S. Supreme Court largely ignored in the 20th century—really relates to another story in constitutional history, the story of the Court's changing interpretation of "equal protection of the laws," a separate clause of the Fourteenth Amendment.[4]

Another part of the caricature of the Court's *Lochner*-era jurisprudence created by Progressive movement scholars and perpetuated by modern liberal scholars has been its identification with "economic substantive due process," and specifically with economic freedom in the labor law context (as in the *Lochner* case itself), to distinguish it from the modern liberal constitutionalism and its protection of "personal" freedoms such as the right to privacy. That caricature is flawed in two important respects. First, it is based on a false distinction between "economic" liberty and "personal" liberty—a distinction that ignores the fact that what some people regard as mere economic freedom is quite "personal" to the individuals who wish to exercise it. The natural right to liberty, as understood by America's Founders, pertained to one basic right—the freedom of individuals to act as they choose—that cannot be easily broken down into economic and noneconomic categories. In protecting liberty of contract as a fundamental right, the Court understood that the word *liberty* as used in the Fifth and Fourteenth Amendments' due process clauses encompassed the broad array of freedoms identified by Justice Peck-ham in his opinion for the Court in *Allgeyer v. Louisiana*, including

> the right of the citizen to be free in the enjoyment of all his faculties; to be free to use them in all lawful ways; to live and work where he will; to earn his livelihood by any law-ful calling; to pursue any livelihood or avocation, and for that purpose to enter into all contracts which may be proper, necessary and essential to his carrying out to a successful conclusion the purposes above mentioned.

Freedom of the parties to an employment contract to decide such terms as the number of hours to work or the employee's wage is but one aspect—arguably, a small aspect—of the broad right to liberty identified in *Allgeyer*.

This suggests the second flaw in the "economic substantive due process" stereotype: that it ignores the full scope of liberty of con-tract as it was protected by the Court during the 1897–1937 period. Through its liberty-of-contract jurisprudence, the Court protected various aspects of liberty, including not only economic freedom in the context of the employer-employee relationship (as in the famous cases of *Lochner v. New York* and *Adkins v. Children's Hospital*) but other important aspects of economic freedom, as well as other aspects of liberty that today would be regarded as "personal" freedom. Moreo-ver, the Court protected not just the wealthy or powerful but also relatively powerless individuals and members of minority groups—as illustrated in its important (but largely overlooked) decisions in *Buchanan v. Warley* (1917) and the two 1920s' "school cases," *Meyer* and *Pierce*.

Finally, it was not the *Lochner*-era Court that was guilty of "judi-cial activism" in protecting liberty of contract. Its liberty-of-contract jurisprudence objectively applied established rules of constitutional law. The activism came, rather, with the Court's abandonment of liberty of contract as a fundamental right following the so-called New Deal Revolution. That activism is evident today in the "dou-ble standard" that the modern Court applies in its substantive due process jurisprudence. Certain "preferred freedoms"—including not only certain rights enumerated in the Bill of Rights such as First Amendment freedom of speech and religion but also the unenumerated "right of privacy"—are more strongly protected than are economic freedom or property rights, the rights stereotypically associated with *Lochner*-era jurisprudence. The irony is that among the aspects of liberty protected today, such as the right to privacy, are the last remaining vestiges of the old Court's liberty-of-contract jurisprudence. Indeed, the great untold story in American constitutional law today is the debt that modern protection of personal freedoms and civil liberties owes to the Court's pre-1937 protection of liberty of contract.

Notes

Introduction

1. Judicial review is the power of American courts—not just the U.S. Supreme Court but all courts, both federal and state—to consider the constitutionality of laws and to refuse to enforce any laws that courts find to be unconstitutional. Although not explicitly found in the U.S. Constitution, judicial review is considered by scholars to be part of the "judicial power" that Article III grants to the Supreme Court and other federal courts. The distinction between judicial review, properly considered, and what many modern scholars condemn as "judicial activism" is discussed in chapter 2.

2. The Fifth Amendment provides, in relevant part, that "[no] person shall. . . be deprived of life, liberty, or property, without due process of law." The relevant portion of the Fourteenth Amendment provides, "[N]or shall any State deprive any person of life, liberty, or property, without due process of law."

3. As discussed in chapter 1, the distinction between substantive and procedural due process is artificial, invented by 20th-century scholars, especially those who were critics of the Court's liberty-of-contract jurisprudence.

4. The Court's protection of liberty of contract began with its decision in *Allgeyer v. Louisiana*, 165 U.S. 578 (1897), and ended with its decision in *West Coast Hotel Co. v. Parrish*, 300 U.S. 379 (1937).

5. Lochner v. New York, 198 U.S. 45 (1905).

6. For example, one of the leading casebooks used in law school constitutional law courses characterizes *Lochner*-era liberty-of-contract decisions as "economic substantive due process," to distinguish them from modern substantive due process decisions. CONSTITUTIONAL LAW 2d ed. 524–40 (Erwin Chemerinsky ed., 2005).

7. Aviam Soifer, *The Paradox of Paternalism and Laissez-Faire Constitutionalism: United States Supreme Court, 1888–1921*, 5 LAW & HIST. REV. 249, 250 (1987); Michael Les Benedict, *Laissez-Faire and Liberty: A Re-Evaluation of the Meaning and Origins of Laissez-Faire Constitutionalism*, 3 LAW & HIST. REV. 293, 295 (1985); WILLIAM M. WIECEK, LIBERTY UNDER LAW: THE SUPREME COURT IN AMERICAN LIFE 124–25 (1988).

8. For classic examples of this view of laissez-faire constitutionalism, see CLYDE E. JACOBS, LAW WRITERS AND THE COURTS: THE INFLUENCE OF THOMAS M. COOLEY, CHRISTOPHER G. TIEDEMAN, AND JOHN F. DILLON UPON AMERICAN CONSTITUTIONAL LAW (1954); ARNOLD M. PAUL, CONSERVATIVE CRISIS AND THE RULE OF LAW: ATTITUDES OF BAR AND BENCH, 1887–1895 (1960); BENJAMIN TWISS, LAWYERS AND THE CONSTITUTION: HOW LAISSEZ-FAIRE CAME TO THE SUPREME COURT (1942). A modern variant of the traditional view sees the *Lochner* era as one in which the Court protected a supposed laissez-faire system of "common law" rights against redistributive legislation. *See* Cass R. Sunstein, *Lochner's Legacy*, 87 COLUM. L. REV. 873 (1987).

9. Among law school casebooks, see, for example, GEOFFREY R. STONE ET AL., CONSTITUTIONAL LAW 755 (5th ed. 2005) (describing the *Lochner* era as one in which the Court "attempted to vindicate, as a matter of constitutional law, a laissez-faire conception of the role of government that could not be sustained"); JESSE H. CHOPER ET AL., CONSTITUTIONAL LAW: CASES, COMMENTS, QUESTIONS 292 (9th ed. 2001) (summarizing the *Lochner*-era as one in which the Court "frequently substituted its judgment for that of Congress and state legislatures on the wisdom of economic regulation"); DANIEL A. FARBER ET AL., CASES AND MATERIALS ON CONSTITUTIONAL LAW: THEMES FOR THE CONSTITUTION'S THIRD CENTURY 18 (2d ed. 1998) (criticizing the *Lochner*-era as "a rather dreary one in the Court's history" in which backward-looking judges used the Fourteenth Amendment as "a shield for businesses"). Among legal and constitutional history textbooks, see, for example, MELVIN I. UROFSKY & PAUL FINKELMAN, A MARCH OF LIBERTY: A CONSTITUTIONAL HISTORY OF THE UNITED STATES 509 (2d ed. 2002) (summarizing the modern view of *Lochner*-era judges as "intellectual prisoners, held captive by the doctrines of laissez-faire and the inverted logic of legal formalism"); DAVID P. CURRIE, THE CONSTITUTION IN THE SUPREME COURT: THE SECOND CENTURY, 1888–1986, 45 (1990) ("liberty of contract found its way into the Constitution by bald fiat"); KERMIT L. HALL, THE MAGIC MIRROR: LAW IN AMERICAN HISTORY 190, 222 (1989) (describing laissez-faire constitutionalism as a combination of "Social Darwinist" laissez-faire ideology and legal formalism empowering "reactionary" appellate judges).

10. *See, e.g.,* ROBERT H. BORK, THE TEMPTING OF AMERICA 46 (1990) (criticizing both *Allgeyer* and *Lochner* as "unjustifiable assumptions of power" by the judiciary); LAURENCE H. TRIBE, CONSTITUTIONAL CHOICES 169 (1985) (maintaining that the demise of *Lochner* coincided with "judicial acceptance of positivist approaches to property and contract rights"). As is typical of modern judicial restraint conservatives, Bork rejects substantive due process altogether as inconsistent with "neutral" judicial decision-making; Tribe, on the other hand, accepts substantive due process protection of certain noneconomic liberty interests, such as the right to privacy. *Compare* BORK, *supra*, at 43, *with* TRIBE, *supra*, at 12–13.

11. *See, e.g,* Griswold v. Connecticut, 381 U.S. 479, 482 (1965) (characterizing the *Lochner*-era as one in which the Court sat "as a super legislature to determine the wisdom, need, and propriety of laws that touch economic problems, business affairs, or social conditions"); Planned Parenthood v. Casey, 505 U.S. 833, 861–62 (1992) (maintaining that the Court's protection of contractual freedom "rested on fundamentally false factual assumptions about the capacity of a relatively unregulated market to satisfy minimal levels of human welfare").

12. For the classic treatment of Progressivism in the history of American political thought, see RICHARD A. HOFSTADTER, THE AGE OF REFORM (1955). A more recent and somewhat fuller account of the Progressive Era may be found in MICHAEL MCGERR, A FIERCE DISCONTENT: THE RISE AND FALL OF THE PROGRESSIVE MOVEMENT IN AMERICA, 1870–1920 (2003). The Progressive movement and its conflict with the classical liberal, or laissez-faire, philosophy in early 20th-century public policy debates are discussed in chapter 3.

13. *See* Learned Hand, *Due Process of Law and the Eight-Hour Day*, 21 HARV. L. REV. 495, 501–03 (1908) (defending an eight-hour law as within the discretion of the legislature to "make more equal the relative economic advantages of the two parties" to the labor contract, and to "promote the 'welfare' of the public"); Roscoe Pound, *Liberty of Contract*, 18 YALE L.J. 454, 457 (1909) (criticizing judicial

protection of freedom of contract as the result of an "individualistic conception of justice," which "exaggerates private right at the expense of public right"); Charles Warren, *The New "Liberty" under the Fourteenth Amendment*, 39 HARV. L. REV. 431, 462 (1926) (predicting that the term "liberty" as used in the Fourteenth Amendment's due process clause and "newly defined" by the Court, in its liberty-of-contract decisions, would "become a tremendous engine for attack on State legislation").

14. GERALD GUNTHER, LEARNED HAND: THE MAN AND THE JUDGE 190 (1994). Hand's efforts on behalf of the movement included helping his good friend Herbert Croly plan *The New Republic* magazine and advising Teddy Roosevelt on antitrust policy and on the "social and industrial" planks of Roosevelt's 1912 platform. *Id.* at 191–202 and 226–27.

15. *Id.* at 209, 249.

16. In *Roe v. Wade*, 410 U.S. 113 (1973), the Supreme Court expanded the constitutional right to privacy to include a right to abortion in the early stages of pregnancy. It is one of the most controversial Court decisions of the last half of the 20th century and, like many of the decisions in the *Lochner* era, has ignited controversy between partisans with firmly held beliefs on both sides.

17. *Lochner*, 198 U.S. at 75–76 (Holmes, J., dissenting).

18. *See, e.g.*, BERNARD SCHWARTZ, A HISTORY OF THE SUPREME COURT 202 (1993) (maintaining that Justice Holmes was "surely correct" in his characterization of Justice Peckham's opinion for the *Lochner* majority); UROFSKY & FINKELMAN, *supra* note 9, at 559 (noting that Holmes "showed up Peckham and the majority for doing just what they claimed not to be doing—writing their personal preferences into law"). *But see* 2 DAVID O'BRIEN, CONSTITUTIONAL LAW AND POLITICS 257–58 (2d ed. 1995) (acknowledging that Justice Harlan's dissent provided a "rival interpretation" critiquing the majority for failing to construe New York's law as a legitimate public health measure).

19. 198 U.S. at 76.

20. Many scholars also ignore the other dissenting opinion in *Lochner*—authored by Justice Harlan, joined by Justices White and Day—which accepted liberty of contract as an important constitutional right but disagreed with the majority's interpretation of the New York law as a violation of that right, as discussed in chapter 3.

21. HALL, *supra* note 9, at 222–23.

22. ALFRED H. KELLY ET AL. THE AMERICAN CONSTITUTION: ITS ORIGINS AND DEVELOPMENT 454 (7th ed. 1991). As the authors further note, by the 1920s there emerged, out of sociological jurisprudence, "a more radical and reform-oriented theory of law"—legal realism—which rejected altogether the idea of law as an objective set of rules and embraced instead a view of law as "a kind of *ad hoc* method of arbitration." *Id.* at 455. For a collection of classic legal realist writings of the 1920s and 1930s, see AMERICAN LEGAL REALISM (William W. Fisher III et al. eds., 1993).

23. OLIVER WENDELL HOLMES, THE COMMON LAW 5 (Mark DeWolfe Howe ed., Little, Brown & Co. 1963) (1881).

24. *See, e.g.*, Calvin Woodard, *Reality and Social Reform: The Transition from Laissez-Faire to the Welfare State*, 72 YALE L. J. 286, 327 (1962) (arguing that the laissez-faire standard "has ceased to comport with reality" in modern industrial society).

25. *See* Bernard H. Siegan, *Rehabilitating* Lochner, 22 SAN DIEGO L. REV. 453 (1985). Other scholars representing a variety of jurisprudential perspectives—conservative, libertarian, as well as left-liberal—have urged a revival of "natural law" in defense of substantive due process protection of unenumerated constitutional rights, includ-

ing (perhaps, but not necessarily) liberty of contract. *See, e.g.*, HADLEY ARKES, THE RETURN OF GEORGE SUTHERLAND: RESTORING A JURISPRUDENCE OF NATURAL RIGHTS (1994); Randy E. Barnett, *Getting Normative: The Role of Natural Rights in Constitutional Adjudication*, 12 CONST. COMMENTARY 93 (1995); Suzanna Sherry, *Natural Law in the States*, 61 U. CIN. L. REV. 171 (1992).

26. *See* Benedict, *supra* note 7, at 293; HOWARD GILLMAN, THE CONSTITUTION BESIEGED: THE RISE AND DEMISE OF *LOCHNER* ERA POLICE POWERS JURISPRUDENCE (1993); Alan Jones, *Thomas M. Cooley and "Laissez-Faire Constitutionalism": A Reappraisal*, 53 J. AM. HIST. 751 (1967).

27. *See* Eric Foner, *Abolitionism and the Labor Movement in Antebellum America, in* POLITICS AND IDEOLOGY IN THE AGE OF THE CIVIL WAR 57 (1980); William E. Forbath, *The Ambiguities of Free Labor: Labor and the Law in the Gilded Age*, 1985 WIS. L. REV. 767; Charles W. McCurdy, *The Roots of Liberty of Contract Reconsidered: Major Premises in the Law of Employment, 1867–1937*, 1984 SUP. CT. HIST. SOC'Y Y.B. 20.

28. GILLMAN, *supra* note 26, at 4. While acknowledging the contributions of scholars such as Benedict, Jones, and McCurdy to his work, Gillman specifically dissociates his interpretation from that of Siegan and other "conservative polemicists" interested in, as he characterizes it, "resurrecting the ghost of *Lochner* by citing some incantation about the importance in our constitutional tradition of rights to property and contract." *Id.* at 11.

29. *See* MICHAEL J. PHILLIPS, THE *LOCHNER* COURT, MYTH AND REALITY: SUBSTANTIVE DUE PROCESS FROM THE 1890s TO THE 1930s (2001) (concluding that the conventional view of *Lochner*-era substantive due process jurisprudence is based on several myths). *See also* STEPHEN B. PRESSER, RECAPTURING THE CONSTITUTION (1994). In this provocative book, which challenges modern constitutional law from a conservative perspective, Professor Presser nevertheless disagrees with some other conservatives, such as Robert Bork, who have criticized *Lochner* as an "activist" decision. Such criticism of the Supreme Court's liberty-of-contract jurisprudence "misses the mark," Presser argues, because *Lochner* was "solidly grounded in a specific and historically defined American natural law tradition of the protection of private property." *Id.* at 142–43. Holmes's dissent in *Lochner* "could not have been more wrong," Presser adds, noting that "the core" of the Founders' philosophy of government was the protection of private property and contract rights. *Id.* at 141–42.

30. *See* David E. Bernstein, *Roots of the "Underclass": The Decline of Laissez-Faire Jurisprudence and the Rise of Racist Labor Legislation*, 43 AM. U. L. REV. 85, 91 (1993) (arguing that liberty of contract "often served to protect the most disadvantaged, disenfranchised workers from monopolistic legislation sponsored by politically powerful discriminatory labor unions"); David E. Bernstein, *Lochner, Parity, and the Chinese Laundry Cases*, 41 WM. & MARY L. REV. 211 (1999) (showing how federal courts' liberty-of-contract jurisprudence protected Chinese laundrymen from discriminatory state legislation). In a recent book, Professor Bernstein has expanded on the thesis of his *American University Law Review* article and other related articles, arguing that the ultimate failure of *Lochner* era jurisprudence—and, with it, the triumph of the post–New Deal regulatory state— not only has strengthened racially exclusive labor unions, but also has contributed to a massive loss of employment opportunities for African Americans. DAVID E. BERNSTEIN, ONLY ONE PLACE OF REDRESS: AFRICAN AMERICANS, LABOR REGULATIONS, AND THE COURTS FROM RECONSTRUCTION TO THE NEW DEAL (2001).

31. *See* Bernstein, *Roots of the "Underclass," supra*, at 88 n.11 (noting scholarship showing that "Social Darwinism actually had minimal influence on American laissez-faire liberal thought, inside or outside legal circles"); Herbert Hovenkamp, *The Political Economy of Substantive Due Process*, 40 STAN. L. REV. 379, 418 (1988) (finding "painfully little evidence that any members of the Supreme Court were Social Darwinists, or for that matter even Darwinian").

32. *See* David N. Mayer, *The Jurisprudence of Christopher G. Tiedeman: A Study in the Failure of Laissez-Faire Constitutionalism*, 55 Mo. L. REV. 93, 99–100 (1990) [hereafter "Mayer, *Tiedeman*"] (arguing that Tiedeman, who was the purest laissez-faire legal treatise writer, grounded his constitutionalism not in formalism but in the German sociological school of jurisprudence).

33. For discussions of the shift in the "worldview" of American intellectuals between the 1880s and 1930s, see SIDNEY FINE, LAISSEZ-FAIRE AND THE GENERAL WELFARE STATE (1956); Woodard, *supra* note 24. Woodard describes the shift from the laissez-faire standard to the welfare state standard as "one of the greatest intellectual and moral upheavals in western history." Woodard, *supra*, at 288.

34. Charles W. McCurdy, *The "Liberty of Contract" Regime in American Law, in* THE STATE AND FREEDOM OF CONTRACT 162–63 (Harry N. Scheiber ed., 1998) (quoting Ernst Freund, *Standards of American Legislation* 22 (1917)). The Supreme Court never used the term "social legislation" until 1940; before then, only a handful of state judges had used the term. McCurdy's LEXIS search uncovered only three decisions in which the term was used before 1940, all state appellate court cases: a New York case in 1914 involving a statute banning night work for female factory workers and another New York case in 1916 and an Ohio case in 1923 involving workers' compensation statutes. *Id.* at 339 n.3.

35. Farnam was an economist and cofounder of the American Association for Labor Legislation who was a lifelong activist for minimum wage laws, social insurance programs, and other social legislation. *Id.* at 188–89. Freund was also active in the AALL and was the author of an influential 1904 treatise advocating a broad "elastic" interpretation of the police power. *Id.* at 192–93; Mayer, *Tiedeman, supra* note 32, at 146–48. As noted in chapter 4, the new majority on the Supreme Court who upheld social legislation and other economic regulatory laws after the so-called New Deal Revolution did so by accepting unquestioningly the assumptions on which those laws were based, as exemplified by Chief Justice Hughes's majority opinion in *West Coast Hotel*.

36. West Coast Hotel v. Parrish, 300 U.S. 379, 397 (1937) (upholding a Washington State minimum wage law). A year after this decision, the Court declared that government regulations of business would be found to violate due process only if they did not rest "upon some rational basis within the knowledge and experience of the legislators." United States v. Carolene Products Co., 304 U.S. 144, 152 (1938).

37. The double standard in modern constitutional law is ably described in JAMES W. ELY JR., THE GUARDIAN OF EVERY OTHER RIGHT: A CONSTITUTIONAL HISTORY OF PROPERTY RIGHTS 132–34 (1992). Ely notes that the double standard became institutionalized through the Court's famous footnote 4 in *Carolene Products Co.*, 304 U.S. at 144. That case and the rise of the double standard are discussed more fully in chapter 4.

Chapter 1

1. Roscoe Pound, *Liberty of Contract*, 18 YALE L.J. 454, 455, 457–58 (1909).

2. JOHN PHILLIP REID, THE CONCEPT OF LIBERTY IN THE AGE OF THE AMERICAN REVOLUTION 1 (1988) [hereafter "REID, LIBERTY"].

3. On English radical Whig thought and its influence on American constitutionalism, see David N. Mayer, *The English Radical Whig Origins of American Constitutionalism*, 70 WASH. U. L.Q. 131 (1992) [hereafter "Mayer, *Whigs*"].

4. *See id.* at 174 (summarizing basic principles of radical Whig constitutionalism), 191 (summarizing the state of nature as described in John Locke's *Second Treatise on Government* and other Whig writers), 193 (noting the connection between protection of rights and the legitimacy of government).

5. GORDON S. WOOD, THE RADICALISM OF THE AMERICAN REVOLUTION 5, 8 (1992). Discussing the "myth" that "the American Revolution was sober and conservative while the French Revolution was chaotic and radical," Wood adds that "only if we measure radicalism by violence and bloodshed can the myth be sustained; by any other measure the American Revolution was radical. . . ." *Id.* at 231.

6. *See, e.g.*, JOHN PHILLIP REID, CONSTITUTIONAL HISTORY OF THE AMERICAN REVOLUTION: THE AUTHORITY OF RIGHTS 9–10 (1986) [hereafter "REID, RIGHTS"] (arguing that the rights regarded as essential by American Whigs during the Revolutionary period were English constitutional rights).

7. WOOD, *supra* note 5, at 145–68 (discussing various ways in which traditional authority was questioned by Americans even before the Revolution).

8. Discussing the transformations in the legal system, Wood concludes that Americans modernized and "republicanized" English paternalism, replacing it with a "new conception of contract as a consensual bargain between two equal parties" (*id.* at 162), the individualistic conception of contract discussed in chapter 2 of this book. By the mid-18th century, Wood notes, "positive written contracts and other impersonal legal instruments were more and more replacing the informal, customary, and personal ways people had arranged their affairs with one another." *Id.* at 163.

9. *See* ERIC FONER, TOM PAINE AND REVOLUTIONARY AMERICA 151–52 (1976). Foner notes that while Patriot leaders such as Franklin and Jefferson had long believed in freedom of trade, it was during the Revolution itself that middle-class Americans, such as the Philadelphia merchants, challenged the "traditional idea that government had a responsibility to regulate trade for the common good" and instead advocated the "new doctrine of laissez-faire," the philosophical underpinnings of which were "articulated most systematically in the writings of Adam Smith." *Id.* at 152–53. Significantly, Foner finds near-universal opposition, on principle, to governmental price controls among both merchants and political writers like Thomas Paine. "Respectable merchant opinion had no use for price-fixing legislation; the maxim that 'trade can best regulate itself' had won virtually universal approval in the mercantile community." *Id.*

10. WOOD, *supra* note 5, at 8. Wood emphasizes that "[i]n a monarchical world of numerous patron-client relations and multiple degrees of dependency, nothing could be more radical than this attempt to make every man independent. What was an ideal in the English-speaking world now became for Americans an ideological imperative." *Id.* at 179.

11. As the next section of this chapter briefly discusses, notwithstanding the constitutional protections of liberty and property rights, courts in early America often upheld various types of government regulations as valid exercises of state police powers.

12. *See, e.g.*, William E. Nelson, Americanization of the Common Law: The Impact of Legal Change on Massachusetts Society, 1760–1830 (1975).

13. Thomas Paine, *Common Sense* (1776), *in* The Essential Thomas Paine 66 (1969).

14. *See* David N. Mayer, The Constitutional Thought of Thomas Jefferson 25–26 (1994) (quoting a letter from Thomas Jefferson to Henry Lee, May 8, 1825). On Jefferson's draft of the Declaration generally, see *id.* at 41–45.

15. On the meaning of "self-evident," see *id.* at 42; *see also* I. Bernard Cohen, Science and the Founding Fathers 122–32 (1995) ("self-evident" as synonymous with axiomatic).

16. Burlamaqui's treatise, *The Principles of Natural and Politic Law*, was first published in French in 1747 and was republished in many English-language editions. On Burlamaqui and his influence on Jefferson and his contemporaries, see Cohen, *supra*, at 112; Morton White, The Philosophy of the American Revolution 37–41 (1978). Burlamaqui's influence on American lawyers and judges extended well into the 20th century. *See, e.g.*, Hadley Arkes, The Return of George Sutherland: Restoring a Jurisprudence of Natural Rights vi (1994) (frontispiece, reproducing a page from George Sutherland's commonplace book, quoting Burlamaqui's definition of "natural liberty," in 1882 (when the future Justice Sutherland was 20 years old)).

17. Although many modern scholars use the terms "natural law" and "natural rights" loosely and interchangeably, they have distinct meanings. As Randy Barnett nicely summarizes the distinction, natural rights "define a moral space or liberty, as opposed to license, in which we may act free from the interference of other persons"; natural law or, more precisely, natural law ethics *"instructs us on how to exercise the liberty that is defined and protected by natural rights."* Randy E. Barnett, *A Law Professor's Guide to Natural Law and Natural Rights*, in *Symposium: Natural Law v. Natural Rights: What Are They? How Do They Differ?* 20 Harv. J.L. & Pub. Pol'y 655, 680–81 (1997) (emphasis in original).

18. Ralph Henry Gabriel, The Course of American Democratic Thought 288 (3d ed. 1986) (quoting Mark Hopkins, *Lectures on Moral Science* 258–59 (1867)). For a modern explanation of why inalienable rights are nevertheless forfeitable, see Randy Barnett, The Structure Of Liberty: Justice and the Rule of Law 77 (1998).

19. For example, Progressive Era legal historian Charles Warren asserted—with no historical evidence to support his position—that "liberty" meant merely "freedom from physical restraint of the person." Charles Warren, *The New "Liberty" under the Fourteenth Amendment*, 39 Harv. L. Rev. 431, 440 (1926). Some modern judicial-restraint conservatives have similarly asserted this narrow view of liberty. *See, e.g.*, Raoul Berger, Government by Judiciary: The Transformation of the Fourteenth Amendment 270 (1977).

20. "Cato," An Enquiry into the Nature and Extent of Liberty (Letter No. 62) (Jan. 20, 1721), *in* 1 John Trenchard & Thomas Gordon, Cato's Letters: Or, Essays on Liberty, Civil and Religious, and Other Important Subjects 3d ed. 244–45, 248 (photo. reprint, New York, Russell & Russell 1969) (1733). On the importance of

this four-volume work in early American political thought, see generally CLINTON ROSSITER, SEEDTIME OF THE REPUBLIC: THE ORIGIN OF THE AMERICAN TRADITION OF POLITICAL LIBERTY 141 (1953).

21. "Cato," *supra* note 20, at 249. The juxtaposition of "liberty" and "slavery" was commonplace in 18th-century radical Whig thought and in the writings of American revolutionaries. *See* REID, LIBERTY, *supra* note 2, at 38–59.

22. "Cato," *supra* note 20, at 245–46, 248.

23. John Locke was perhaps the most famous and influential of the English radical Whig philosophers in early American political thought. In his most important work of political philosophy, his *Second Treatise of Government*, Locke posited a "state of nature" in which individuals have "perfect freedom" to order their actions and dispose of their persons and property as they see fit, "within the bounds of the Law of Nature." That law, Locke maintained, was "Reason, which teaches mankind that, "being all equal and independent, no one ought to harm another in his life, health, liberty, or possessions." JOHN LOCKE, TWO TREATISES OF GOVERNMENT 269–71 (Peter Laslett ed., Cambridge Univ. Press 1988) (1690) (book 2, chapter 2, §§ 4–6).

24. JEAN JACQUES BURLAMAQUI, THE PRINCIPLES OF NATURAL AND POLITIC LAW 225–26, 228 (Columbus, Ohio, Joseph H. Riley 1859). Burlamaqui's view of natural liberty—like the concept of liberty in *Cato's Letters*—was strikingly similar to the view adopted by classical liberal thinkers in the 19th century, particularly Herbert Spencer and his "law of equal freedom," discussed in chapter 2 of this book.

25. *See generally* REID, LIBERTY, *supra* note 2, at 70–73 (discussing property as "the security of liberty"); LAWRENCE H. LEDER, LIBERTY AND AUTHORITY: EARLY AMERICAN POLITICAL IDEOLOGY, 1689–1763 125 (1968).

26. EDMUND S. MORGAN, THE CHALLENGE OF THE AMERICAN REVOLUTION 55 (1978).

27. LEDER, *supra* note 25, at 125 (quoting *New York Weekly Journal*, June 16, 1735 (no. 84)); REID, LIBERTY, *supra* note 2, at 119 (emphasis in original).

28. On Jefferson's use of the phrase "pursuit of happiness" in drafting the Declaration, see MAYER, *supra* note 14, at 77–80 (discussing Jefferson's theory of rights and particularly his view of property rights). Jefferson followed Burlamaqui in regarding the basic right to property—that is, the right to acquire, possess, and protect property generally—as a natural right, albeit a secondary-level natural right because it was "adventitious," that is, dependent on civil law for its full realization. *Id.* at 80. On Burlamaqui's treatment of property rights, see WHITE, *supra* note 16, at 215–28.

29. Virginia Declaration of Rights (1776), art. I, *in* 1 THE BILL OF RIGHTS: A DOCUMENTARY HISTORY 234 (Bernard Schwartz ed. 1971) (emphasis added). Jefferson had access to Mason's declaration of rights while writing the Declaration of Independence; the famous clause he drafted in the second paragraph of the Declaration expressed the same ideas as Mason's declaration, but more concisely. Thus, instead of the awkwardly long phrase "[rights] of which, when they enter into a state of society, they cannot, by any compact, deprive or divest their posterity"—the phrase omitted in the place of the ellipsis in the quotation in the main text—Jefferson substituted the single word "inalienable." Similarly, Jefferson's phrase "pursuit of happiness" was a more concise expression of the rights elaborated by Mason here and in other early state constitutions. *See* MAYER, *supra* note 14, at 78.

30. Pennsylvania Declaration of Rights (1776), art. I, *in* 1 THE BILL OF RIGHTS: A DOCUMENTARY HISTORY, *supra*, at 264 ("That all men are born equally free and independent, and have certain natural, inherent and inalienable rights, amongst which

are, the enjoying and defending life and liberty, *acquiring, possessing and protecting property*, and pursuing and obtaining happiness and safety") (emphasis added); Massachusetts Declaration of Rights (1780), art. I, *in id.* at 340 ("All men are born free and equal, and have certain natural, essential, and unalienable rights; amongst which may be reckoned the right of enjoying and defending their lives and liberties; that of *acquiring, possessing, and protecting property*; in fine, that of seeking and obtaining their safety and happiness") (emphasis added); New Hampshire Bill of Rights (1783), art. II, *in id.* at 375 ("All men have certain natural, essential, and inherent rights—among which are, the enjoying and defending life and liberty; *acquiring, possessing, and protecting property*; and, in a word, of seeking and obtaining happiness") (emphasis added).

31. *E.g.*, Ohio Constitution of 1851, sec. 1, *in* 1 DOCUMENTS OF AMERICAN CONSTITUTIONAL AND LEGAL HISTORY 354 (Melvin I. Urofsky & Paul Finkelman eds., 2002) ("All men are, by nature, free and independent, and have certain inalienable rights, among which are those of enjoying and defending life and liberty, *acquiring, possessing, and protecting property*, and seeking and obtaining happiness and safety") (emphasis added). The bill of rights in Ohio's 1851 constitution was based on Ohio's original 1802 constitution; a similar provision was included in the Illinois constitution of 1818. *See* JAMES W. ELY JR., THE GUARDIAN OF EVERY OTHER RIGHT: A CONSTITUTIONAL HISTORY OF PROPERTY RIGHTS 56–57 (1992).

32. WILLI PAUL ADAMS, THE FIRST AMERICAN CONSTITUTIONS: REPUBLICAN IDEOLOGY AND THE MAKING OF THE STATE CONSTITUTIONS IN THE REVOLUTIONARY ERA 193 (1980).

33. On Madison's essays, see IRVING BRANT, JAMES MADISON: FATHER OF THE CONSTITUTION, 1787–1800 334–36 (1950). These essays generally helped define the Republican opposition to Treasury Secretary Alexander Hamilton's measures. *See* LANCE BANNING, THE SACRED FIRE OF LIBERTY: JAMES MADISON AND THE FOUNDING OF THE FEDERAL REPUBLIC 348 (1995). In the opinion of another Madison biographer, however, Madison's essays had a tone "so scholarly that they provided no excitement for readers itching for a fight with the Hamilton crowd" (ROBERT A. RUTLAND, JAMES MADISON: THE FOUNDING FATHER 108 (1987))—an attribute probably illustrated nicely by this particular essay.

34. James Madison, "Property" (Mar. 27, [1792]), *in* 14 THE PAPERS OF JAMES MADISON 266–68 (Robert Rutland et al. eds., 1983) (emphasis in original). Being no anarchist, Madison added, "Where an excess of liberty prevails, the effect is the same, tho' from an opposite cause." *Id.* at 266. His ideal, in short, was a limited government, exercising only those powers necessary to secure individual rights.

35. *Id.* at 267. One modern scholar has noted that Madison's language here "anticipates substantive due process review of economic legislation." ELY, *supra* note 31, at 55. Indeed, the same type of "arbitrary restrictions" or "monopolies" Madison here condemned were considered unconstitutional under the Fourteenth Amendment by Justice Field and other dissenters in the *Slaughterhouse Cases* 83 U.S. (16 Wall.) 36 (1873), and by the majority of the Supreme Court in *Allgeyer v. Louisiana*, 165 U.S. 578 (1897), as discussed later in this chapter.

36. With regard to taxation, Madison noted:

> A just security to property is not afforded by that government, under which unequal taxes oppress one species of property and reward another species: where arbitrary taxes invade the domestic sanctuaries of the rich, and excessive taxes grind the faces of the poor; where the keenness and competitions of want are deemed an insufficient spur to labor, and taxes are again applied, by an unfeeling policy, as another spur. . . .

Madison, "Property," *supra* note 34, at 267.

37. *Id.* (emphasis in original).

38. Turpin v. Locket, 10 Va. (6 Call) 113 (1804) (holding that an 1802 statute divesting the Episcopal Church of some of its property violated section 1 of the Virginia Declaration of Rights); Herman v. State, 8 Ind. 545 (1855) (holding that the state liquor prohibition law was an unconstitutional deprivation of "the right of liberty and pursuing happiness secured by the constitution"). The Virginia court decision was invalidated, however, when the judge who had written the opinion died the night before he was to deliver it. After a replacement judge was appointed and the case reargued, an equally divided court upheld the confiscation. *Turpin*, 10 Va. (6 Call) at 186–87; *see also* Suzanna Sherry, *Natural Law in the States*, 61 U. CIN. L. REV. 171, 192–93 (1992). The Virginia case was one of a series of early state court decisions recognizing, in various ways, constitutional protection for natural rights through both written and unwritten constitutional limitations on government power. *See generally* Sherry, *supra*.

39. Magna Carta (1215), cl. 39, *in* 1 SOURCES OF ENGLISH CONSTITUTIONAL HISTORY 115, 121 (Carl Stephenson & Frederick George Marcham eds., rev. ed. 1972).

40. *E.g.*, Virginia Declaration of Rights (1776), sec. 8 ("that no man be deprived of his liberty except by the law of the land, or the judgment of his peers"); Pennsylvania Declaration of Rights (1776), sec. IX ("nor can any man be justly deprived of his liberty except by the laws of the land, or the judgment of his peers"); Massachusetts Declaration of Rights (1780), sec. XII ("no subject shall be arrested, imprisoned, despoiled, or deprived of his property, immunities, or privileges, put out of the protection of the law, exiled, or deprived of his life, liberty, or estate, but by the judgment of his peers, or the law of the land."); *in* 1 THE BILL OF RIGHTS: A DOCUMENTARY HISTORY, *supra* note 29, at 235, 265, 342. For a discussion of these state constitutional provisions, see Robert E. Riggs, *Substantive Due Process in 1791*, 1990 WIS. L. REV. 941, 974–75.

41. *See, e.g.*, ROBERT H. BORK, THE TEMPTING OF AMERICA 32 (1990); BERGER, *supra* note 19, at 193–95, 204 n.36. The claim that due process—and specifically, the due process clause of the Fourteenth Amendment—was limited to procedural requirements may have originated with Justice Miller's opinion for the majority of the Supreme Court in *Davidson v. New Orleans*, 96 U.S. 97, 104 (1877) (complaining that "the docket of this court is crowded with cases" challenging state laws under "some strange misconception" of the scope of due process). *See* A. E. DICK HOWARD, THE ROAD FROM RUNYMEDE: MAGNA CARTA AND CONSTITUTIONALISM IN AMERICA 363–64 (1968). Miller's analysis in this case, like his opinion for the Court in the *Slaughterhouse Cases*, reflected the majority's desire to narrow the scope of the Fourteenth Amendment to minimize federal review of state laws, as discussed in the last part of this chapter.

42. *See* G. Edward White, *Revisiting Substantive Due Process and Holmes' Lochner Dissent*, 63 BROOK. L. REV. 87, 108 (1997); James W. Ely Jr., *The Oxymoron Reconsidered: Myth and Reality in the Origins of Substantive Due Process*, 16 CONST. COMMENT. 315, 319 (1999).

43. *See* Gary D. Rowe, *The Legacy of* Lochner: Lochner *Revisionism Revisited*, 24 L. & SOC. INQUIRY 221, 244–45 (1999).

44. *See* Roger Pilon, *Legislative Activism, Judicial Activism, and the Decline of Private Sovereignty*, *in* ECONOMIC LIBERTIES AND THE JUDICIARY 183, 197–99 (James A. Dorn & Henry G. Manne eds., 1987). Pilon argues that "[w]hile procedural correctness is a *necessary* condition for due process, it is not a *sufficient* condition," for due process of law also requires "substantive correctness." *Id.* at 197 (emphasis in original). "Due

process of law," he concludes, "is more than mere process; and it is more than process plus any substance. It is process plus that substance that tells us when we may or may not deprive a person of his life, liberty, or property." *Id.* at 199. Pilon gives a simple example: "We have no right to hang a man simply because he is a Jew, even if a substantial majority of the legislature says that we may." Due process of law requires recognition of the principle that "no man may be hanged unless he has done something to alienate his right against being hanged." *Id.* at 198–99.

45. *See* J. A. P. JONES, KING JOHN AND MAGNA CARTA 53, 83 (1971).

46. ELY, *supra* note 31, at 78. Ely cites Alexander Hamilton, who had argued in 1787 that the words "due process" had a technical meaning applicable to court proceedings—historical evidence also cited by Raoul Berger, who also emphasized that the early law-of-the-land clauses in state constitutions typically appeared in sections dealing with criminal trials. BERGER, *supra* note 19, at 194, 199–200. Except for *Dred Scott*, however, Berger ignores the other early 19th-century cases, discussed here, showing use of law-of-the-land or due process clauses as limitations on legislative powers.

47. ELY, *supra* note 31, at 78.

48. *See generally* Riggs, *supra* note 40. Even Hamilton's oft-quoted statement, when viewed in full context, supported the proposition that the due process clause prohibited the legislature from depriving persons of their legally protected rights. *See id.* at 989–90.

49. *E.g.,* Bowman v. Middleton, 1 S.C.L. (1 Bay) 252, 254–55 (1792) (invalidating a 1712 act transferring property from one owner to another, holding that "it was against common right, as well as against *magna charta*, to take away the freehold of one man and vest it in another, . . . without any compensation, or even a trial by a jury of the country, to determine the right in question"); University of North Carolina v. Foy, 5 N.C. (1 Mur.) 58 (1805) (holding that the repeal of an act granting land to university trustees violated the "law of the land" clause in the state constitution). Two other South Carolina cases from the 1790s are instructive as to the meaning of "law of the land" clauses: *Zylstra v. Corporation of Charleston,* 1 S.C.L. (1 Bay) 382 (1794); and *Lindsay v. Commissioners,* 2 S.C.L. (2 Bay) 38 (1796). Although the court in neither case declared a law unconstitutional (the *Zylstra* court reversed a conviction under a city bylaw on procedural grounds, and in *Lindsay* an equally divided court rejected a challenge to the taking of land for building a road), the judges' opinions in both cases understood the state constitution's "law of the land" clause as a protection of substantive common-law rights, even against statutes duly passed by the legislature. *See* Sherry, *supra* note 38, at 216–19; Riggs, *supra* note 40, at 980–81.

50. Herman v. State, 8 Ind. 545, 558 (1855). This was the one decision conceded by Charles Warren, in his 1926 *Harvard Law Review* article, to be an exception to his claim that in early American history, "liberty" meant only the freedom of the person from physical restraint. Warren, *supra* note 19, at 444–45.

51. Wynehamer v. People, 13 N.Y. 378, 399 (1856); ELY, *supra* note 31, at 79. In another essay, Ely calls attention to the 1805 North Carolina case, *University of North Carolina,* 5 N.C. He cites that decision as well as the *Wynehamer* decision to show that "antebellum courts employed due process as a device to safeguard economic interests." James W. Ely Jr., *Economic Due Process Revisited* (reviewing PAUL KENS, JUDICIAL REVIEW AND REFORM POLITICS: THE ANATOMY OF LOCHNER V. NEW YORK (1990)), 44 VANDERBILT L. REV. 213, 220 & n.45 (1991).

52. Murray's Lessee v. Hoboken Land & Improvement co. 59 U.S. 272, 276 (1856). Ely observes that although *Murray's Lessee* turned on a procedural issue, the opinion "suggested a larger measure of judicial authority that could easily provide a basis for substantive review of congressional legislation." ELY, *supra* note 31, at 79.

53. Dred Scott v. Sandford, 60 U.S. (19 Howard) 393, 450 (1857). Although Taney wrote for only a minority of the justices in other parts of his opinion for the Court (including the first, and perhaps most controversial, part declaring that African Americans were not citizens), in this part of the opinion he wrote for a majority of six justices and thus expressed the true holding of the Court. *See generally* DON E. FEHRENBACHER, THE DRED SCOTT CASE: ITS SIGNIFICANCE IN AMERICAN LAW AND POLITICS 322–34 (1978).

54. The Antislavery Planks of the Republican National Platform (1856), *in* SOURCES IN AMERICAN CONSTITUTIONAL HISTORY 99 (Michael Les Benedict ed., 1996). The 1860 Republican platform repeated this plank and also, without referring directly to the *Dred Scott* decision, decried "the new dogma that the Constitution, of its own force, carries Slavery" into the territories, calling the idea "a dangerous political heresy" at odds with the Constitution itself. The Republican Party Platform (May 16, 1860), *in* 1 DOCUMENTS OF AMERICAN HISTORY 363, 364 (Henry Steele Commager ed., 9th ed. 1973).

55. *See* BERNARD H. SIEGAN, THE SUPREME COURT'S CONSTITUTION 71–72 (1987). Two anti-slavery third parties, the Liberty Party in its 1843 platform and the Free Soil Party in its 1848 and 1852 platforms, also declared that the Fifth Amendment's due process clause secured the inalienable rights enumerated in the Declaration of Independence. *Id.*

56. A seven-justice majority of the *Dred Scott* Court held that, under Missouri law, Dred Scott was still a slave—arguably making irrelevant the holding on the Missouri Compromise restriction. FEHRENBACHER, *supra* note 53, at 324–25. "*Obiter dictum*" was "the Republican battle cry in the war upon the Dred Scott decision." *Id.* at 439.

57. In his first inaugural address, Abraham Lincoln criticized third parties' use of Supreme Court decisions "for political purposes." Without specifically mentioning *Dred Scott*, he denied that the Court's decisions "in ordinary litigation between parties in personal actions" could determine for Congress or the president "the policy of the government, upon vital questions affecting the whole people." Lincoln, First Inaugural Address (Mar. 4, 1861), *in* 1 DOCUMENTS OF AMERICAN HISTORY, *supra* note 54, at 387.

58. *In re Jacobs*, 98 N.Y. 98 (1885). The statute applied only to cities having over 500,000 inhabitants—which at the time meant only two cities, New York City and Brooklyn. *Id.* at 104.

59. *Id.* at 106–07. The court noted that the police power, "however broad and extensive," was "not above the Constitution," *id.* at 108, and that "in its exercise the legislature must respect the great fundamental rights guaranteed by the Constitution," *id.* at 110. The court also reaffirmed its judicial review power, maintaining that if the legislature "passes an act ostensibly for the public health, and thereby destroys or takes away the property of the citizen, or interferes with his personal liberty, then it is for the courts to scrutinize the act and see whether it really relates to and is convenient and appropriate to promote the public health." *Id.*

60. *Id.* at 114. The court took judicial notice of "the nature and qualities of tobacco," finding no evidence that its preparation and manufacture into cigars was "even injurious

to the health of those who deal in it, or are engaged in its production or manufacture," let alone dangerous to the health of the public. *Id.* at 113. "It is plain that this is not a health law," the court concluded. *Id.* at 114.

61. *Id.* at 115. In stating its holding, the court also clearly identified the standard of review it was applying to the statute: "When a health law is challenged in the courts as unconstitutional on the ground that it arbitrarily interferes with personal liberty and private property without due process of law, the courts must be able to see that it has at least in fact some relation to the public health, that the public health is the end actually aimed at, and that it is appropriate and adapted to that end. This we have not been able to see in this law, and we must, therefore, pronounce it unconstitutional and void." *Id.* Earlier in the opinion, the court also found that the statute deprived persons of their property without due process of law, by depriving inhabitants of tenement houses of the right to work at a lawful trade therein. *Id.* at 105–06.

62. People v. Marx, 99 N.Y. 377, 2 N.E. 29 (1885).

63. The court asked, "If the argument of the respondents in support of the absolute power of the legislature to prohibit one branch of industry for the purpose of protecting another with which it competes can be sustained, why could not the oleomargarine manufacturers, should they obtain sufficient power to influence or control the legislative councils, prohibit the manufacture or sale of dairy products?" *Id.*, 99 N.Y. at 386, 2 N.E. at 33–34.

64. *Id.*, 99 N.Y. at 386, 2 N.E. at 33. The court cited the U.S. Supreme Court's decision in the *Slaughterhouse Cases*, although its view that the right to pursue any lawful industrial pursuit was "one of the fundamental rights and privileges of every American citizen" was the view adopted by the *Slaughterhouse* dissenters, not the majority.

65. Ritchie v. People, 155 Ill. 98, 102, 40 N.E. 454, 455 (1895).

66. *Id.*, 155 Ill. at 104–05, 40 N.E. at 455–56.

67. *Id.*, 155 Ill. at 111–12, 40 N.E. at 458. The court rejected the state's rationale that the statute fell within the traditional scope of the police power, as "a measure for the promotion of the public health" and "designed to protect woman on account of her sex and physique"—the rationale accepted by the U.S. Supreme Court as justification for a maximum-hours law applied to women in *Muller v. Oregon*, discussed in chapter 4.

68. Ely, *supra* note 31, at 60.

69. For example, in his opinion for the majority of the Court in *Lochner*, Justice Peckham described the police power as "relating to the safety, health, morals and general welfare of the public." *Lochner*, 198 U.S. at 53.

70. Scott M. Reznick, *Empiricism and the Principle of Conditions in the Evolution of the Police Power: A Model for Definitional Scrutiny*, 1978 Wash. U.L.Q. 2, 4.

71. 4 William Blackstone, Commentaries *162.

72. Thomas M. Cooley, A Treatise on the Constitutional Limitations which Rest upon the Legislative Power of the States of the American Union 704 (6th ed. 1890).

73. Commonwealth v. Alger, 61 Mass. (7 Cush.) 53, 84–85 (1851).

74. *See* Thorpe v. Rutland & Burlington R.R., 27 Vt. 140, 153 (1854) (upholding a statute requiring railroads to construct and maintain fences as cattle guards along their routes, as a valid application of the police power according to the *sic utere* maxim, "in regard to those whose business is dangerous and destructive to other persons' property or business"); State v. Paul, 5 R. I. 185, 191 (1858) (sustaining conviction under

a criminal statute prohibiting the sale and keeping of intoxicating liquors as a valid exercise of the police power, which the court declared "exists in great part for the very purpose of changing the [common law] adjustment [of rights] from time to time, as the relative circumstances of the community and individuals may require").

75. U.S. CONST. art. 1, § 10, cl. 1. The clause was modeled after a provision in the Northwest Ordinance that "no law ought ever to be made, or have force in the said territory, that shall, in any manner whatever, interfere with or affect private contracts or engagements, *bona fide*, and without fraud, previously formed." 1 DOCUMENTS OF AMERICAN HISTORY, *supra* note 54, at 131 (The Northwest Ordinance, July 13, 1787, art. 2).

76. Henry G. Manne, *Inequality and the Constitution*, 9 HARV. J. LAW & PUB. POL'Y 31, 32 (1986).

77. Champion v. Casey (Cir. Ct. R.I. 1792) (unreported), cited in ELY, *supra* note 31, at 62–63.

78. ELY, *supra* note 31, at 64. Ely regards the contract clause as "the centerpiece of Marshall Court jurisprudence" and "a powerful bulwark to property interests." *Id.* at 63–64. Noting the scholarly dispute about the scope of the contract clause—whether it was meant to apply only to contracts between private individuals or whether it extended to contracts made by state governments—he finds historical evidence in favor of the latter view confirmed by a series of significant Marshall Court decisions, including *Fletcher v. Peck*, 10 U.S. (6 Cranch) 87 (1810), *New Jersey v. Wilson*, 11 U.S. (7 Cranch) 164 (1812), and *Dartmouth College v. Woodward*, 17 U.S. (4 Wheat.) 518 (1819). *Id.* at 45, 64–66.

79. 10 U.S. (6 Cranch) at 139 (emphasis added). The case is ably discussed in C. PETER McGRATH, YAZOO: THE CASE OF *FLETCHER V. PECK* (1966). Justice William Johnson, one of Jefferson's appointees to the Court and the only justice to challenge Marshall's opinions with some frequency, wrote a concurring opinion relying exclusively on natural law principles. *Id.* at 63, 80 (quoting 6 Cranch 87, 143–48 (Johnson, J., concurring)).

80. On the vested rights doctrine, see ELY, *supra* note 31, at 63.

81. *Id.* (quoting Vanhorne's Lessee v. Dorrance, 2 Dallas 304, 310 (1795)).

82. *Id.* (quoting Calder v. Bull, 3 Dallas 386, 388 (1798)).

83. Turpin v. Locket, 10 Va. (6 Call) 113 (1804), and Herman v. State, 8 Ind. 545 (1855), discussed *supra* notes 38 & 50. *See generally* Sherry, *supra* note 38; Riggs, *supra* note 40; *see also* STEPHEN B. PRESSER, RECAPTURING THE CONSTITUTION 142 (1994).

84. HOWARD GILLMAN, THE CONSTITUTION BESIEGED: THE RISE AND DEMISE OF LOCHNER ERA POLICE POWERS JURISPRUDENCE 49 (1993). An early example cited by Gillman was a Massachusetts Supreme Court case decided the same year Andrew Jackson was first elected president, involving a Boston bylaw that prohibited any person not licensed by the mayor and aldermen from removing "any house-dirt, refuse, offal, filth or animal or vegetable substance" from houses. Although the court affirmed the conviction and thus upheld the challenged law, it cited an English precedent as an example of an illegitimate law: a London bylaw that prohibited carmen from operating their carts within the precincts of a hospital without license from the wardens of the hospital. Such a law, the Massachusetts court observed, would be held "void" and "unreasonable," both "because it was in restraint of the liberty of the trade of the carman" and "because it went to the private benefit of the wardens of the hospital, and was in the nature of a monopoly." *Id.* at 51 (quoting Vadine's Case, 6 Pick (23 Mass.) 187, 187–92 (1828)). Note that the Boston bylaw fit within one of the traditional categories of the police power, the protection of public health.

85. LOCKE, *supra* note 23, at 304 (book 2, chapter 2, § 54) (emphasis in original). Citing this passage from Locke in support of the "libertarian" conception of equality, Bernard Siegan has argued that Representative John Bingham, the author of the original version of the Fourteenth Amendment, understood the equal protection provision of the amendment in this way. "For him, equality before the law meant that all laws should apply equally, and that no person or persons would be favored or denied. When government limits liberties of certain individuals, it also denies them equality with others not so incapacitated." Bernard H. Siegan, *Rehabilitating* Lochner, 22 SAN DIEGO L. REV. 453, 469 (1985).

86. James Madison, *Memorial and Remonstrance* (1785), *in* THE MIND OF THE FOUNDER 8–9 (Marvin Meyers ed., rev. ed. 1981). This argument was part of point 4 of Madison's petition to the General Assembly protesting against a proposed bill to support the Christian religion. Thus, the equality principle was part of Madison's case for religious freedom or, specifically, in opposition to government establishment of religion.

87. GILLMAN, *supra* note 84, at 35–40, 54–55. Gillman describes Jacksonian democracy as "an ideology of market freedom protected specifically by a core value of political equality." *Id*. at 35. For more on Jacksonian ideology and the radical wing of the Jeffersonian Republican party from which it derived, see RICHARD E. ELLIS, THE JEFFERSONIAN CRISIS: COURTS AND POLITICS IN THE YOUNG REPUBLIC (1971); MARVIN MEYERS, THE JACKSONIAN PERSUASION: POLITICS AND BELIEF (1960).

88. GILLMAN, *supra* note 84, at 47–49. The classic example of the Taney Court's shift away from the Marshall Court's vested rights doctrine, especially in its contract clause jurisprudence, is the Court's decision in *Charles River Bridge v. Warren Bridge*, 36 U.S. (11 Pet.) 420 (1837), ably discussed in STANLEY I. KUTLER, PRIVILEGE AND CREATIVE DESTRUCTION: THE CHARLES RIVER BRIDGE CASE (1971).

89. *See, e.g.*, Wally's Heirs v. Kennedy, 2 Yerger (10 Tenn.) 554, 555–56 (1831) (invalidating a law authorizing the state judiciary to dismiss certain kinds of Indian reservation cases, on the grounds that it was not "a general public law" but a "partial, or private law"); Bank v. Cooper, 2 Yerger (10 Tenn.) 599, 606–07 (1831) (invalidating an act creating a special court to handle all lawsuits brought against the Bank of the State of Tennessee, because the law was not "general in its operation, affecting all alike"); and Durkee v. City of Janesville, 28 Wis. 464, 470 (1871) (invalidating a law exempting the city of Janesville from the obligation to pay court costs in a previous case, because "the clause 'law of the land,' is held to mean a general public law, equally binding upon every member of the community"), cited in GILLMAN, *supra* note 84, at 53–54 & 229 nn.111–12, 59 & 230 n.130.

90. GILLMAN, *supra* note 84, at 55 and at 95 (quoting Charles Chauncy Binney's article, "Restrictions upon Local and Special Legislation in the United States," in the *American Law Register* in the 1890s). Much of the impetus behind such provisions in antebellum state constitutions was the reaction against state subsidies for roads and canals—what a modern legal historian has called the "erosion of faith in the active state." KERMIT L. HALL, THE MAGIC MIRROR: LAW IN AMERICAN HISTORY 102–03 (1989).

91. GILLMAN, *supra* note 84, at 55.

92. *Id*. at 54. Gillman identifies this principle as "a jurisprudence of *public purpose*," which he contrasts with modern constitutional jurisprudence and its "theory of *preferred freedoms*." *Id*. (emphasis in original).

93. COOLEY, *supra* note 72, at 483. He explained that "every one has a right to demand that he be governed by general rules, and a special statute which, without his consent, singles his case out as one to be regulated by a different law from that which is applied in all similar cases, would not be legitimate legislation, but would be such an arbitrary mandate as is not within the province of free governments." *Id.*

94. People v. Salem, 20 Mich. 487 (1870), *quoted in* GILLMAN, *supra* note 84, at 56. *Id.* Cooley's own abhorrence of subsidies was rooted in his background as a "Locofoco" Democrat, one of the more radical anti-privilege wings of the Jacksonian party. GILLMAN, *supra* note 84, at 38, 55–56 (citing Alan Jones, *Thomas M. Cooley and "Laissez-Faire Constitutionalism": A Reconsideration*, 53 J. AM. HIST. 751 (1967)). Alan Jones discusses Cooley's background in Locofoco Democracy more fully in his doctoral dissertation, "The Constitutional Conservatism of Thomas McIntyre Cooley: A Study in the History of Ideas" (University of Michigan, 1960), published by Garland in 1987.

95. *See* GILLMAN, *supra* note 84; Michael Les Benedict, *Laissez-Faire and Liberty: A Re-Evaluation of the Meaning and Origins of Laissez-Faire Constitutionalism*, 3 LAW & HIST. REV. 293 (1985).

96. GILLMAN, *supra* note 84, at 10. Although he recognizes that judicial standards during this era "were not illegitimate creations of unrestrained free-market ideologues" and thus rejects the Holmesian orthodox view, Professor Gillman is explicitly unsympathetic to *Lochner*-era jurisprudence, which he sees as grounded in early American constitutional principles that were "anachronistic" in industrialized America, where economic conditions "might justify special government protections for dependent classes." *Id.* In other words, he accepts unquestioningly the rationale that Progressives gave in support of early 20th-century "social legislation."

97. *Id.* at 88, 92.

98. *Id.* at 126–29.

99. In a recent reply to his critics, Gillman admits that his revisionist account was intended to show that modern "fundamental rights" jurisprudence was "a completely different sort of thing" from *Lochner* era "public purpose" jurisprudence—in order to defend modern substantive due process decisions, particularly *Roe v. Wade*, against conservative critiques. *See* Howard Gillman, *De-Lochnerizing* Lochner, 85 BOSTON U. L. REV. 859, 862 n.17 (2005).

100. COOLEY, *supra* note 72, at 484. Significantly, this statement appeared in the section dealing with "Unequal and Partial Legislation." Cooley added, "To forbid to an individual or a class the right to the acquisition or enjoyment of property in such manner as should be permitted to the community at large, would be to deprive them of *liberty* in particulars of primary importance to their 'pursuit of happiness,'" citing among other sources Burlamaqui's definition of "natural liberty" as "the right which nature gives to all mankind of disposing of their persons and property after the manner they judge most consonant to their happiness. . . and so as not to interfere with an equal exercise of the same rights by other men." *Id.* at 484–85 & n.2. As one modern property-rights scholar has noted, the "Cooley synthesis" thus linked the Jacksonian principles of equal rights and hostility to class legislation with substantive due process protection of individual rights. ELY, *supra* note 31, at 342–43.

101. *Compare, e.g.*, David E. Bernstein, Lochner *Era Revisionism, Revised:* Lochner *and the Origins of Fundamental Rights Constitutionalism*, 92 GEO. L.J. 1 (2003) [hereafter "Bernstein, *Revisionism*"], *with* Barry Cushman, *Some Varieties and Vicissitudes of Lochnerism*, 85 BOSTON U. L. REV. 881 (2005) (defending Gillman's class legislation thesis against Bernstein's critique).

102. *See* Bernstein, *Revisionism, supra,* at 13–21, 27–30. Moreover, a legal scholar who has comprehensively surveyed the Court's decisions during the *Lochner* era has found that class legislation rhetoric—the terms "class legislation," "class law," "partial legislation," or "partial law"—was infrequently used in early 20th-century decisions; he found no cases during the years 1902–1932 in which the concept was critical to the Court's decision. MICHAEL J. PHILLIPS, THE *LOCHNER* COURT, MYTH AND REALITY: SUBSTANTIVE DUE PROCESS FROM THE 1890S TO THE 1930S, 114 (2001).

103. Thorpe v. Rutland & Burlington R.R., 27 Vt. 140, 147, 153 (1854).

104. *See, e.g.,* HALL, *supra* note 90, at 94–102 (discussing the "active state" and "mixed economy" in antebellum America, with state governments promoting and regulating economic activity in various ways).

105. *See* ELY, *supra* note 31, at 62. Ely cites several examples of restrictions on the use of property that were sustained as valid police power regulations; these include "requirements that owners of urban lots construct buildings with inflammable materials, regulations of privately owned wharves in harbors, measures prohibiting the sale of liquor without a license, and statutes requiring railroads to institute safety features such as cattle guards." *Id.* at 61. With regard to controls over business activities, he cites the states' continuation of colonial schemes to control the quality of export commodities, such as South Carolina's tobacco-inspection laws. "Although many of these controls did impose costs on businesses or property owners, their objective was to safeguard the general public interest," he notes. *Id.* at 62.

106. The "social legislation" advocated by Progressive activists is discussed more fully in chapter 2.

107. U.S. CONST. amend. XIV, § 1. The other important provision is Section 5, which grants Congress the power "to enforce, by appropriate legislation," these limits on the states.

108. Charles Fairman, *Does the Fourteenth Amendment Incorporate the Bill of Rights?* 2 STAN. L. REV. 5 (1949). As Richard Aynes has shown, Fairman's analysis supported the conclusion of his mentor at Harvard Law School, Justice Felix Frankfurter, who, in his famous concurring opinion in *Adamson v. California,* 332 U.S. 46 (1947), took the position that the amendment applied against the states none of the specific rights guaranteed by the federal Bill of Rights. Richard J. Aynes, *On Misreading John Bingham and the Fourteenth Amendment,* 103 YALE L. J. 57, 64–65 & n.44 (1993).

109. *Compare, e.g.,* BERGER, *supra* note 19 (arguing that Congress intended to give the Fourteenth Amendment a relatively narrow scope), *and* JAMES E. BOND, NO EASY WALK TO FREEDOM: RECONSTRUCTION AND THE RATIFICATION OF THE FOURTEENTH AMENDMENT (1997) (finding in the ratification debates in Southern states little evidence that Section 1 was intended to incorporate the Bill of Rights), *with* MICHAEL KENT CURTIS, NO STATE SHALL ABRIDGE: THE FOURTEENTH AMENDMENT AND THE BILL OF RIGHTS (1986) (finding in the congressional debates and other historical sources ample evidence supporting full incorporation), *and* Aynes, *supra* note 108 (concluding that the amendment's framers indeed did intend to incorporate the Bill of Rights). In the first chapter of his book on the amendment, William Nelson has nicely summed up the scholarly debate, characterizing it as largely an "interpretivist game." *See* WILLIAM E. NELSON, THE FOURTEENTH AMENDMENT: FROM POLITICAL PRINCIPLE TO JUDICIAL DOCTRINE 5 (1988).

110. For example, Berger interprets the three restrictions imposed on the states in the first section of the amendment as but three facets of one design: the protection of certain "fundamental rights" (the privileges or immunities clause) from diminishment except by "due course of law" or "laws of the land" (the due process clause) applying to all alike (the equal protection clause). BERGER, *supra* note 19, at 18, 208–09, 213. The authors of a more recent study of the Fourteenth Amendment's original meaning have concluded that "it was the Privileges or Immunities Clause that was expected to be the principal source for rights" protected against state abridgement by the amendment. Kimberly C. Shankman & Roger Pilon, *Reviving the Privileges or Immunities Clause to Redress the Balance among States, Individuals, and the Federal Government*, 3 TEXAS REV. L. & POLITICS 1, 26 (1998).

111. The Black Codes severely restricted black persons' rights, particularly their economic freedom, in an apparent attempt to hold them in a status of quasi-slavery. See DAVID HERBERT DONALD, LIBERTY AND UNION: THE CRISIS OF POPULAR GOVERNMENT, 1830–1870, 193 (1978); ERIC FONER, RECONSTRUCTION: AMERICA'S UNFINISHED REVOLUTION, 1863–1877, 199–205 (1988). The first of these codes, adopted by the Mississippi legislature, prohibited black persons from renting or leasing "any lands or tenements except in incorporated cities or towns." South Carolina's code excluded them from practicing "the art, trade, or business of an artisan, mechanic or shopkeeper, or any other trade, employment or business (besides that of husbandry, or that of a servant)"; and Louisiana's code required freedmen who were agricultural laborers to enter into long-term contracts and "to obey all proper orders" of their employers, subject to fines or dismissal for insubordination. Despite these restrictions on their freedom to earn a living, in most of the Southern states black persons who were unemployed were liable for criminal punishment, by imprisonment or hard labor, for vagrancy. Moreover, they were forbidden from exercising essential civil rights that white persons enjoyed: for example, they could not purchase or carry firearms, nor could they assemble after sunset. Black Codes of Mississippi and Louisiana (1865) *in* 1 DOCUMENTS OF AMERICAN HISTORY, *supra* note 54, at 452–56.

112. The act declared that persons born in the United States were citizens of the United States and provided, in relevant part, that

> such citizens, of every race and color, without regard to any previous condition of slavery or involuntary servitude, . . . shall have the same right, in every State and Territory in the United States, to make and enforce contracts, to sue, be parties, and give evidence, to inherit, purchase, lease, sell, hold, and convey real and personal property, and to full and equal benefit of all laws and proceedings for the security of persons and property, as is enjoyed by white citizens, and shall be subject to like punishment, pains and penalties, and to none other.

To remove all doubt that the act was meant to nullify the Black Codes, Congress added the phrase "any law, statute, ordinance, regulation, or custom, to the contrary notwithstanding." Act of April 9, 1866, ch. 31, § 1, 14 Stat. 27, *reprinted in* 1 DOCUMENTS OF AMERICAN HISTORY, *supra* note 54, at 464.

113. Shankman & Pilon, *supra* note 110, at 25.

114. Veto of the Civil Rights Act (Mar. 27, 1866), *in* 1 DOCUMENTS OF AMERICAN HISTORY, *supra* note 54, at 465–66.

115. Bingham was a member of the 15-man Joint Committee on Reconstruction and the principal author of the amendment; Justice Hugo Black called him "the Madison of the first section of the Fourteenth Amendment." Adamson v. California, 332 U.S. 46, 74 (1947) (Black, J., dissenting). For a discussion of Bingham's legal theory, which defends him against the charge by Fairman and other scholars that his views were idiosyncratic, see Aynes, *supra* note 108, at 74–94.

116. The original resolution proposed by Representative Bingham in February 1866 proposed that "Congress shall have power to make all laws which shall be necessary and proper to secure to the citizens of each State all privileges and immunities of citizens in the several States, and to all persons in the several States equal protection in the rights of life, liberty, and property." The Reconstruction Amendments Debates 149–50 (Virginia Commission on Constitutional Government, 1967) [hereinafter, "Debates"] (reprinting speech of Rep. Bingham, Feb. 26, 1866).

117. The evolution of the language of the first section into what became the second sentence of the Fourteenth Amendment, as adopted, is a complicated story. Put simply, after some debate, the House voted on February 28, 1866, by a vote of 110–37, to postpone consideration of Bingham's original proposed amendment until the second week of April. The measure was never taken up again because, by early May, the Joint Committee on Reconstruction reported back to the House and the Senate a proposed five-section amendment that, with some additional changes, became the Fourteenth Amendment as adopted by Congress and sent to the states for ratification. Those changes included the addition of the first sentence of Section 1, declaring all persons "born or naturalized in the United States" to be "citizens of the United States and of the State wherein they reside," to overrule that part of Chief Justice Taney's opinion in *Dred Scott* that denied citizenship to black persons (descendants of African slaves, whether enslaved or free). See Curtis, *supra* note 109, at 173; Siegan, *supra* note 85, at 468. A fairly detailed account of the evolution of the amendment's text is given in Nelson, *supra* note 109, at 49–58.

118. *See* Siegan, *supra* note 85, at 468; Nelson, *supra* note 109, at 55.

119. *See* Foner, *supra* note 111, at 257 ("Unlike the Civil Rights Act, which listed numerous rights a state could not abridge, the Amendment used only the broadest language. Clearly, Republicans proposed to abrogate the Black Codes and eliminate any doubts as to the constitutionality of the Civil Rights Act. Yet to reduce their aims to this is to misconstrue the difference between a statute and a constitutional amendment. . . ."). The final version of Section 1 adopted by the joint committee abandoned a narrower formulation proposed by Representative Robert Dale Owen Jr.—which would have merely prohibited "discrimination. . . as to the civil rights of persons because of race, color, or previous condition of servitude"—and instead substituted the language proposed by Bingham, with its three familiar clauses: the privileges or immunities clause, the due process clause, and the equal protection clause. Nelson, *supra* note 109, at 55–56. As Curtis notes, the inclusion of these clauses shows that the amendment was intended to do more than merely protect black persons from racially discriminatory state laws. *See* Curtis, *supra* note 109, at 118–19.

120. The amendment's opponents, on the other hand, warned that it would destroy federalism. For example, Representative Andrew Jackson Rogers (D-N.J.) called it "the embodiment of centralization and the disfranchisement of the States of those sacred and immutable State rights which were reserved to them by the consent of our

fathers in our organic law." DEBATES, *supra* note 116, at 149 (speech of Rep. Rogers, Feb. 26, 1866).

121. *Id.* at 217 (speech of Rep. Bingham, May 10, 1866) (emphasis added). Bingham added that the amendment "takes from no State any right that ever pertained to it. No State ever had the right. . . to deny to any freeman the equal protection of the laws or to abridge the privileges or immunities of any citizen of the Republic." *Id.*

122. For example, Representative William Higby argued that the amendment was "already embraced in the Constitution" but was "so scattered through different portions of it" that it was ineffectual. Adoption of the amendment would only "give vitality and life to portions of the Constitution" that have been ignored and "have become as dead letter in that instrument," he maintained—with obvious reference to the Article IV privileges and immunities clause. *Id.* at 152 (speech of Rep. Higby, Feb. 26, 1866). Higby was a radical Republican from California. CURTIS, *supra* note 109, at 68. Messages from governors transmitting the proposed amendment for ratification to their state legislatures generally described it as protecting citizens' "rights" or "liberty" without interfering with the lawful authority of the states. *See id.* at 145–47.

123. DEBATES, *supra* note 116, at 220 (speech of Sen. Howard, May 23, 1866).

124. *Id.* at 219–20.

125. 1 WILLIAM BLACKSTONE, COMMENTARIES *125.

126. DEBATES, *supra* note 116, at 219 (speech of Sen. Howard, May 23, 1866).

127. Corfield v. Coryell, 6 F. Cas. 546, 551–52 (C.C.E.D. Pa. 1823) (No. 3230). Justice Washington, who served on the Supreme Court from 1798 to 1829, decided the case in his capacity as circuit judge.

128. DEBATES, *supra* note 116, at 219 (speech of Sen. Howard, May 23, 1866). On the 19-century hierarchical view of rights, and particularly the distinction between civil rights and political rights, see BOND, *supra* note 109, at 255–56. The provision in Section 2 of the Fourteenth Amendment, which sought to encourage states to grant voting rights to black men by proportionately depriving them of their representation in Congress if they failed to do so, as well as the later protection for voting rights in the Fifteenth Amendment, provides textual support that suffrage was not intended to be among the rights protected by Section 1.

129. Bingham shared Howard's broad understanding of "privileges" and "immunities," equating the body of rights protected by Article IV, Section 2, with the body of rights protected by Section 1 of the Fourteenth Amendment, both in his original proposal and in its final version; and he saw that body of rights as including, but not limited to, the particular rights guaranteed by the first eight amendments of the Constitution. Among those rights were the rights of liberty and property that were protected substantively by the due process clause. *See* Aynes, *supra* note 108, at 68–71; CURTIS, *supra* note 109, at 64, 91. As Bernard Siegan has noted, in summarizing the debates over the amendment, "most of the Republicans probably regarded privileges and immunities as encompassing all fundamental liberties secured in the Constitution, which necessarily would include those set forth in the first eight amendments." SIEGAN, *supra* note 55, at 68.

130. DEBATES, *supra* note 116, at 219 (speech of Sen. Howard, May 23, 1866); Aynes, *supra* note 108, at 72 (citing CONG. GLOBE, 39th Cong., 1st Sess. 1089–90 (speech of Rep. Bingham, Feb. 28, 1866)). Thus, Bingham and Howard saw the states' obligation to obey the Bill of Rights as "legally unenforceable—just as the Court had treated other obligations of article IV, section 2 as unenforceable." CURTIS, *supra* note 109, at

100. Notwithstanding the U.S. Supreme Court's refusal to apply the Bill of Rights to the states, in *Barron v. Baltimore*, 32 U.S. (7 Pet.) 243 (1833), and other decisions, some state supreme courts had held that state legislatures were limited by provisions in the federal Bill of Rights, including the Second Amendment's right to bear arms and the due process protections of the Fifth Amendment. CURTIS, *supra* note 109, at 24–25.

131. ELY, *supra* note 31, at 220 (quoting Herbert Hovenkamp, *The Political Economy of Substantive Due Process*, 40 STAN. L. REV. 379, 395 (1988)).

132. In the first two federal court decisions interpreting the Fourteenth Amendment—the 1870 circuit court decision in the *Slaughterhouse Cases* (later reversed by the Supreme Court) and an 1871 federal district court decision in Alabama—Supreme Court Justice Joseph P. Bradley, in his capacity as circuit judge, and Judge William Woods, a future Supreme Court justice, found that the amendment protected against state impairment such fundamental rights as the right to pursue a lawful occupation without interference by "odious monopolies" and the right of freedom of speech. Aynes, *supra* note 108, at 97–98 (discussing Live-Stock Dealers' & Butchers' Ass'n v. Crescent City Live-Stock Landing & Slaughter-House Co., 15 F. Cas. 649 (C.C.D. La. 1870) (No. 8408) (opinion of Bradley and Woods, JJ.); United States v. Hall, 26 F. Cas. 79 (S. D. Ala. 1871) (No. 15, 282)).

133. Butchers' Benevolent Association v. Crescent City Livestock Landing and Slaughterhouse Co., 83 U.S. (16 Wall.) 36 (1873). The law was billed as a public health measure, but evidence that it was really the product of political corruption—including bribes paid by the Crescent City Company to Louisiana legislators, the governor, and the owners and editors of two newspapers—surfaced in a shareholders' suit against the company and was reported in rival papers, including the *New Orleans Picayune* and *Bee*. CHARLES FAIRMAN, RECONSTRUCTION AND REUNION, 1864–88, 1321–44 (1971). The authors of a recent exhaustive study of the *Slaughterhouse Cases* have concluded that "although the claims of bribery and corruption remain uncertain," the historical evidence shows that the Crescent City Company "obtained [its] franchise by means that left a good deal to be desired" and that "it was feasible for [courts] to conclude that the act had been obtained by bribery." RONALD M. LABBÉ & JONATHAN LURIE, THE SLAUGHTERHOUSE CASES: REGULATION, RECONSTRUCTION, AND THE FOURTEENTH AMENDMENT 84, 96–97, 102 (2003).

134. Aynes, *supra* note 108, at 98–99 & n.266 (noting that lawyers for the butchers challenging the Crescent City monopoly had submitted portions of Bingham's congressional speeches, along with those of other members of Congress, in their brief to the Court).

135. 83 U.S. (16 Wall.) at 71. By most accounts, the butchers who were challenging the Crescent City monopoly were white; therefore, they could be said to be outside the class of persons whom Justice Miller considered the intended beneficiaries of the Fourteenth Amendment's protections. As noted *supra*, text at note 111, however, some of the most important rights denied freedmen by the Black Codes were economic rights, including the freedom to pursue a lawful occupation unrestrained by a state-granted monopoly—the very right asserted by the plaintiffs in the *Slaughterhouse Cases*. Thus, as noted below, Justice Field was right in criticizing the majority decision for being logically inconsistent or hypocritical.

136. The first sentence of Section 1 provided that "[a]ll persons born or naturalized in the United States and subject to [its] jurisdiction" were both "citizens of the United States" and citizens "of the State wherein they reside"; it thus redefined state

citizenship in terms of federal citizenship. Although noting this clear purpose of the provision, Justice Miller drew a distinction between the two types of citizenship and maintained that because the second sentence of Section 1 referred to "the privileges or immunities of citizens of the United States," only those rights—and not any of the rights protecting "a citizen of a State from the legislative power of his own State"—were protected by the clause. 83 U.S. (16 Wall.) at 73–74. After relying heavily on Justice Washington's opinion in *Corfield v. Coryell* to describe the "privileges and immunities of citizens of the several States" protected by Article IV, Justice Miller concluded that because these rights "belong to citizens of the States as such," they were "left to the State governments for security and protection, and not by this article [the Fourteenth Amendment] placed under the special care of the Federal government." *Id.* at 78. That conclusion, of course, overlooked the essential purpose of the amendment, as stated in the congressional debates by its framers.

137. *Id.* at 79–80. Needless to say, none of the rights identified by Justice Miller was jeopardized by the Black Codes that prompted Congress to pass the 1866 Civil Rights Act or to consider the need for the Fourteenth Amendment. As Justice Field observed in his dissent, explaining why the majority's interpretation rendered the Fourteenth Amendment a "vain and idle enactment": "With privileges and immunities thus designated or implied no State could ever have interfered by its laws, and no new constitutional provision was required to inhibit such interference. The supremacy of the Constitution and the laws of the United States always controlled any State legislation of that character." *Id.* at 96 (Field, J., dissenting).

138. *Id.* at 97 (Field, J., dissenting) (emphasis in original). "[G]rants of exclusive privileges," such as the Crescent City monopoly, "are opposed to the whole theory of free government, and it requires no aid from any bill of rights to make them void," Field concluded. "That only is a free government, in the American sense of the term, under which the inalienable right of every citizen to pursue his happiness is unrestrained, except by just, equal, and impartial laws." *Id.* at 111. Field recognized that the state, by valid police regulations to protect public health, could restrict the slaughtering business by general laws regulating the places where animals were slaughtered or requiring their inspection before being slaughtered—as other parts of the Louisiana statute, not challenged in this case, provided. "But under the pretence of prescribing a police regulation," he added, "the State cannot be permitted to encroach upon any of the just rights of the citizen, which the Constitution intended to secure against abridgement." *Id.* at 87.

139. *Id.* at 96. Field recognized that the first clause of the amendment redefined citizenship, making irrelevant the distinction on which Miller relied. "The citizen of a State is now only a citizen of the United States residing in that State. The fundamental rights, privileges, and immunities which belong to him as a free man and a free citizen, now belong to him as a citizen of the United States, and are not dependent upon his citizenship of any State." *Id.* at 95. Thus, as Field interpreted the Constitution, what the privileges and immunities clause of Section IV did for "the protection of the citizens of one State against hostile and discriminating legislation of other States," the Fourteenth Amendment did for "the protection of every citizen of the United States against hostile and discriminating legislation against him in favor of others, whether they reside in the same or different States." *Id.* at 100–01.

140. *Id.* at 113–14, 116 (Bradley, J., dissenting). Monopolies over commodities or "ordinary callings or pursuits," exclusive privileges granted by government to com-

panies like Crescent City, thus were "an invasion of the rights of others to choose a lawful calling, and an infringement of personal liberty." *Id.* at 120. Like Field also, Bradley distinguished the monopoly created under the Louisiana law from valid police regulations to protect public health. He regarded the monopoly as "one of those arbitrary and unjust laws made in the interest of a few scheming individuals, by which some of the Southern states have, within the past few years, been so deplorably oppressed and impoverished." *Id.* at 120.

141. For example, James Bradley Thayer, the respected professor at Harvard Law School, told his students that "so far as it relates to the construction of the 14th amend[ment]. . . the minority. . . seem to be the sounder." Nelson, *supra* note 109, at 159 (quoting Thayer's teaching notes for his constitutional law class). Other critical comments by members of Congress and other commentators, including some later justices of the Court, are quoted in Aynes, *supra* note 108, at 99–101; and in Curtis, *supra* note 109, at 177.

142. Justice Miller gave scant attention to the rights claimed by the butchers who challenged the Louisiana law, blithely stating that the majority of justices were "of opinion that the rights claimed by these plaintiffs in error, if they have any existence, are not privileges or immunities of citizens of the United States" within the meaning of the Fourteenth Amendment. 83 U.S. (16 Wall.) at 80. He summarily disposed of challenges under the other clauses of Section 1. With regard to the due process clause, he simply asserted that "under no construction of that provision that we have seen, or any that we deem admissible," can the Crescent City monopoly be regarded as a deprivation of the other butchers' property. *Id.* at 81. With regard to the equal protection clause, he noted that in light of his previous discussion of the " pervading purpose" of the post–Civil War amendments, "[w]e doubt very much whether any action of a State not directed by way of discrimination against the negroes as a class, or on account of their race, will ever be held to come within the purview of this provision"—thus limiting its scope to class legislation that overtly discriminated against black persons. *Id.*

143. *Id.* at 78. The dissenters did not share this fear. Justice Field frankly considered the amendment to have "a profound significance and consequence." *Id.* at 96. Justice Bradley believed "it was the intention of the people of this country in adopting the amendment to provide National security against violation by the States of the fundamental rights of the citizen," *id.* at 122; and in response to the majority's concern about opening the floodgates to challenges of state laws, he forecast "but a slight accumulation of business in the Federal courts," adding that if he was wrong, "[t]he National will and National interest are of far greater importance" than the "inconvenience" to the federal judiciary from an increase in its caseload. *Id.* at 124. Justice Swayne wrote a separate dissent, in part, to express his view that the post–Civil War amendments indeed were "a new departure" from antebellum federalism and "mark an important epoch in the constitutional history of the country." *Id.* at 125.

144. This concern for federalism also explains the Court's early narrow reading of the Sherman Act of 1890, the first federal antitrust law. *See, e.g.,* United States v. E.C. Knight Co., 156 U.S. 1 (1895) (Chief Justice Fuller's opinion for the Court finding that a monopoly in manufacturing was not in commerce "among the States" and thus not subject to federal regulation under the commerce clause but rather left within the jurisdiction of the police power of the states).

145. Bradwell v. Illinois, 83 U.S. (16 Wall.) 130 (1873). Only Chief Justice Salmon P. Chase dissented, maintaining that the Illinois Supreme Court's refusal to admit Myra Bradwell to the bar violated her rights under the Fourteenth Amendment. The other three *Slaughterhouse* dissenters concurred with the majority decision, with Justice Bradley writing the opinion for them, maintaining that under the valid exercise of the police power, the legislature could "prescribe regulations founded on nature, reason, and experience for the due admission of qualified persons to professions and callings demanding special skill and confidence." In Bradley's view, "[t]he natural and proper timidity and delicacy which belongs to the female sex evidently unfits it for many of the occupations of civil life," including the practice of law. *Id.* at 139 (Bradley, J., concurring).

146. Chief Justice Waite's opinion for the Court in *Munn* borrowed from English law sources—specifically, from Sir Matthew Hale's 17th-century treatise, *De Portibus Maris*, which maintained that the king had broad authority to regulate ports, for the common good—as the basis for the "business affected with a public interest" doctrine. Munn v. Illinois, 94 U.S. 113, 125–26 (1877). Justice Field, in a dissenting opinion concurred in by Justice Strong, accepted the doctrine but maintained that under common law the only businesses whose rates could be regulated under it were those either "dedicated by the owner to public uses" or de jure monopolies, that is, those that held exclusive privileges granted by law—neither of which applied to the supposed de facto monopoly involved in this case. *Id.* at 139–40 (Field, J., dissenting).

Although the Court generally upheld state regulation of railroad rates, it did hold in a series of decisions in the 1880s that the Fourteenth Amendment limited the exercise of police powers and authorized federal courts to invalidate regulations that were unequal or unreasonable, arbitrarily depriving businesses of property or liberty without due process of law. *See, e.g.,* Stone v. Farmers' Loan & Trust Co., 116 U.S. 307, 331 (1886) (upholding a Mississippi law empowering a commission to regulate railroad rates but warning that its authority would be abused if it deprived a railroad of its ability to earn a profit); Chicago, Milwaukee & St. Paul Ry. Co. v. Minnesota, 134 U.S. 418 (1890) (holding that the reasonableness of a rate set by a state commission must be subject to judicial review). In addition, when state regulation of railroad rates interfered with interstate commerce, the Court limited the exercise of police powers under what is now called the "dormant commerce clause." *See, e.g.,* Wabash, St. Louis & Pacific Ry. Co. v. Illinois, 118 U.S. 557 (1886) (finding unconstitutional an Illinois law prohibiting "long haul–short haul" rate discrimination, a prohibition eventually incorporated in the federal Interstate Commerce Act of 1887).

147. Mugler v. Kansas, 123 U.S. 623 (1887). Although the Court sustained the prohibition law as a valid use of the police power to protect public health and morals, Justice Harlan in his opinion for the Court cautioned that there were "limits beyond which legislation cannot rightfully go" and that courts could "look at the substance of things" to determine whether the legislature had gone outside the valid scope of the police power. *Id.* at 661. As one modern scholar notes, the significance of the decision was that it signaled that the Court would not blithely accept legislation billed as police power regulations at face value; rather, Harlan's caveat asserted potentially "far-reaching federal judicial supervision of state economic legislation." Ely, *supra* note 31, at 89.

148. Powell v. Pennsylvania, 127 U.S. 678 (1888). Pennsylvania was one of 22 states that by the mid-1880s had passed laws targeting oleomargarine—an artificial substitute for butter, derived from animal or vegetable fats—through prohibitions,

discriminatory taxes, or coloring or labeling requirements. Although rationalized by their proponents as necessary to protect public health or to prevent consumer fraud, the oleomargarine laws were "protectionism, pure and simple, enacted only because of the political influence of large dairy interests." GILLMAN, *supra* note 84, at 73–74. Justice Harlan's majority opinion in *Powell* upheld the Pennsylvania law as a valid police-power regulation "to protect the public health and to prevent the adultera-tion of dairy products and fraud in the sale thereof." 127 U.S. at 683–84. Justice Field, the lone dissenter, found the law to be an unconstitutional deprivation of economic liberty, citing *In re Jacobs* and *People v. Marx*, the New York Court of Appeals decisions protecting liberty of contract, discussed *supra* notes 58–64. Following *Mugler's* sanc-tion "to look at the substance of things," Field concluded, as the New York court had in *Marx* when it invalidated that state's oleomargarine law, that the law really had nothing to do with protecting public health or safety but rather was "nothing less than an unwarranted interference with the rights and liberties of the citizen." 127 U.S. at 695 (Field, J., dissenting).

149. Budd v. New York, 143 U.S. 517 (1892). The majority opinion, by Justice Blatch-ford, followed *Munn* in holding grain elevators to be "business affected with a public interest," even though the New York elevator industry—which included "floating" elevators, or boats, in harbors, as well as stationary elevators on land—had nothing like the character of the de facto monopoly the Court had found in the Illinois case. Emphasizing this difference, Justice Brewer's dissent (joined by Justices Brown and Field) assailed the majority's "radically unsound" application of the doctrine to a free market of competing private businesses. "[T]here are no exclusive privileges given to these elevators. They are not upon public ground. If the business is profitable, any one can build another; the field is open for all the elevators, and all the competition that may be desired," Justice Brewer observed, adding his own fears about the rise of socialism: "The paternal theory of government is to me odious. The utmost liberty to the individual, and the fullest possible protection to him and his property, is both the limitation and duty of government. If it may regulate the price of one service, which is not a public service, or the compensation for the use of one kind of property which is not devoted to a public use, why may it not with equal reason regulate the price of all service, and the compensation to be paid for the use of all property? And if so, 'Looking Backward' is nearer than a dream." 143 U.S. at 548, 551 (Brewer, J., dissent-ing). Brewer's reference to *Looking Backward*, Edward Bellamy's novel about a social-ist future, typified the justice's propensity to be, in the words of one scholar, "not shy about expressing his fear of, and disgust for, socialism"—a fear that he shared with many of his contemporaries. Bernstein, *Revisionism, supra* note 101, at 41 n.217.

150. United States v. Cruikshank, 92 U.S. 542 (1876) (with only Justice Clifford dissenting, finding that the First Amendment right to assemble and the Second Amendment right to bear arms applied only against the national government); Walker v. Sauvinet, 92 U.S. 90 (1876) (with Justices Clifford and Field dissenting, finding that the Seventh Amendment right to a jury trial in civil cases did not apply to the states); Hurtado v. California, 110 U.S. 516 (1884) (with only Justice Harlan dissenting, finding that the Fifth Amendment right to a grand jury indictment was not required by the due process clause of the Fourteenth Amendment).

151. CURTIS, *supra* note 109, at 191. The six justices identified by Curtis are Woods, before his elevation to the Court (in his circuit court opinions before *Slaughterhouse*); Bradley and Swayne, dissenting in *Slaughterhouse*; and Field, Brewer, and Harlan, dissenting in *O'Neil v. Vermont*, 144 U.S. 323, an 1892 decision affirming a conviction

under Vermont's prohibition law of a New York liquor merchant selling across state lines. (The merchant had challenged his conviction, in part, as contrary to the Eighth Amendment's ban on "cruel and usual" punishments.)

152. As observed *supra*, text at note 135, Justice Miller's opinion for the *Slaughterhouse* majority confined the scope of the equal protection clause to laws "directed by way of discrimination against the negroes as a class, or on account of their race." By the 1880s, the Court was considering challenges to various state laws under the equal protection clause, including challenges arguing that laws regulating railroads were invalid as "special" or "class" legislation. Nevertheless, unlike state courts, the Supreme Court enforced only relatively narrow restrictions on class legislation; it rejected the class legislation challenges to railroad laws just as it failed to take seriously such a claim in *Powell*, the oleomargarine case. Bernstein, *Revisionism, supra* note 101, at 17–20.

153. *See* Yick Wo v. Hopkins, 118 U.S. 356 (1886) (holding that a San Francisco ordinance prohibiting operation of a laundry in a wooden building without the consent of the Board of Supervisors, which was enforced by the board in a way that discriminated against Chinese-owned laundries, violated the equal protection clause). Scholars disagree about whether *Yick Wo* was an aberration, in an era when the Court's equal protection jurisprudence seemed to be typified more by its decision upholding "Jim Crow" segregation laws in *Plessy v. Ferguson*, 163 U.S. 537 (1896). David Bernstein, who has studied other decisions from the period involving Chinese laundries, concludes that the Court was far less willing than state courts to invalidate laws as class legislation. Bernstein, *Revisionism, supra* note 101, at 17–19; David Bernstein, Lochner, *Parity, and the Chinese Laundry Cases*, 41 Wm. & Mary L. Rev. 211 (1999), and *Two Asian Laundry Cases*, 24 J. Sup. Ct. Hist. 95 (1999).

154. Peckham was nominated to the Court by President Grover Cleveland, his friend and fellow New York Democrat. Although sometimes called by scholars an "ultra-" or "arch-conservative" (*see, e.g.*, Curtis, *supra* note 109, at 192), Peckham is more accurately described as a limited-government conservative with a high regard for economic liberty. As a judge on New York's highest court, the New York Court of Appeals, between 1886 and 1895 he became known for his lucid and well-reasoned opinions. Perhaps the most illuminating of these was his dissent in *People v. Budd*, 117 N.Y. 1 (1889), in which he regarded the rate-fixing laws for grain elevators that the majority had upheld, under the "affected with a public interest" doctrine, as paternalistic anachronisms that had no place in modern free-market societies. *See* Richard Skolnik, *Rufus Peckham, in* 3 The Justices of the United States Supreme Court, 1789–1969: Their Lives and Major Opinions 1685, 1688–95 (Leon Friedman & Fred L. Israel eds., 1969).

155. Warren, *supra* note 19, at 439. For more on congressional Republicans' intent regarding the Fourteenth Amendment's due process clause, see Siegan, *supra* note 85, at 485–92.

Chapter 2

1. As this chapter shows, however, that inconsistency can be explained by the limited scope of the Court's protection of liberty of contract.

2. Lochner v. New York, 198 U.S. 4, 75 (1905) (Holmes, J., dissenting).

3. Lawrence M. Friedman, A History of American Law 203 (3d ed. 2005). Friedman notes, for example, that although land law remained important, "land dealings were more and more treated contractually." *Id.*

4. John V. Orth, *Contract and the Common Law, in* The State and Freedom of Contract 44, 48–49, 51 (Harry N. Scheiber ed., 1998). Orth notes:

> In the entire four-volume *Commentaries*, extending over two thousand printed pages, labor law (such as it is) occupies ten pages in Book I, on the "rights of persons." A chapter on "master and servant" leads off a series of chapters on what Blackstone calls "the great relations in private life," including, in addition to the employment relationship, familial relationships such as "husband and wife" and "parent and child" and the substituted family of "guardian and ward."

Id. at 51 (quoting 1 William Blackstone, Commentaries *410).

5. Sir Henry Maine, Ancient Law 141 (London, 1861) (emphasis in original).

6. Friedrich A. Hayek, The Constitution of Liberty 154 (1960).

7. *Id.*; James Willard Hurst, Law and the Conditions of Freedom in the Nineteenth-Century United States 6 (1956).

8. Budd v. New York, 143 U.S. 517, 524–25 (1892) (argument for plaintiffs in error). Although the majority of justices on the U.S. Supreme Court rejected this argument in *Budd*, it received a far more sympathetic response from the New York Court of Appeals when it decided to strike down the law—the decision overturned by the U.S. Supreme Court ruling. In his opinion for New York's highest court, Judge Peckham declared that continued adherence to the old ideas and practices of paternal government (like rate-fixing laws) would "wholly ignore the later and, as I firmly believe, the more correct ideas which an increase of civilization and a fuller knowledge of the fundamental laws of political economy, and a truer conception of the proper functions of government have given us at the present day." Richard Skolnik, *Rufus Peckham, in* 3 The Justices of The United States Supreme Court, 1789–1969: Their Lives and Major Opinions 1685, 1692–93 (Leon Friedman & Fred L. Israel eds., 1969) (quoting from People v. Budd, 117 N.Y. 1 (1889)).

9. *In re Jacobs*, 98 N.Y. 98, 114–15 (1885).

10. Sumner has been regarded as the Herbert Spencer of the United States, "the American champion of *laissez faire*" whose book *What Social Classes Owe to Each Other* was "a restatement in the American vernacular of the great English classicists." Ralph Henry Gabriel, The Course of American Democratic Thought 231–32 (3d ed. 1986).

11. William Graham Sumner, What Social Classes Owe to Each Other 22–23 (Caxton Printers 1986) (1883).

12. *Id.* at 23–24.

13. Alexis de Tocqueville, Democracy in America 506, 508 (J. P. Mayer ed., 1969) (part 2, chapter 2).

14. Thanks to his father's hard work, wise management, and frugal living, Sumner received a college education. After serving first as a clergyman, Sumner moved to academics in 1872 and became professor of political economy at Yale. He was a pioneer in the emerging field of sociology. Gabriel, *supra* note 10, at 231–32.

15. Sumner, *supra* note 11, at 33–34.

16. *Id.* at 136–37, 145.

17. *Id.* at 11, 141–42 (emphasis in original).

18. *Id.* at 30 (emphasis in original).

19. *Id.* at 98. Sumner emphasized self-responsibility because, as noted below, he was especially critical of social reformers who did not "mind their own business" and instead sought to take care of others—and to use the coercive powers of government to achieve their paternalistic ends.

20. *Id.* at 104 (emphasis in original).

21. The phrase "laissez faire," which has become a famous libertarian rallying cry, legendarily originated among a group of 18th-century French philosophers known as the Physiocrats (derived from the Greek words *physis* (nature) and *kratos* (rule)) who advocated freeing economic markets from government control so that markets could be ordered by their own "natural laws." When asked by Louis XV "How can I help you," a group of merchants was said to have responded with the Physiocratic argument, "*Laissez-nous faire, laissez-nous passer. Le monde va de lui-même.*" ("Let us do, leave us alone. The world runs by itself.") DAVID BOAZ, LIBERTARIANISM: A PRIMER 38–39 (1997).

22. The term "liberal" underwent a change in the early 20th century when people on the left side of the traditional political spectrum—that is, people who advocated more government control over economic markets—started calling themselves "liberals." Economist Joseph Schumpeter noted, "As a supreme, if unintended, compliment, the enemies of private enterprise have thought it wise to appropriate its label." Thus, modern libertarians refer to the philosophy of individualism, free markets, and limited government as "classical liberalism," although as libertarian writer David Boaz observes, "[I]n this era of historical illiteracy, if you call yourself a classical liberal, most people think you're an admirer of Teddy Kennedy!" *Id.* at 23.

23. LUDWIG VON MISES, HUMAN ACTION: A TREATISE ON ECONOMICS v (3d rev. ed. 1966). *See also* LUDWIG VON MISES, LIBERALISM IN THE CLASSICAL TRADITION (3d ed. 1985) [hereafter "MISES, LIBERALISM"].

24. BOAZ, *supra* note 21, at 2, 16. *See also* DAVID CONWAY, CLASSICAL LIBERALISM: THE UNVANQUISHED IDEAL 10 (1995) (basing the classical liberal "system of natural liberty" on individualism with respect to both ends and means). Among the key concepts of modern libertarianism that Boaz identifies, in addition to individualism, are limited government (the legitimate function of government as limited to the protection of natural rights); the rule of law (a society of liberty under law in which individuals are free to pursue their own lives so long as they respect the equal rights of others); free-market capitalism (including the principle of spontaneous order and the concept of a natural harmony of interests among peaceful, productive people in a just society); and nonaggression, or peace (the principle that it is wrong to initiate the use of force as a means to achieve social or political goals). BOAZ, *supra* note 21, at 16–17.

25. On the no-harm principle generally, see T. PATRICK BURKE, NO HARM: ETHICAL PRINCIPLES FOR A FREE MARKET (1993). Burke explains that the classical liberal conception of *harm* requires, first, that a person "harmed" by some action "must be worse off after the action than he was before it," that is, have "some *deterioration* in his condition"; and second, that "the action in question must have *caused* the harm, that is, *produced* it." Thus, for example, under the classical liberal conception of "harm," a worker is not "harmed" by accepting an offer of employment at low wages. *Id.* at 46–47 (emphasis in original). Moreover, because neither force nor fraud induced acceptance of the offer, the no-harm principle is not violated. Similarly, a successful businessman does not violate the no-harm principle by competing fairly, on the merits—that is, by selling better-qual-

ity goods or services at better prices than his competitors—even if he harms a competitor, by driving him out of business.

26. BOAZ, *supra* note 21, at 36. Although Boaz traces the roots of libertarianism as far back as the Old Testament's book of Samuel and sees the "first stirrings of clearly protoliberal ideas" in the English Revolution of the 1640s, he dates "the birth of liberalism" to the Glorious Revolution and specifically to the publication of Locke's *Second Treatise of Government* in 1690. *Id.* at 28, 35–37. On the radical Whig tradition generally, see David N. Mayer, *The English Radical Whig Origins of American Constitutionalism*, 70 WASH. U. L. Q. 131 (1992) [hereafter "Mayer, *Whigs*"].

27. On the 18th-century radical Whigs and their support for both American independence and British parliamentary reform, see Mayer, *Whigs, supra*, at 164–74, 189–96. *See also* ROBERT E. TOOHEY, LIBERTY & EMPIRE: BRITISH RADICAL SOLUTIONS TO THE AMERICAN PROBLEM, 1774–1776 (1978); CAROLINE ROBBINS, THE EIGHTEENTH-CENTURY COMMONWEALTHMAN (1959).

28. *See* Eric Foner, *Radical Individualism in America*, LITERATURE OF LIBERTY 5 (Cato Institute, July–Sept. 1978).

29. HERBERT SPENCER, SOCIAL STATICS 95 (reprint, New York, Robert Schalkenbach Foundation, 1970) (London, 1877) (emphasis in original). Spencer regarded this law as the "first principle," or "the *primary* law of right relationship between man and man," and maintained it was "the prerequisite to normal life in society," just as freedom was "the prerequisite to normal life in the individual." *Id.* at 79, 95.

30. JOHN STUART MILL, ON LIBERTY, IN JOHN STUART MILL, THREE ESSAYS (ON LIBERTY, REPRESENTATIVE GOVERNMENT, THE SUBJECTION OF WOMEN) 15 (Oxford 1975).

31. *See* BOAZ, *supra* note 21, at 82–87 (distinguishing utilitarians from neo-natural rights philosophers among modern libertarians). Albert Venn Dicey, the preeminent constitutional authority in late Victorian and Edwardian Britain, associated classical liberalism, insofar as it related to British law, with the utilitarianism of Jeremy Bentham and his disciples among the group of philosophers called the Radicals, including James Mill and John Stuart Mill. Nevertheless, he recognized that important "speculative differences" distinguished the "utilitarian individualism" of such thinkers as J. S. Mill from the "absolute individualism" of Spencer. ALBERT VENN DICEY, LECTURES ON THE RELATION BETWEEN LAW AND PUBLIC OPINION IN ENGLAND DURING THE NINETEENTH CENTURY 17 (photo. reprint, New Brunswick, NJ, Transaction Books 1981) (2d ed. 1914).

32. MISES, LIBERALISM, *supra* note 23, at 52. Mises added, "Everything that goes beyond this is an evil"; a government that infringes these rights rather than protects them would be "altogether bad." *Id.*

33. The qualifier "at most" recognizes the general split among modern libertarians between anarchist libertarians (sometimes called "anarcho-capitalists"), who deny the legitimacy of government altogether, and minimal-government libertarians, or minarchists. *See* RANDY E. BARNETT, THE STRUCTURE OF LIBERTY: JUSTICE AND THE RULE OF LAW (1998); BRUCE L. BENSON, THE ENTERPRISE OF LAW: JUSTICE WITHOUT THE STATE (1990).

34. BOAZ, *supra* note 21, at 2. The libertarian "no-harm," or nonaggression, principle views fraud as a form of theft, tantamount to the initiation of physical force against others' property. *Id.* at 74–75 (explaining, in simple terms, why fraud is a form of theft: "If I promise to sell you a Heineken for a dollar, but I actually give you a Bud Light, I have stolen your dollar").

35. *See* John Hospers, *Libertarianism and Legal Paternalism, in* THE LIBERTARIAN READER 135 (Tibor R. Machan ed., 1982) (defining "legal paternalism" as the view supporting the use of legislation to protect people from themselves). Libertarians oppose all paternal legislation, except for laws protecting those persons who cannot take care of themselves: namely, infants and children, the senile, and mentally incompetent persons. *Id.* at 136–37. Thus, libertarians would oppose laws that prohibit competent adults from using narcotic drugs, committing or attempting to commit suicide, gambling, engaging in prostitution, or other so-called victimless crimes. *See, e.g.,* GILBERT GEIS, NOT THE LAW'S BUSINESS: AN EXAMINATION OF HOMOSEXUALITY, ABORTION, PROSTITUTION, NARCOTICS, AND GAMBLING IN THE UNITED STATES (1979); PETER MCWILLIAMS, AIN'T NOBODY'S BUSINESS IF YOU DO: THE ABSURDITY OF CONSENSUAL CRIMES IN A FREE SOCIETY (1993).

36. Among these principles, of course, is the traditional concept of the police power and the constitutional limits that constrained it. As discussed in the next section of this chapter, laissez-faire theorists would change traditional police-power jurisprudence at least as much as would Progressive-Era reformers.

37. *See, e.g.,* Cass R. Sunstein, *Lochner's Legacy,* 87 COLUM. L. REV. 873, 874, 888 n.49 (1987) (identifying the common law with the "allocation of rights of use, ownership, transfer, and possession of property associated with 'laissez-faire' systems'" and arguing that judges during the *Lochner* era measured the constitutionality of state action against a free-market/common-law "baseline").

38. In a devastating critique of Sunstein's article, David Bernstein has argued that Sunstein misrepresented both the Supreme Court's understanding of common-law rules and the Court's decisions concerning constitutional limitations on the police power during the *Lochner*-era. David E. Bernstein, Lochner's *Legacy's Legacy,* 82 TEX. L. REV. 1 (2003) [hereafter "Bernstein, *Legacy*"]. With regard to the former, he shows that, contrary to Sunstein's claim that the Court treated common-law rules as "natural and immutable," the Court rather regarded them as mutable and contingent; for example, the Court consistently upheld federal and state workers' compensation statutes even though they replaced common-law rights and duties with new statutory schemes that included many novel features. *Id.* at 23–32. With regard to police powers, Bernstein also shows that the Court rarely interfered with redistributive legislation claimed to be within the states' police power. *Id.* at 34–42. Moreover, he shows that the Court's "civil liberties" decisions—including its protection for liberty of contract—during the *Lochner* era cannot be explained by the theory that the Court was protecting common-law distributions of wealth; rather, the Court used substantive due process "to protect what it considered the fundamental liberties of Americans from arbitrary or unreasonable legislation." *Id.* at 47. Thus, he concludes, Sunstein's article "shows the danger of applying an ideological construct to constitutional history for presentist purposes, while ignoring or neglecting contrary evidence." *Id.* at 63. What Bernstein is describing is the vice that legal historians condemn as "lawyers' history."

39. SUMNER, *supra* note 11, at 20–22.

40. *Id.* at 110, 119, 130. Noting how women had entered the workforce by the late 19th century, Sumner added, "We must not overlook the fact that the Forgotten Man is not infrequently a woman." *Id.* at 126. To Sumner, "the Forgotten Man and the Forgotten Woman are the real productive strength of the country," the people who work and vote—and generally pray—but whose "chief business in life," thanks to the social reformers, is "to pay." *Id.* at 128–29.

41. The coalitions that formed the temperance and prohibition movements, culminating in the Eighteenth Amendment to the U.S. Constitution, are nicely summarized in RICHARD B. BERNSTEIN & JEROME AGEL, AMENDING AMERICA 170–77 (1993).

42. *See, e.g.*, DAVID HERBERT DONALD, LIBERTY AND UNION: THE CRISIS OF POPULAR GOVERNMENT, 1830–1870, 233–34 (1978). Donald notes that in the late 19th century the tariff issue was "seldom debated in terms of free trade versus protectionism." He adds, "Except for a few doctrinaire economic theorists, everybody recognized some tariff barrier was required to protect some American industries." *Id*. at 233. Needless to say, Sumner was one of those "doctrinaire theorists" who disagreed.

43. SUMNER, *supra* note 11, at 115. Explaining why the punishment of vice was best left to the natural order of things, Sumner writes: "Nature's remedies against vice are terrible" and "without pity." Sumner himself was without pity with regard to alcohol abuse: "A drunkard in the gutter is just where he ought to be, according to the fitness and tendency of things." *Id*. at 113–14.

44. *Id*. at 120, 122.

45. Mugler v. Kansas, 123 U.S. 623 (1887).

46. *See, e.g.*, WILLIAM W. FREEHLING, PRELUDE TO CIVIL WAR: THE NULLIFICATION CONTROVERSY IN SOUTH CAROLINA, 1816–1836 (1966).

47. SUMNER, *supra* note 11, at 82–83.

48. *Id*. at 83.

49. *Id*. at 75.

50. *Id*. at 80. Although he maintained that "a strike is a legitimate resort at last," and that it is "like war, for it is war," he also doubted whether strikes for higher wages were "expedient." *Id*.

51. *Id*. at 83. In calling unions "right and useful," Sumner recognized workers' rights of freedom of association and saw unions' value in raising workers' wages. He also saw them as useful in other ways: "to spread information, to maintain *esprit de corps*, to elevate the public opinion of the class." Without saying so explicitly, Sumner's view that "it may be that [unions] are necessary" was his answer to the argument that employers and employees had unequal bargaining strength. He did regard unions as "an exotic and imported institution" and saw many of their rules and methods, "having been developed in England to meet English circumstances," as "out of place" in America; hence, he argued, unions needed "development, correction, and perfection" in the United States. *Id*. at 82–84.

52. *See, e.g.*, Arthur F. McEvoy, *Freedom of Contract, Labor, and the Administrative State*, *in* THE STATE AND FREEDOM OF CONTRACT 198, 214–16 (Harry N. Scheiber ed., 1998) (summarizing courts' use of labor injunctions against even peaceful union activity).

53. For more on the Progressive movement, see RICHARD A. HOFSTADTER, THE AGE OF REFORM (1955); and MICHAEL MCGERR, A FIERCE DISCONTENT: THE RISE AND FALL OF THE PROGRESSIVE MOVEMENT IN AMERICA, 1870–1920 (2003). *See also* James W. Ely Jr., *Melville W. Fuller Reconsidered*, 1988 J. SUP. CT. HIST. 35, 36 (observing that the Progressives "championed greater governmental intervention in American life and constructed a version of constitutional history serviceable for their purpose").

54. THE QUOTABLE CONSERVATIVE 145 (Rod L. Evans & Irwin M. Berent eds., 1995) (quoting Mencken in the [Baltimore] *Evening Sun*, Jan. 19, 1926).

55. Albert Venn Dicey suggested this parallel in his classic work, *Law and Public Opinion in England during the Nineteenth Century*, which divided the century into three periods based on the dominant public opinion in each: the period of "Old Toryism

or Legislative Quiescence" (1800–1830), characterized by traditionalism; the period of "Benthamism or Individualism" (1825–1870), characterized by utilitarian classical liberal reforms; and the period of "Collectivism" (1865–1900), characterized by the forms of state intervention favored by socialist reformers. DICEY, *supra* note 31, at 62–65. As Dicey saw it, the brief mid-century period in which classical liberal reform ideas dominated gave way to the collectivism of the late Victorian period. That collectivism curtailed freedom of contract "as surely as individualism [had] extend[ed it]," *id.* at 264; and by using collective action on behalf of the interests of organized labor—for example, in the Combination Act (Conspiracy and Protection of Property Act of 1875) and Trade Union Acts (1871–1876)—it used government power to favor unions just as the earliest Combination Act (1800) had favored employers by outlawing unions. Dicey contrasted the combination laws of both the early and late 19th century (the laws of 1800 and 1875) with the "Benthamite" legislation of 1825, which he viewed as neutral with regard to employer-worker disputes and consistent with the dominant spirit of individualism in mid-century Britain: the 1825 law "was intended to establish free trade in labour, and allowed, or tolerated, trade combinations, only in so far as they were part of and conducive to such freedom of trade." *Id.* at 270. Late-Victorian laws, like the 1875 Combination Act and other labor laws, echoed the "Tory paternalism" of the first third of the century, which was in turn based on England's centuries-old tradition of paternal government. *Id.* at 101–02.

56. As discussed more fully in chapter 3, so-called protective laws for women were, in the words of one scholar, "as much as anything designed to keep them *out* of the labor market; at a minimum, their underlying premise was that women properly belonged in the private sphere and were constitutionally unsuited for the wage-labor market." McEvoy, *supra* note 52, at 218.

57. On the term "social legislation," see Charles W. McCurdy, *The "Liberty of Contract" Regime in American Law*, in THE STATE AND FREEDOM OF CONTRACT 162–63 (Harry N. Scheiber ed., 1998). On social legislation as unconstitutional class legislation, see HOWARD GILLMAN, THE CONSTITUTION BESIEGED: THE RISE AND DEMISE OF LOCHNER ERA POLICE POWERS JURISPRUDENCE 158–59 (1993) (discussing the unprecedented nature of minimum wage legislation).

58. David N. Mayer, *The Jurisprudence of Christopher G. Tiedeman: A Study in the Failure of Laissez-Faire Constitutionalism*, 55 MO. L. REV. 93, 117–18 (1990) [hereafter "Mayer, *Tiedeman*"] (quoting CHRISTOPHER G. TIEDEMAN, THE UNWRITTEN CONSTITUTION OF THE UNITED STATES 79–80 (1890)); John F. Dillon, Presidential Address to the American Bar Association (1892), *in* SOURCES IN AMERICAN CONSTITUTIONAL HISTORY 143 (Michael Les Benedict ed., 1996).

59. Self-described "liberals" and "Progressives" who might oppose such a free-market policy as "reactionary" are the true reactionaries, from the libertarian perspective. As Isabel Paterson, the great 20th-century laissez-faire writer, observed, "If you go back 150 years you are a reactionary; but if you go back 1,000 years, you are in the foremost ranks of progress." Isabel Paterson, *A Paterson Collection*, 7 LIBERTY 39, (1993).

60. *See* DICEY, *supra* note 31, at 37 (defining "counter-current" as "a body of opinion, belief, or sentiment more or less directly opposed to the dominant opinion of a particular era").

61. As observed at the beginning of chapter 1, Roscoe Pound rejected the prevalent view that in protecting liberty of contract, judges were deciding cases according to their

own "personal, social, and economic views," even though he criticized liberty of contract as based on what he regarded as an outmoded jurisprudence. On the Progressives' reshaping of constitutional interpretation and history to advance their political agenda, see RICHARD A. EPSTEIN, HOW PROGRESSIVES REWROTE THE CONSTITUTION (2006).

62. Arthur D. Hellman, *Judicial Activism: The Good, the Bad, and the Ugly*, 21 MISS. C. L. REV. 253 (2002). After discussing various definitions of judicial activism, the author proposes one of his own, inspired by Judge Richard Posner: "decisions that expand the power of the judiciary over political institutions." *Id.* at 253, 264. The problem with that definition is that it equates activism with judicial review, for any decision declaring a law passed by a legislature unconstitutional may be seen as an "outcome adverse to the result reached through the political process."

63. Some modern libertarian scholars during the late 1980s, at the height of the controversy over Robert Bork's failed nomination to the Supreme Court, sought to defend a broad judicial protection of liberty rights as a "principled judicial activism." *See* Randy E. Barnett, *Judicial Conservatism v. A Principled Judicial Activism*, 10 HARV. J. L. & PUB. POL'Y 273 (1987); STEPHEN MACEDO, THE NEW RIGHT V. THE CONSTITUTION (1987). Of course, by calling it "principled" they were really saying that it was not activism at all but rather justifiable—albeit vigorous—use of the judicial review power to protect legitimate constitutional rights. More recently, taking note of how some leftists have criticized the conservative decisions of the Rehnquist Court as "activist," Barnett has argued that the term, "while clearly pejorative, is generally empty." Randy E. Barnett, *Is the Rehnquist Court an "Activist" Court? The Commerce Clause Cases*, 73 U. COLO. L. REV. 1275, 1276 (2002).

64. The first recorded use of the term "judicial activism" occurred in a popular magazine, *Fortune*, in a 1947 article by historian Arthur Schlesinger Jr., profiling all nine justices on the Supreme Court at that time. Schlesinger characterized Justices Black, Douglas, Murphy, and Rutledge as the "Judicial Activists," who were willing to let the Court use its judicial review powers for "wholesome social purposes," such as "to protect the underdog or to safeguard basic human rights." He called Justices Frankfurter, Jackson, and Burton the "Champions of Self-Restraint," who were skeptical of individual judges' notions of justice and who preferred to defer to the legislative will. The other two members of the Court, Justice Reed and Chief Justice Vinson, he regarded as a middle group. Keenan D. Kmiec, *The Origin and Current Meaning of "Judicial Activism*,*"* 92 CAL. L. REV. 1441, 1445–49 (2004) (summarizing Arthur M. Schlesinger Jr., *The Supreme Court: 1947*, FORTUNE, Jan. 1947). Publication of Schlesinger's article preceded the famous dialogue between Justices Black and Frankfurter in their dissenting and concurring opinions, respectively, in *Adamson v. California*, 332 U.S. 46 (1947), over the incorporation of Bill of Rights guarantees against the states through the Fourteenth Amendment.

65. *See, e.g.*, Edwin Meese III, *Construing the Constitution*, 19 U. CAL. DAVIS L. REV. 22–30 (1985) (explaining the Reagan administration's preferred "jurisprudence of original intention" as an antidote to the result-oriented "chameleon" jurisprudence of the activist Warren Court).

66. This definition combines elements of three of the five different meanings of "judicial activism" identified by Keenan Kmiec: "judicial legislation," "departures from accepted interpretive methodology," and "result-oriented judging." Kmiec, *supra* note 64, at 1471–76.

67. Laurence H. Silberman, *Will Lawyering Strangle Democratic Capitalism? A Retrospective*, 21 HARV. J. L. & PUB. POL'Y 607, 618 (1998). Judge Silberman identifies policy issues as "those questions of public concern on which the body politic or political institutions have free range of choice"; those questions are resolved by legislatures or constitutional conventions when they "crystallize" the majority view into rules. "If a judge exercises policy choice when deciding what these rules mean," that judge is an "activist," according to Silberman. *Id.*

68. *See, e.g.*, Kmiec, *supra* note 64, at 1471 (quoting former president George W. Bush, as reported in *Newsday*, Mar. 29, 2002, saying he planned "to appoint strict constructionists who would hew closely to the law rather than judicial activists whom he said were prone to 'legislate from the bench'": "'We want people to interpret the law, not try to make law and write law,' he said.").

69. This definition of "judicial activism," properly understood, may be contrasted with "judicial restraint," which in its strict sense stands for the idea that the judge applies the relevant law, and only the law, in the case before him—he "restrains" any inclination to do otherwise. I thank Roger Pilon for helping me clarify these definitions, especially in light of the loose way in which some modern conservative scholars misuse both "judicial activism" and "judicial restraint." One common misuse of the latter term, as employed by some modern conservatives, confuses legitimate judicial restraint with the erroneous notion that "judicial restraint" requires judges to be deferential to the political branches despite constitutional limitations on government power. A judge who refrains from enforcing constitutional limitations, or from protecting rights (whether enumerated or unenumerated) meant to be protected by the Constitution, is just as "lawless" a judge (as Pilon calls him) as one who is "activist," properly speaking. *See* Roger Pilon, *Lawless Judging: Refocusing the Issue for Conservatives*, 2 GEO. J. L. & PUB. POL'Y 5, 15 (2001) (criticizing "lawless judging" in either direction, whether "active" or "restrained"). Richard Epstein has similarly condemned what he calls "excessive judicial restraint," arguing that it is as much an abuse of the judicial power as judicial activism, properly considered. EPSTEIN, *supra* note 61, at 132 (citing as an example the Supreme Court's decision in the 2005 eminent-domain case, *Kelo v. City of New London*, 545 U.S. 469 (2005)).

70. On the nonjusticiability doctrine generally, see JOHN E. NOWAK & RONALD D. ROTUNDA, CONSTITUTIONAL LAW 125–37 (7th ed. 2004). One of the clearest and most frequently cited examples of the Supreme Court's violating this doctrine is the *Dred Scott* decision of 1857, when a majority of the justices took it upon themselves to decide the controversial political question of slavery in the western territories. By holding that the Fifth Amendment's due process clause required Congress to permit slavery in the territories—and by rejecting the equally plausible reading of the Fifth Amendment urged by Republicans, that it required Congress to forbid slavery in the territories—the Court, under the guise of constitutional interpretation, had decided a nonjusticiable question of policy and hence was guilty of judicial activism, at least as Republicans at the time saw it. See the discussion in chapter 1, *supra*, text at notes 54–57.

71. For example, the Ohio Supreme Court, in a series of decisions beginning in 1997, has held that the state's system for funding public schools violates the provision in the Ohio Constitution empowering the legislature to fund "a thorough and efficient system of common schools throughout the State." Chief Justice Thomas J. Moyer, writing the opinion for the three dissenting justices in the second of these deci-

sions, accused the majority of violating the nonjusticiability doctrine by attempting to decide the policy question of what constitutes a "thorough and efficient" system. "[D]ecisions regarding the level of educational quality to be made available to Ohio school children are dependent upon policy decisions—political, budgetary, and value judgments—that require a balancing of interests that is not appropriately struck in the Supreme Court of Ohio. 'The judicial branch is simply neither equipped nor empowered to make these kinds of decisions,'" Moyer noted. DeRolph v. Ohio, 89 Ohio St. 3d 1, 48, 728 N.E. 2d 993, 1029 (2000) (Moyer, C.J., dissenting).

72. On activist decisions by the Supreme Court upholding state or federal laws challenged as being unconstitutional, *see generally* Robert A. Levy & William Mellor, The Dirty Dozen: How Twelve Supreme Court Cases Radically Expanded Government and Eroded Freedom 215–24 (2008). Indeed, as chapter 4 will more fully argue, the Court's post-1937 decisions upholding federal and state New Deal legislation—and abandoning all but minimal "rational basis" substantive due process protection for economic liberty—better fit the model of activist jurisprudence than do its pre-1937 decisions protecting liberty of contract. Chief Justice Hughes's opinion for the majority in *West Coast Hotel v. Parrish*, 300 U.S. 379 (1937), for example, was based largely on the justices' agreement with the policy arguments advanced by the state in favor of minimum-wage laws.

73. Because this book focuses on what the Court actually did in protecting liberty of contract, arguing that it did not follow the "laissez-faire constitutionalism" caricature created by the Holmesian orthodox view of the *Lochner*-era, it does not address the question of whether a true model of laissez-faire constitutionalism really would have been "activist," in the sense described above. That is an open question because it is not clear that consistent and rigorous protection of liberty, as defined by the classical liberal philosophy, would have required judges to disregard the law. Indeed, it could certainly be argued that a true laissez-faire constitutionalism would have been a more objective, and less activist, protection of liberty under the due process clause than the Court's post-1937 substantive due process jurisprudence, with its "double standard" and various, inconsistent tests for the protection of certain rights, as discussed in chapter 4.

74. Lochner, 198 U.S. at 75–76 (Homes, J., dissenting).

75. Jacobson v. Massachusetts, 197 U.S. 11, 31 (1905). Only two justices—the most libertarian members of the Court at that time, Justices Breyer and Peckham—dissented, without opinions. Modern scholars might debate whether such a compulsory vaccination law, at least under the real threat of a public epidemic, truly violates libertarian principles; or, put another way, whether one's freedom not to be vaccinated and thus to be potentially a carrier of infectious disease falls within the legitimate scope of liberty as defined under the no-harm principle.

76. For a short biographical sketch of Christopher Gustavus Tiedeman (1857–1903), see Mayer, *Tiedeman, supra* note 58, at 102–03. Tiedeman's unique jurisprudential views were shaped by two important early influences on his intellectual life: his youth in Charleston, South Carolina, and his legal studies in Germany at a time when the German sociological school of jurisprudence was rising in influence. *See id.* at 102–08. These dual influences were reflected in, among other things, Tiedeman's views regarding "unwritten law" and the limitations it put on government powers, which he discussed in his treatise *The Unwritten Constitution of the United States* (1890). *See id.* at 108–25. Tiedeman's jurisprudence thus defies the stereotype associating laissez-faire constitutionalism with a rigid, formalistic conception of the law; rather, Tiedeman grounded

his laissez-faire views on the newer, sociological theories of jurisprudence—and particularly the German school, which saw the law as resulting from "the prevalent sense of right" (*Rechsgefuehl*), as it evolves in society. *See id.* at 109, 124–25.

77. *Id.* at 97–98. Tiedeman's work, first published in 1886 under the title *A Treatise on the Limitations of Police Power in the United States*, was published again in 1900 as a two-volume work, in an expanded second edition, under the title *A Treatise on State and Federal Control of Persons and Property in the United States*.

78. 1 CHRISTOPHER G. TIEDEMAN, A TREATISE ON STATE AND FEDERAL CONTROL OF PERSONS AND PROPERTY IN THE UNITED STATES at ix (1900).

79. Although Progressive movement scholars such as Clyde Jacobs and Benjamin Twiss usually identified both Tiedeman and Cooley as leading laissez-faire writers, even they recognized that Cooley at most only anticipated the purer laissez-faire constitutionalism of Tiedeman. *See* CLYDE E. JACOBS, LAW WRITERS AND THE COURTS: THE INFLUENCE OF THOMAS M. COOLEY, CHRISTOPHER G. TIEDEMAN, AND JOHN F. DILLON UPON AMERICAN CONSTITUTIONAL LAW 62 (1954); BENJAMIN TWISS, LAWYERS AND THE CONSTITUTION: HOW LAISSEZ-FAIRE CAME TO THE SUPREME COURT (1942). Comparing Cooley's treatise to Tiedeman's, one historian has noted that Tiedeman's narrow interpretation of the police power "revealed a much more extreme laissez-faire bias than Cooley's treatise." SIDNEY FINE, LAISSEZ-FAIRE AND THE GENERAL WELFARE STATE 154 (1956). This comparison can be illustrated by Cooley's and Tiedeman's different conclusions regarding the constitutionality of usury laws, discussed *infra* note 87.

80. Tiedeman's list of provisions in the U.S. Constitution that limited government power, state or federal, included Article I, Sections 9 and 10; the Bill of Rights; and the Civil War amendments. 1 TIEDEMAN, *supra* note 78, § 4, at 18–20. Citing approvingly Justice Chase's opinion in *Calder v. Bull*, 3 U.S. (3 Dall.) 386 (1798), that "certain vital principles in our free republican governments" also limited the legislative power, Tiedeman added that no law could be enforced that does not "conform to the fundamental principles of free government" or which "violates reason and offends against the prevalent conceptions of right and justice" in the United States. *Id.*, § 2, at 8–11.

81. *Id.*, § 1, at 4–5.

82. *Id.* § 1, at 5. Tiedeman added that such a law is "a governmental usurpation," violating "the principles of abstract justice, as they have been developed under our republican institutions." *Id.*

83. In the first edition of his treatise on the police power, Tiedeman defined "liberty" as "that amount of personal freedom, which is consistent with a strict obedience" to the *sic utere* rule. He also explained why that definition led logically to Spencer's Law of Equal Freedom:

> "That man is free who is protected from injury," and his protection involves necessarily the restraint of other individuals from the commission of the injury. In the proper balancing of the contending interests of individuals, personal liberty is secured and developed; any further restraint is unwholesome and subversive of liberty. As Herbert Spencer has expressed it, "every man may claim the fullest liberty to exercise his faculties compatible with the possession of like liberty by every other man."

CHRISTOPHER TIEDEMAN, TREATISE ON THE LIMITATIONS OF POLICE POWER IN THE UNITED STATES § 30 (1886) (quoting Herbert Spencer, *Social Statics*).

84. In the 14-year interval between the publications of the two editions of the work, case law had so expanded that Tiedeman required two volumes to "corral every important adjudication, which has been made by the State and Federal courts," on the various branches of the subject. 1 TIEDEMAN, *supra* note 78, at ix. The change in the title of the treatise, from *Limitations of Police Power* to *State and Federal Control of Persons and Property*, also reflected the growth of national government powers, especially through the commerce clause. *See* Mayer, *Tiedeman, supra* note 58, at 128–29.

85. Significantly, Tiedeman organized his treatise not in terms of types of regulations, but rather in terms of the types of rights restricted or burdened, with a threefold general classification: personal rights (including personal security, liberty, and private property), relative rights (arising between husband and wife, parent and child, guardian and ward, or master and servant), and statutory rights. 1 TIEDEMAN, *supra* note 78, § 5, at 20–21.

86. On laws regulating wages, see *id.* §§ 99, 100, at 316–30; on laws regulating hours, see *id.* §102, at 333–38. *See also* Mayer, *Tiedeman, supra* note 58, at 139–44.

87. On usury laws, see 1 TIEDEMAN, *supra* note 78, § 106, at 351–53. "Free trade in money is as much a right as free trade in merchandise," Tiedeman maintained, because "[i]nterest is nothing more than the price asked for the use of money," and price is determined by the law of supply and demand." *Id.* at 351. Tiedeman noted that usury laws originated in medieval England, where the lending of money was a special privilege, conferred by Parliament, in the days when the common law condemned as usury any taking of money for the use of money. He rejected this rationale as obsolete in the modern era, when the lending of money on interest was "in no sense a privilege"; he also disagreed with Thomas M. Cooley, who similarly had found this form of government price regulation difficult to defend on principle but who nevertheless took the view (as summarized by Tiedeman) that "long acquiescence in such laws preclude[ed] an inquiry into their constitutionality," a view that Tiedeman rejected. *Id.* at 352–53.

88. On the protective tariff, see *id.* § 93, at 292–94.

89. On anti-miscegenation laws, see 2 TIEDEMAN, *supra* note 78, § 188, at 894–95. Tiedeman also condemned as unconstitutional laws against polygamy, at least insofar as these laws violated the religious freedom of Mormons. *See id.* § 189, at 897.

90. On laws prohibiting vices generally, see 1 TIEDEMAN, *supra* note 78, § 60, at 179–87.

91. *Id.* at 180–81, 184–85. Although Tiedeman acknowledged that one person's addiction to vices, even trivial ones, might be harmful to others in society, he regarded those evils as "indirect and remote," not involving "trespasses upon rights." Indeed, such evils are "so remote that many other causes co-operate to produce the result," making it "difficult, if not impossible, to ascertain what is the controlling and real cause." *Id.* at 181. Tiedeman would apply to constitutional analysis a rule akin to the rule of proximate causation in tort law—a rule he regarded as "deduced from the accumulated experience of ages, . . . a law of nature, immutable and invarying." *Id.* at 184. To make acts criminal that did not result in trespasses upon others—acts that would not be actionable in tort because the damages they caused were too remote—would be an unconstitutional deprivation of liberty, without due process of law, he argued. *Id.*

92. *Id.* § 121, at 510. One court nearly accepted Tiedeman's distinction between vice and crime. In *Ah Lim v. Territory of Washington*, 1 Wash. 156 (1890), the Washington territorial court considered the defendant's challenge to his conviction under a statute that prohibited the smoking of opium. Although a majority of three out of five judges upheld the conviction as a legitimate exercise of the government's power to control "the moral, mental, and physical condition of its citizens," the dissenting judges maintained that the statute was void, as an impermissible exercise of the police power, because it was "altogether sweeping in its terms." By prohibiting all smoking of opium, even when done only in private and harming directly only one's own person, the statute was "an unwarranted infringement of individual rights," wrote one of the dissenting judges. *See* Mayer, *Tiedeman, supra* note 58, at 134–36.

93. 1 TIEDEMAN, *supra* note 78, § 121, at 508–10.

94. As Tiedeman understood it, the constitutional guarantee of liberty of contract was "intended to operate equally and impartially upon both employer and employee." *Id.* § 98, at 316. Statutes that determined the hours of labor, either directly by prohibiting labor above a proscribed maximum or indirectly by requiring extra compensation for overtime, violated the constitutional liberty of contract of persons who were sui juris. *Id.* § 102, at 333–34. Tiedeman exempted children from the general rule because they were not sui juris; and he exempted government employees because government, as a party to the contract, had the right to limit the hours of employment. *Id.* at 335, 338. But he applied the guarantee of liberty of contract equally to women, married or single, as well as to men—citing with approval the Illinois Supreme Court's recognition of women's contract rights in *Ritchie v. People*, 155 Ill. 98, 40 N.E. 454 (1895), discussed in chapter 1, *supra*, text at notes 65–67. 1 Tiedeman, *supra* note 78, § 102, at 336. Nor did he exempt from his general rule "unwholesome employments"; in his view, the danger to the health of the employee from working long hours, regardless of the type of occupation, was not a constitutional justification for interference with liberty of contract. *Id.* at 337–38. Tiedeman had a generally positive attitude toward labor unions, regarding them as legitimate means of reducing the disparity in bargaining strength between employer and employee—and therefore of helping to maintain a standard of wages and to control the terms of the labor contract, consistent with liberty of contract. *Id.* § 114, at 419–24.

95. Tiedeman regarded regulations that were "reasonable safeguards" of the health and safety of workers as legitimate exercises of the police power, provided the regulations were not in opposition to "the old common law theory of the non-liability of the employer for injuries sustained by the employee, either through accident or the carelessness or negligence of the fellow-servant." *Id.* § 103, at 339; *see also* 2 TIEDEMAN, *supra* note 78, at 736–49 (discussing the constitutionality of regulations of "unwholesome and objectionable trades," and of the regulations of mines).

96. Allgeyer v. Louisiana, 165 U.S. 578, 589 (1897).

97. "[I]t may be conceded," Peckham wrote, "that this right to contract in relation to persons or property or to do business within the jurisdiction of the State may be regulated and sometimes prohibited when the contracts or business conflict with the policy of the State as contained in its statutes. . . ." *Id.* at 591.

98. *Ritchie*, 155 Ill. at 106, 40 N.E. at 456. The court then noted some of these limitations: those "imposed by the obligation to so use one's own as not to injure another, by the character of property as affected with a public interest or devoted to a public use, by the demands of public policy or the necessity of protecting the public from

fraud or injury, by the want of capacity, by the needs of the necessitous borrower as against the demands of the extortionate lender." But, as the court added, "the power of the legislature to thus limit the right to contract must rest upon some reasonable basis, and cannot be arbitrarily exercised." *Id.* Later in the opinion, the Illinois court also noted that laws passed in pursuance of the police power "must have some relation to the ends sought to be accomplished"—to the "health, comfort, safety, and welfare of society"—and "cannot invade the rights of persons and property under the guise of a mere police regulation, when it is not such in fact." *Id.,* 155 Ill. at 111, 40 N.E. at 458.

99. Adkins v. Children's Hospital, 261 U.S. 525 (1923) (holding that a law fixing minimum wages for women in the District of Columbia was an unconstitutional deprivation of the liberty protected by the Fifth Amendment). Although not as famous as *Lochner, Adkins* is arguably the best-reasoned and most paradigmatic liberty-of-contract decision. The author of the Court's majority opinion in *Adkins,* Justice George Sutherland, has been regarded by many scholars as the most distinguished of the so-called Four Horsemen, the block of conservative justices on the Court in the 1920s and 1930s. *See generally* G. Edward White, The American Judicial Tradition: Profiles of Leading American Judges 178–99 (expanded ed. 1988). And as observed in the introduction, it was the reversal of *Adkins* in the 1937 *West Coast Hotel* decision that marked the end of the Court's protection of liberty of contract as a fundamental right.

100. 261 U.S. at 546. Among those "great variety of restraints" were the numerous exceptions to the general rule of liberty that Sutherland identified as valid exercises of the police power, discussed more fully in chapter 4.

101. *Id.* at 554.

102. Randy Barnett has argued that courts ought to apply "a general Presumption of Liberty" as a way to enforce both the Ninth Amendment's protection of unenumerated constitutional rights and the privileges or immunities clause of the Fourteenth Amendment. Randy E. Barnett, Restoring the Lost Constitution: The Presumption of Liberty 259–69 (2004); Randy E. Barnett, *Implementing the Ninth Amendment, in* 2 The Rights Retained by the People: The History and Meaning of the Ninth Amendment 1, 10–19 (Randy E. Barnett ed., 1993); Randy E. Barnett, *Reconceiving the Ninth Amendment,* 74 Cornell L. Rev. 1 (1988).

103. Mugler v. Kansas, 123 U.S. 623, 661 (1887).

104. Lochner v. New York, 198 U.S. 45, 56 (1905).

105. *Id.* at 57–58.

106. *See* Gillman, *supra* note 57, at 72–73 (arguing that *arbitrary* characterized "factional politics" while *reasonableness* denoted "class-neutral policies that advanced a public purpose"). Ironically, the very example Gillman cites to illustrate his interpretation of this distinction, *Mugler v. Kansas,* disproves his thesis. The Court upheld a Kansas liquor prohibition law—a measure that, by singling out a particular industry, could be considered special-interest or class legislation—because it regarded the law as a valid use of the police power to protect public health and morals. Moreover, the test articulated by Justice Harlan in that case asked explicitly whether the challenged law truly "protected the public health, the public morals, or the public safety" and had a "real or substantial relation to those objects," not whether the law was class-neutral.

107. As David Bernstein and Michael Phillips have shown, Gillman's thesis fails to account for several significant *Lochner*-era decisions upholding laws that would seem

obvious pieces of class legislation, among them *Powell v. Pennsylvania*, 127 U.S. 678 (1888) (oleomargarine ban), and *Holden v. Hardy*, 169 U.S. 366 (1898) (maximum-hours law for miners). David E. Bernstein, Lochner *Era Revisionism, Revised:* Lochner *and the Origins of Fundamental Rights Constitutionalism*, 92 GEO. L.J. 1, 18–23 (2003) [hereafter "Bernstein, *Revisionism*"]; MICHAEL J. PHILLIPS, THE LOCHNER COURT, MYTH AND REALITY: SUBSTANTIVE DUE PROCESS FROM THE 1890s TO THE 1930s, 108 (2001). Moreover, *Lochner* itself shows that the Court did not use class-legislation arguments to invalidate labor regulations. The maximum-hours law at issue in *Lochner* "could have been construed as class legislation on two grounds," Bernstein observes: first, because it applied only to bakers; and second, because it was "arguably special-interest legislation that benefited established, unionized German-American bakers at the expense of more recent immigrants." Yet, as even Gillman acknowledges, "*Lochner* 'does not explicitly rely on the language of unequal, partial, or class legislation.'" Bernstein, *Revisionism, supra*, at 23–24 (quoting GILLMAN, *supra* note 57, at 128). Finally, as observed in chapter 1, Gillman's thesis fails to take into account many significant liberty-of-contract decisions outside the labor law context. *See also* PHILLIPS, *supra*, at 111–12 (criticizing Gillman's failure to emphasize the old Court's decisions striking down restrictions on entry, "some of which are class legislation through and through," citing *Louis K. Liggett Co. v. Baldridge*, 278 U.S. 105 (1928); and *New State Ice Co. v. Liebman*, 285 U.S. 262 (1932)).

108. PHILLIPS, *supra* note 107, at 4, 164. Under a means-ends analysis, the Court upholds a challenged law as constitutional "if it promotes some appropriate goal (the end) in a sufficiently direct or effective way (the means)." *Id.* at 4. Noting that, as applied by the modern Court, means-ends tests "vary considerably in their stringency"—ranging from "strict scrutiny" to the weak "rational basis" test—Phillips characterizes the test applied by Justice Peckham in *Lochner* as "fairly rigorous" rational-basis review, in contrast with the weak substantive test implied by Justice Holmes's dissent. *Id.* at 4, 164.

109. Chapter 4 discusses more fully the modern tests: on the one hand, the minimal rational basis test used by the Court in reviewing economic regulations; and on the other, the strict scrutiny test requiring laws to be "necessary" to achieve a "compelling" government purpose, used by the Court in reviewing laws restricting certain "preferred freedoms." Phillips argues that the old Court "applied a smorgasbord of standards and nonstandards when government action was challenged on due process grounds, but never to my recollection did it require that laws restricting economic rights be 'necessary' to achieve a 'compelling' government purpose or anything of the kind." In this respect, he maintains that "the supposedly doctrinaire and extremist *Lochner* Court in fact was considerably more moderate than its modern counterpart." PHILLIPS, *supra* note 107, at 192–93.

110. Citing such decisions, David Bernstein persuasively argues that "liberty of contract was consistently limited by the invocation of common law doctrines that restricted individual freedom for the perceived social good." Bernstein, *Revisionism, supra* note 107, at 46 & n.255 (citing, inter alia, Jacobson v. Massachusetts, 197 U.S. 11 (1905) (upholding compulsory smallpox vaccination law); Champion v. Ames, 188 U.S. 321 (1903) (upholding federal law barring lottery tickets from interstate commerce); Hennington v. Georgia, 163 U.S. 299 (1896) (upholding a Sunday law)). Michael Phillips discerns a similar pattern of deference when the old Court considered measures aimed at promoting public morality. PHILLIPS, *supra* note 107, at 48

& 79 nn.124–25 (citing, inter alia, Eberle v. Michigan, 232 U.S. 700 (1914) (upholding a local option law prohibiting sale of liquor within a county); Butler v. Perry, 240 U.S. 328 (1916) (upholding a law requiring able-bodied men to work on public roads); Waugh v. Board of Trustees, 237 U.S. 589 (1915) (upholding a ban on fraternities in state schools); Murphy v. California, 225 U.S. 623 (1912) (upholding a ban on billiard halls); Marvin v. Trout, 199 U.S. 212 (1905) (upholding a law prohibiting gambling)).

Chapter 3

1. Allgeyer v. Louisiana, 165 U.S. 578, 589 (1897).

2. Slaughterhouse Cases, 83 U.S. (16 Wall.) 36, 97, 109, 110 (1873) (Field, J., dissenting).

3. *See, e.g.,* Lochner v. New York, 195 U.S. 45 (1905) (invalidating a New York maximum-hours statute applicable to workers in bakeries); Adkins v. Children's Hospital, 261 U.S. 525 (1923) (invalidating a federal minimum-wage statute applicable to female workers in the District of Columbia).

4. *See, e.g.,* Arnold M. Paul, Conservative Crisis and The Rule Of Law: Attitudes Of Bar and Bench, 1887–1895, 67 n.15 (1960) (observing that liberty of contract, although the juristic equivalent of economic liberty generally, was "associated almost exclusively with judicial decisions concerning labor laws").

5. 1 Christopher G. Tiedeman, A Treatise On State and Federal Control Of Persons and Property in the United States § 98, at 315 (1900).

6. As discussed in the introduction and chapter 1, wage and hour regulations and other forms of so-called social legislation not only were unprecedented, in that they did not fall within the traditional scope of the police power, but also would be considered unconstitutional under 19th-century prohibitions of "partial" or "class" legislation, for by promoting the special interests of certain economic classes, they perfectly fit the traditional definition of such invalid class laws.

7. *Allgeyer,* 165 U.S. at 589.

8. Ritchie v. People, 155 Ill. 98, 111, 40 N.E. 454, 458 (1895).

9. David E. Bernstein, *The Story of* Lochner v. New York: *Impediment to the Growth of the Regulatory State, in* Constitutional Law Stories 325, 328–34 (Michael C. Dorf ed., 2004) [hereafter "Bernstein, *Lochner*"]; Paul Kens, Judicial Power and Reform Politics: The Anatomy of Lochner V. New York 44–59 (1990). The text of the Bakeshop Act may be found in Appendix B of the Kens book. Kens, *supra,* at 169–70.

10. Bernstein, *Lochner, supra* note 9, at 329–31.

11. On the scholarly debate over the factual background of *Lochner,* see Michael J. Phillips, The Lochner Court, Myth and Reality: Substantive Due Process from the 1890s to the 1930s, 147–50 (2001) (comparing the account given by Bernard Siegan, who in his 1980 book *Economic Liberties and the Constitution* argued that the maximum-hours law was designed to give larger unionized bakeries an advantage over their smaller competitors, with the account given by Kens, *supra* note 9, which downplays the special-interest impetus behind the act).

12. Bernstein, *Lochner, supra* note 9, at 331, 334–35, 339–41.

13. In addition to Justice Peckham, the majority consisted of Chief Justice Melville Fuller and Justices David Brewer, Henry Brown, and Joseph McKenna. Justice Brewer's vote was not surprising as he and Peckham clearly were the two most libertarian justices on the Court during the early part of the *Lochner*-era. Chief Justice Fuller had

joined with Brewer and Peckham in dissenting from the Court's most recent major labor regulation case, *Atkin v. Kansas*, 191 U.S. 207 (1903). The surprise to Court watchers of the time was that the majority had picked up the votes of Justices Brown and McKenna, "neither of whom had previously voted to invalidate a state labor regulation for infringing Fourteenth Amendment rights." Bernstein, *Lochner*, *supra* note 9, at 343. Some commentators believe that, but for a possible last-minute switch in the vote of one of the justices, *Lochner* would have been decided the other way: some evidence suggests that Peckham's majority opinion was originally written as a dissent, and that Justice John Marshall Harlan's dissenting opinion was originally the opinion of the Court. *Id.*; KENS, *supra* note 9, at 117–18.

14. *Lochner*, 198 U.S. at 56–58.

15. *Id.* at 57–58.

16. *Id.* at 59–61 (comparing bakers to a wide range of other occupations). The brief filed with the Court by Lochner's attorneys, Field and Weismann, contained an appendix, which one scholar has called "an incipient 'Brandeis Brief,'" that provided statistics about the health of bakers, comparisons of bakers to other occupations, and articles from various medical journals recommending sanitary and ventilation reforms but not shorter hours. Peckham's conclusions about the comparable healthfulness of the baking trade "clearly relied on" the evidence provided in Lochner's brief, but "to the detriment of his reputation," Peckham did not explicitly cite it. Bernstein, *Lochner*, *supra* note 9, at 344.

17. *Lochner*, 198 U.S. at 58, 61.

18. *Id.* at 61, 64.

19. Bernstein, *Lochner*, *supra* note 9, at 340–41; KENS, *supra* note 9, at 101–03.

20. *Lochner*, 198 U.S. at 75 (Holmes, J., dissenting).

21. As chapter 2 discusses, the Court's protection of liberty of contract under such a moderate means-ends analysis—in effect, a general presumption in favor of liberty that could be overcome by a showing that the challenged law fit within the legitimate exercise of the police power—differed substantially from a true "laissez-faire" constitutionalism that would protect liberty absolutely, for example, by applying Spencer's Law of Equal Freedom to define the scope of the right.

22. *Id.* at 75–76 (Holmes, J., dissenting).

23. *Id.* 198 U.S. at 65–66 (Harlan, J., dissenting). Justices Edward White and William Day joined in Harlan's dissent.

24. *Id.* Harlan cited medical treatises and statistics that supported the claim that "more than ten hours' steady work each day, from week to week, in a bakery or confectionery establishment, may endanger the health, and shorten the lives of the workmen, thereby diminishing their physical and mental capacity to serve the State, and to provide for those dependent upon them"—thereby accepting the logic of what the majority regarded as an argument *ad absurdum*, under which rationale the state could regulate virtually everyone's hours. *Id.* at 72. As David Bernstein notes, it is unclear where Harlan came across his medical data "because they do not appear in New York's brief," which was only 19 pages long and contained nothing like the wealth of physiological evidence contained in Lochner's brief. Bernstein, *Lochner*, *supra* note 9, at 342, 345–46.

25. Holden v. Hardy, 169 U.S. 366, 397 (1898). Justices Brewer and Peckham dissented without opinion.

26. Charles W. McCurdy, *The "Liberty of Contract" Regime in American Law*, in THE STATE AND FREEDOM OF CONTRACT 178–79 (Harry N. Scheiber ed., 1998). *Holden* also shows the general unwillingness of the Supreme Court to invalidate laws as class legislation, as David Bernstein has shown in response to Howard Gillman's thesis in his book *The Constitution Besieged*. *See* David E. Bernstein, Lochner *Era Revisionism, Revised:* Lochner *and the Origins of Fundamental Rights Constitutionalism*, 92 GEO. L.J. 1, 22–23 (2003) [hereafter "Bernstein, *Revisionism*"].

27. Muller v. Oregon, 208 U.S. 412 (1908).

28. On the harmful effects of "protective" legislation on women's employment, see Joan Kennedy Taylor, *Protective Labor Legislation*, in FREEDOM, FEMINISM, AND THE STATE: AN OVERVIEW OF INDIVIDUALIST FEMINISM 2d ed. 187, 190 (Wendy McElroy ed., 1991) ("Protective legislation for women actually diminishes the employment opportunities of women."). *See also* David E. Bernstein, Lochner's *Feminist Legacy*, 101 MICH. L. REV. 1960 (2003) (reviewing scholarship concerning women's rights during the *Lochner*-era); Elisabeth M. Landes, *The Effect of State Maximum-Hours Laws on the Employment of Women in 1920*, 88 J. POL. ECON. 476 (1980) (an empirical study of the 1920s, showing that maximum-hours laws significantly reduced female employment in manufacturing).

29. The National Consumers' League, the special-interest group that hired Brandeis to write a brief defending the Oregon law, was an umbrella organization that lobbied for industrial standards for workers, especially female workers. Brandeis's famous brief consisted of hundreds of pages of documents, a "hodgepodge" of evidence that was anecdotal and unscientific: such things as reports of factory or health inspectors, testimony of physicians or social workers before legislative committees, and quotes from medical journals—all purporting to show the deleterious effects that long hours of work had on women's health and reproductive capability. Bernstein, Lochner's *Feminist Legacy*, *supra* note 28, at 1968.

30. *Muller*, 208 U.S. at 421.

31. Ritchie & Co. v. Wayman, 244 Ill. 509, 91 N.E. 695 (1910) (upholding a 1909 law limiting the employment of women in factories or laundries to no more than 10 hours a day, reversing Ritchie v. People, 155 Ill. 98, 40 N.E. 454 (1895)).

32. Adkins v. Children's Hospital, 261 U.S. 525 (1923).

33. *Id.* at 539–43. Application of the law to minors was not challenged in the case.

34. *Id.* at 542–43; HADLEY ARKES, THE RETURN OF GEORGE SUTHERLAND: RESTORING A JURISPRUDENCE OF NATURAL RIGHTS 13 (1994).

35. Sutherland was nominated to the Court in 1922 by President Warren G. Harding. The other three were Justices Willis Van Devanter, nominated in 1910 by President William H. Taft; James C. McReynolds, nominated in 1914 by President Woodrow Wilson; and Pierce Butler, also nominated in 1922 by President Harding. On the so-called Four Horsemen generally, see G. EDWARD WHITE, THE AMERICAN JUDICIAL TRADITION: PROFILES OF LEADING AMERICAN JUDGES 178–99 (expanded ed. 1988). On Sutherland's jurisprudence, see ARKES, *supra* note 34.

36. *Adkins*, 261 U.S. at 545. In addition to Justices Sutherland, Van Devanter, McReynolds, and Pierce, Justice McKenna joined in the majority. Chief Justice Taft dissented, in an opinion joined by Justice Sanford. Justice Holmes wrote a separate dissent, while Justice Brandeis did not participate.

37. *Id.* at 544.

38. *Id.* at 545–46.

39. *Id.* at 546–54. The various categories Sutherland reviewed are discussed more fully in chapter 4.

40. *Id.* at 554–55. Sutherland's description of the harmful effects of the law explicitly referred to the *Lyons* case. *Id.* at 555 n.1.

41. Sutherland was "highly visible" in the women's suffrage movement. The Republican U.S. senator from Utah had introduced in the Senate the suffrage amendment, also called the Anthony Amendment, named after Susan B. Anthony. ARKES, *supra* note 34, at 3–4, 13.

42. *Adkins*, 261 U.S. at 553.

43. Sutherland maintained there was "an essential difference" between laws regulating the hours of labor, which could fall within the legislature's valid exercise of the police power to protect health, and laws fixing wages, which did not fit within any traditional exercise of the police power and indeed generally had been frowned on in American law. *Id.* Chief Justice Taft, in dissent, disagreed, regarding restrictions on hours and wages as having equivalent economic effects and maintaining that the majority had "exaggerate[d] the importance of the wage term of the contract of employment as more inviolate than its other terms." *Id.* at 564 (Taft, C.J., dissenting). Justice Holmes, in his separate dissent, wrote that he also "[did] not understand the principle on which the power to fix a minimum for the wages of women can be denied by those who admit the power to fix a maximum for their hours of work." He added, pithily, "It will need more than the Nineteenth Amendment to convince me that there are no differences between men and women, or that legislation cannot take those differences into account." *Id.* at 569–70 (Holmes, J., dissenting).

44. *Id.* at 553. Another somewhat difficult precedent was *Bunting v. Oregon*, 243 U.S. 426 (1917), which had upheld a maximum-hours law mandating time-and-a-half overtime payments, and which both Chief Justice Taft and Justice Holmes, in their dissents, maintained had effectively overruled *Lochner*. As summarized by Sutherland, the law at issue in *Bunting* was a valid health law, "necessary for the preservation of the health of employees" in the industries affected by the law (mills, factories, and manufacturing establishments), and thus technically was distinguishable from the law at issue in *Lochner*. *Adkins*, 261 U.S. at 550–51. The *Bunting* case is more fully discussed in chapter 4.

45. *Adkins*, 261 U.S. at 555–56. Sutherland cited some of the wage levels set by the board to illustrate the arbitrary application of the standard. Apparently, according to the board, a woman working in a mercantile establishment required a wage of $16.50 per week to sustain her health and morals, while a woman working in a printing establishment could do so with $15.50, that is, $1 per week less; and a beginner working in a laundry presumably could support herself and her morals with only $9 per week. *Id.* at 556.

46. *Id.* at 557. In response to this point, Justice Holmes in his dissent observed that the law "does not compel anybody to pay anything," adding, "It is safe to assume that women will not be employed at even the lowest wages allowed unless they earn them, or unless the employer's business can sustain the burden." *Id.* at 570. Holmes was probably right about this: as Willie Lyons's circumstances show, the probable effect of the law was to prompt employers to hire men in lieu of women. The law was passed by Congress in 1918, shortly before the end of World War I, at a time when many women had moved into jobs traditionally done by men. It is probable that, like

other so-called protective laws, discussed *supra* note 29, the real economic effect of the law was not to protect but to harm women by pricing their labor out of the market.

47. *Id*. at 558–59.

48. ARKES, *supra* note 34, at 21.

49. Charles Wolff Packing Co. v. Court of Industrial Relations, 262 U.S. 522, 544 (1923).

50. *Id*. at 534.

51. *Id*. at 536. As discussed in chapter 1, text *supra* at notes 146 and 149, the Court was divided in its decisions in *Munn* (1877) and a subsequent "public interest" case, *Budd v. New York*, 143 U.S. 517 (1892). In *Budd*, the Court followed *Munn* and upheld a New York law fixing maximum charges for grain elevators as a legitimate exercise of the police power over a business affected with a public interest. Justice Brewer in dissent, joined by Justices Field and Brown, argued that the doctrine of "public interest," as used in *Munn*, was "radically unsound." He questioned the appropriateness of applying the doctrine to any free, competitive businesses—that is, in the absence of a true monopoly, with legal or natural barriers to entry. *Id*. at 548 (Brewer, J., dissenting).

52. *Wolff Packing*, 262 U.S. at 535. With regard to the second category, Taft elaborated later in the opinion that "in the days of the early common law an omnipotent parliament did regulate prices and wages as it chose, and occasionally a colonial legislature sought to exercise the same power." But he apparently recognized the effect of the free-market movement in early American law, discussed in chapter 1, *supra*, and thus added that "nowadays one does not devote one's property or business to the public use or clothe it with a public interest merely because one makes commodities for, and sells them to, the public" in common callings like those he mentioned in the opinion. *Id*. at 537.

53. *Id*. at 537–38.

54. *Id*. at 540.

55. Adair v. United States, 208 U.S. 161 (1908) (invalidating a federal law prohibiting interstate carriers from discriminating against union members in various ways); Coppage v. Kansas, 236 U.S. 1 (1915) (invalidating a Kansas statute forbidding yellow-dog contracts).

56. *See, e.g.*, PHILLIPS, *supra* note 11, at 140–41 (maintaining that both *Adair* and *Coppage* were incorrectly decided, even under the liberty-of-contract paradigm, because unionism helped alleviate unequal bargaining power between employers and employees: "Because unionism was necessary to make freedom of contract meaningful, . . . a pro-union measure should not have fallen on freedom-of-contract grounds."). As noted in chapter 2 *supra*, laissez-faire writers such as William Graham Sumner and Christopher Tiedeman generally supported the right of workers to join labor unions, viewing unions as a kind of free-market solution to the problem of unequal bargaining strength, even if neither would compel employers to bargain with unions. As emphasized above, however, the Court's protection of liberty of contract did not follow the "laissez-faire constitutionalism" paradigm and hence in many ways departed from a consistently libertarian jurisprudential model.

57. 1 WILLIAM BLACKSTONE, COMMENTARIES *415 (noting, however, that Parliament may limit this right by statute). On the right to pursue an occupation generally, see Timothy Sandefur, *The Right to Earn a Living*, 6 CHAPMAN L. REV. 207, 207–27 (2003); Wayne McCormack, *Economic Substantive Due Process and the Right of Liveli-*

hood, 82 KY. L.J. 397, 399–400 (1993–94). As Sandefur has shown, English judges and commentators, particularly Sir Edward Coke, identified various aspects of this right that received protection in early American court decisions. *See* Sandefur, *supra*, at 225, 263–66 (Appendix A, listing approximately 60 reported cases between 1823 and 1873 in which state courts discussed or protected the common-law right to earn a living).

58. *See* PHILLIPS, *supra* note 11, at 52 (concluding that "the old Court almost always upheld occupational licensing laws," but was "much tougher on other kinds of entry restrictions"). As Michael Phillips notes, there are many valid economic criticisms of occupational licensing schemes: among others, that they "'limit consumer choice, raise consumer costs, increase practitioner income, limit practitioner mobility, deprive the poor of adequate services, and restrict job opportunities for minorities.'" *Id.* at 98 (quoting S. DAVID YOUNG, THE RULE OF EXPERTS: OCCUPATIONAL LICENSING IN AMERICA 1 (1987)). Phillips adds that occupational licensing has these effects "because it exists less to protect the public than to advance private economic interests by restricting entry into the business and thus limiting competition." *Id.* That is true; but, unfortunately, the Court did not recognize that underlying reality and instead, following the traditional conception of the police power, upheld most occupational licensing laws, failing to see that they abridged fundamental rights as much as the other forms of entry restriction the Court did find invalid.

59. Allgeyer v. Louisiana, 165 U.S. 578 (1897).

60. PHILLIPS, *supra* note 11, at 52.

61. Adams v. Tanner, 244 U.S. 590, 594 (1917).

62. *Id.* at 596–97. The Court's opinion was written by Justice James B. McReynolds. In his opinion for the Court in *Meyer v. Nebraska*, discussed *infra*, McReynolds would identify, as part of the liberty protected by due process, the freedom "to engage in any of the common occupations of life."

63. Louis K. Liggett Co. v. Baldridge, 278 U.S. 105, 113–14 (1928). Sutherland observed: "It is a matter of public notoriety that chain drug stores in great numbers, owned and operated by corporations, are to be found throughout the United States. They have been in operation for many years. We take judicial notice of the fact that the stock in these corporations is bought and sold upon the various stock exchanges of the country and, in the nature of things, must be held and owned to a large extent by persons who are not registered pharmacists." *Id.* Justices Holmes and Brandeis dissented, maintaining that a drugstore's ownership had sufficient effect on the safety with which it operates to bring the law within the valid scope of police regulation. *Id.* at 114–15 (Holmes, J., dissenting). The *Liggett* case was not overturned until 1973, when a unanimous Court upheld a nearly identical law regulating pharmacies in North Dakota. North Dakota State Bd. of Pharmacy v. Snyder's Drug Stores, 414 U.S. 156 (1973).

64. New State Ice Co. v. Liebmann, 285 U.S. 262, 273–78 (1932). Sutherland called it "a business as essentially private in its nature as the business of the grocer, the dairyman, the butcher, the baker, the shoemaker, or the tailor, each of whom performs a service which, to a greater or less extent, the community is dependent upon and is interested in having maintained; but which bears no such relation to the public as to warrant its inclusion in the category of businesses charged with a public use." *Id.* at 278. Sutherland sought to adhere to the standard defining a "business affected with a public interest" that Chief Justice Taft had articulated in *Wolff Packing*, discussed

supra, by essentially showing through an argument *ad absurdum* that if the state could restrict entry into the ice business, then it could do so for any "ordinary business."

65. *Id.* at 278–79. Sutherland's reference to "the dairyman" is ironically prescient, for it anticipated the Court's decision in *Nebbia v. New York*, 291 U.S. 502 (1934), discussed more fully in chapter 4 *infra*, which upheld a New York law setting minimum prices for the dairy industry, marking the end of the Court's adherence to the traditional definition of business "affected with a public interest."

66. Justice Brandeis's dissent famously championed experimentation: "There must be power in the States and the Nation to remould, through experimentation, our economic practices and institutions to meet changing social and economic needs." *New State Ice Co.*, 285 U.S. at 310–11 (Brandeis, J., dissenting). Michael Phillips presents a devastating critique of Brandeis's attempt to defend the Oklahoma entry restriction, showing that "this supposed master policy scientist failed either to justify Oklahoma's entry restriction or to undermine Sutherland's arguments against it," and in fact "lent crucial support to Sutherland's position." Phillips, *supra* note 11, at 101–5.

67. 285 U.S. at 280.

68. Adair v. United States, 208 U.S. 161, 173 (1908) (quoting *Cooley on Torts*, at 278).

69. Since the enactment of modern antitrust and unfair competition statutes, the law generally distinguishes individual refusals to deal—which are still considered "privileged," or part of one's general freedom of contract—and concerted refusals, which may be actionable as either antitrust violations or "unfair" methods of competition. Put another way, an individual's refusal to deal generally is not unlawful unless it is accomplished by unlawful conduct or agreement or is conceived in monopolistic purpose or market control. *See generally* 54 Am. Jur. 2d *Monopolies and Restraints of Trade* § 113 (2006). Nevertheless, the general common-law right of an individual to refuse to engage in business with another person for any reason has been abrogated by a number of statutes, including anti-discrimination laws such as the Civil Rights Act of 1964, 42 U.S.C. §2000a (1974) (prohibiting discrimination on the basis of race in public accommodation). *See generally* Edward W. Kitch & Harvey S. Perlman, Intellectual Property and Unfair Competition 364–66 (5th ed. 1998).

70. *Adair*, 208 U.S. at 168–69. William Adair, an agent of the Louisville and Nashville Railroad Company, had been convicted of violating the law—and fined $100 (the minimal punishment under the statute)—for firing O. B. Coppage, a railroad employee, "because of his membership" in a labor union, the Order of Locomotive Firemen. *Id.* at 170–71.

71. Justices McKenna and Holmes wrote separate dissents; Justice Moody did not participate in the decision of this case.

72. *Id.* at 174–75. Thus, Harlan added, under the facts of this case, "[i]t was the legal right of the defendant Adair—however unwise such a course might have been—to discharge Coppage, because of his being a member of a labor organization, as it was the legal right of Coppage, if he saw fit to do so—however unwise such a course on his part might have been—to quit the service in which he was engaged, because the defendant employed some persons who were not members of a labor organization." *Id.* at 175.

73. Richard A. Epstein, *Religious Liberty in the Welfare State*, 31 Wm. & Mary L. Rev. 375, 377 (1990). Title II of the Civil Rights Act of 1964 forbids private businesses that are engaged in interstate commerce and accommodate the public from discriminating on the ground of race, color, religion, or national origin. 78 Statutes at Large 241,

§ 201 (1964). Because of the way it thus limits freedom of contract or association, the Civil Rights Act may be seen as "a gross infringement of individual rights." *See, e.g.,* Ayn Rand, *Racism, in* THE VIRTUE OF SELFISHNESS 156 (Ayn Rand ed., 1964). *See also* Roger Pilon, *The Right to Do Wrong, in* THE LIBERTARIAN READER 197, 200 (David Boaz ed., 1997) ("For if we do have a right to be free, to plan and live our own lives as we choose, limited only by the equal right of others, then we have a right to associate, or refuse to associate, for whatever reasons we choose, or for no reason at all. That is what freedom is all about. Others may condemn our reasons—that too is a right. But if freedom and personal sovereignty mean anything, they mean the right to make those kinds of decisions for ourselves, even when they offend others.")

74. Bruce Ramsey, *"A Naked, Arbitrary Exercise,"* LIBERTY (November 1998), at 47, 68–69.

75. Griswold v. Connecticut, 381 U.S. 419 (1965) (striking down an 1897 statute prohibiting the use of any drug or device to prevent conception and prohibiting any person from advising or providing contraceptive materials, as an unconstitutional interference with the "right of privacy" of married couples and their physicians).

76. Justice Douglas's opinion for the majority of the Court grounded the right of privacy in various "penumbras, formed by emanations" from such Bill of Rights guarantees as the Third Amendment prohibition against the quartering of soldiers, the Fourth Amendment's prohibition of unreasonable searches and seizures, and the Fifth Amendment's protection against self-incrimination. 381 U.S. at 484. Douglas apparently was reluctant to base the right of privacy directly on substantive due process protection of liberty—or to place it among the unenumerated rights protected by the Ninth Amendment, as Justice Goldberg suggested in his concurring opinion—because he feared a return to the *Lochner* era, a time when (as he characterized it) the Court sat "as a super-legislature to determine the wisdom, need, and propriety of laws that touch economic problems, business affairs, or social conditions." In this case, however, he emphasized that the law in question "operates directly on an intimate relation of husband and wife and their physician's role in one aspect of that relation." *Id.* at 482.

77. WILLIAM M. WIECEK, LIBERTY UNDER LAW: THE SUPREME COURT IN AMERICAN LIFE 177–78 (1988).

78. Meyer v. Nebraska, 262 U.S. 390 (1923); Pierce v. Society of the Sisters of the Holy Names of Jesus and Mary, 268 U.S. 510 (1925). Each case was "an easy one, striking down indefensible legislation," William Wiecek asserts. WIECEK, *supra,* at 178. Nevertheless, the statutes at issue in the cases seem "indefensible" only to modern-day eyes; at the time, it could be argued, they were the kind of laws "purporting to advance public morality and communal solidarity" that the old Court tended to uphold, unless they conflicted with liberty of contract rights. *See* PHILLIPS, *supra* note 11, at 48. Noting that Justice James C. McReynolds authored the Court's opinion in both *Meyer* and *Pierce,* Wiecek further argues that McReynold's conception of noneconomic substantive due process rights remained dormant until the post–World War II era, when it emerged, indirectly, in *NAACP v. Alabama,* 357 U.S. 449 (1958) (protecting right of association) and, directly, in *Griswold.* WIECEK, *supra* note 77, at 178. For other constitutional scholars' views on the link between these cases and the modern right to privacy, see, for example, JOHN E. NOWAK & RONALD D. ROTUNDA, CONSTITUTIONAL LAW 916 (7th ed. 2004) (discussing *Meyer* and *Pierce* as antecedents); LAURENCE H. TRIBE, CONSTITUTIONAL CHOICES 25, 286 n.28 (1985) (citing *Meyer* and

Pierce among other privacy cases, as examples of constitutional protection of "individual autonomy").

79. *See, e.g.,* WILLIAM G. ROSS, FORGING NEW FREEDOMS: NATIVISM, EDUCATION, AND THE CONSTITUTION, 1917–1927, at 133 (1994).

80. In a companion case, the Court followed the authority of *Meyer* to strike down a similar English-only law passed by the Iowa legislature. Bartels v. Iowa, 262 U.S. 404, 409–11 (1923). Justice Holmes dissented in both cases, finding the requirement that young children be taught in English to be "reasonable" and therefore "not an undue restriction" of liberty. Surprisingly, Justice Sutherland concurred in Holmes's dissent. *Id.* at 412–13.

81. In addition to being, in the words of one modern scholar, "the New Deal's most implacable foe on the Court," McReynolds has been described by a friendly biographer as a man who "'discriminated against blacks, patronized women, and disliked Jews.'" PHILLIPS, *supra* note 11, at 48 (quoting JAMES EDWARD BOND, I DISSENT: THE LEGACY OF JUSTICE JAMES CLARK MCREYNOLDS 135 (1992)).

82. *Meyer*, 262 U.S. at 399–400.

83. *Id.* at 401, 403. McReynolds cited the Court's previous decision in *Adams v. Tanner*, invalidating the Washington State law that prohibited employment agencies from charging fees for their services, to show "that mere abuse incident to an occupation ordinarily useful is not enough to justify its abolition." *Id.* at 403.

84. On the Klan's influence, see PHILIP HAMBURGER, SEPARATION OF CHURCH AND STATE 415–19 (2002).

85. *Pierce*, 268 U.S. at 529–33.

86. *Id.* at 534–35.

87. *Id.* at 535–36.

88. Buchanan v. Warley, 245 U.S. 60 (1917).

89. For example, although Kermit Hall does mention *Buchanan v. Warley* in *The Magic Mirror*, his history of American law, he cites it erroneously as a case decided "on equal-protection grounds." Moreover, he mentions the case not at all in his discussion of "laissez-faire constitutionalism," but rather discusses it only in the context of the National Association for the Advancement of Colored People's campaign of litigation that culminated in *Brown v. Board of Education* (1954). KERMIT L. HALL, THE MAGIC MIRROR: LAW IN AMERICAN HISTORY 264–65 (1989). (It should be noted, however, that the second edition of Hall's book, revised by Peter Karsten, does correctly identify *Buchanan v. Warley* as a case decided "on due process grounds." KERMIT L. HALL & PETER KARSTEN, THE MAGIC MIRROR: LAW IN AMERICAN HISTORY 288 (2d ed. 2009).) Other scholars—see, for example, PHILLIPS, *supra* note 11, at 157–58—omit the case from their lists of liberty-of-contract decisions because they regard it as a "property rights" case, although the right to acquire or dispose of property that was involved in the case was a right also to enter into a contract for its sale.

90. *Buchanan*, 245 U.S. at 70–71, 73. The historical background of the Louisville ordinance and of the case (which was a test case brought by William Warley, an active African-American member of the Louisville NAACP) is ably discussed in David Bernstein, *Philip Sober Controlling Philip Drunk:* Buchanan v. Warley *in Historical Perspective*, 51 VANDERBILT L. REV. 797, 839–56 (1998) [hereafter "Bernstein, *Buchanan*"].

91. 245 U.S. at 79 (citing Plessy v. Ferguson, 163 U.S. 537 (1896)).

92. Justice Holmes drafted a dissent in *Buchanan* that he ultimately chose not to deliver. *See* Bernstein, *Buchanan*, *supra* note 90, at 855.

93. *Buchanan*, 245 U.S. at 74, 82.

94. *Id.* at 81. Other police-power rationales argued by Kentucky were that the law would promote the public peace by preventing race conflict and that the law was necessary to prevent the depreciation in the value of property owned by white people when black persons became their neighbors. *Id.* at 80–82. *See also* Bernstein, *Buchanan, supra* note 90, at 844–45, 847–50 (discussing the overtly racist arguments in Kentucky's briefs), and 853–84 (summarizing Justice Day's disposition of the state's police-power arguments).

95. 245 U.S. at 81. Justice Day also held that the Fourteenth Amendment operated "to qualify and entitle a colored man to acquire property without state legislation discriminating against him because of color." *Id.* at 79.

96. On Storey's role in the founding of the NAACP, see Hall, *supra* note 89, at 260–65; on Storey's role in the *Buchanan* case, see Bernstein, *Buchanan, supra* note 90, at 842–43, 846–47.

97. Bernstein, *Buchanan, supra* note 90, at 856 (quoting a biography of Storey).

98. *Id.* at 856–58.

99. David Bernstein notes, "Relying on *Buchanan*, the NAACP persuaded the Supreme Court to invalidate segregation ordinances in New Orleans. . . and Richmond," and "[l]ocal branches of the NAACP successfully challenged laws passed in Indianapolis, Norfolk, and Dallas." *Id.* at 858 n.360 (citations omitted). Bernstein also credits *Buchanan* for opening up white neighborhoods to African Americans, at least in the short run; for establishing the NAACP as an important player on the American legal scene; and for marking the positive turning point in the history of African-American litigation before the Supreme Court. *Id.* at 859–61, 871–72.

100. In the long run, *Buchanan* failed to invalidate segregation laws outside the residential housing context because of the narrowness of its holding and the continued validity of *Plessy v. Ferguson*. The decision had limited longer-term effects on de facto segregation in housing because white persons were eventually able to use barriers other than explicit racial zoning to keep black persons out of their neighborhoods; these devices included facially neutral zoning laws and restrictive covenants. *See id.* at 861–66.

101. *Id.* at 870–71. Bernstein notes that W. E. B. Du Bois reportedly credited *Buchanan* with "the breaking of the back of segregation," and that Leon Higginbotham has argued that if the decision had come out the other way, the living conditions of black Americans in many southern states and perhaps many other parts of America could have been akin to those of black South Africans. *Id.* Bernstein himself suggests that "the road not taken," if the Court's decision had gone the other way in *Buchanan*, might have led to de jure segregation in not only housing but also occupations. *Id.* at 869–70.

102. *Plessy*, 163 U.S. at 559 (Harlan, J., dissenting).

103. James W. Ely Jr., *Reflections on* Buchanan v. Warley, *Property Rights, and Race*, 51 Vanderbilt L. Rev. 953, 972 (1998). Discussing the significance of *Buchanan*, Ely maintains that the decision "exemplifies the historic tendency of constitutional law to encourage the dynamic and creative aspects of property ownership rather than just uphold the status quo. By placing a high value on the acquisition and use of property, the Justices tried to keep open the channels of change even for racial minorities." *Id.* at 965. In addition to the minority interests protected in *Meyer* and *Pierce*, Ely also points to decisions such as *New State Ice Co.* that, by voiding anti-competitive entry barriers, vindicated the rights of fledgling entrepreneurs. *Id.* at 972.

104. Summarizing Bernstein's findings about the Progressives' hostile reaction to the *Buchanan* decision, Ely notes how the Progressive movement, with its fondness for planning and reliance on experts, "looked with disfavor on judicial efforts to enforce constitutional limits on governmental authority." *Id.* at 961. It was not just property rights that were adversely affected by Progressive ideology, Ely notes; Progressives displayed little interest in other rights—for example, free speech, during the years preceding World War I. *Id.* (citing a First Amendment scholar who has found that most prominent early 20th-century proponents of economic regulation also supported federal and state speech regulations). Indeed, he adds, Progressives also "placed great faith in the use of government to police moral norms. . . . The Progressive Era saw an outpouring of morals regulation designed to strengthen the community by eliminating social problems. In areas of personal behavior, individual freedom was subordinated to the perceived needs of the society. Drawing no distinction between economic and other liberties, the Progressives viewed with suspicion all claims of individual right." *Id.* at 962.

Chapter 4

1. *See, e.g.,* Calvin Woodard, *Reality and Social Reform: The Transition from Laissez-Faire to the Welfare State,* 72 YALE L. J. 286, 305–11 (1962) (explaining the demise of the "laissez-faire standard" by pointing to "a clash with reality," the reality of an industrial society).

2. The concept of "neutral principles"—the idea that judicial decisionmaking should be based on principles that transcend the specific issue presented to the Court—has been developed by modern jurists to help justify judicial review and to reconcile it with the American commitment to democracy, or popular sovereignty. *See, e.g.,* R. Kent Greenawalt, *The Enduring Significance of Neutral Principles,* 78 COLUM. L. REV. 982 (1978); Herbert Wechsler, *Toward Neutral Principles of Constitutional Law,* 73 HARV. L. REV. 1 (1959). In his classic 1959 *Harvard Law Review* article, Professor Wechsler identified a "genuinely principled" decisionmaking process as one "resting with respect to every step that is involved in reaching judgment on analysis and reasons quite transcending the immediate result that is achieved." Wechsler, *supra,* at 9, 15.

3. *See* Stephen A. Siegel, Lochner *Era Jurisprudence and the American Constitutional Tradition,* 70 N. C. L. REV. 1, 9 (1991); David E. Bernstein, Lochner *Era Revisionism, Revised:* Lochner *and the Origins of Fundamental Rights Constitutionalism,* 92 GEO. L.J. 1, 10–11 (2003) [hereafter "Bernstein, *Revisionism*"].

4. Bernstein, *Revisionism, supra* note 3, at 10 & n.31.

5. *Id.* at 10 & n.32.

6. *Id.* at 10 & n.33; Barry Cushman, *The Secret Lives of the Four Horsemen,* 83 VA. L. REV. 559, 566 & n.56 (1997).

7. Charles Warren's crude empirical study of Supreme Court decisions in the years 1887 to 1911 found that, out of over 560 decisions based on the due process and equal protection clauses of the Fourteenth Amendment, the Court invalidated only a handful of state statutes that he called "social justice legislation." *See* Charles Warren, *The Progressiveness of the United States Supreme Court,* 13 COLUMBIA L. REV. 294, 295 (1913); *see also* 3 CHARLES WARREN, THE SUPREME COURT IN UNITED STATES HISTORY 463–78 (1923). Two other studies from the 1930s and 1940s, however, credited the Court with a more aggressive enforcement of Fourteenth Amendment limitations on state police

powers. A study by B. F. Wright, originally published in 1942 (and reissued in paperback in 1967) but still cited in some constitutional history texts, maintained that the Court invalidated state laws on Fourteenth Amendment grounds in nearly 200 cases during the 1899–1937 period. *See* BENJAMIN F. WRIGHT, THE GROWTH OF AMERICAN CONSTITUTIONAL LAW 148–79 (Phoenix Book paperback 1967). Another important study by Felix Frankfurter, also still cited today, identified 220 decisions from the 1897–1938 period that invalidated state laws on Fourteenth Amendment grounds. FELIX FRANKFURTER, MR. JUSTICE HOLMES AND THE SUPREME COURT 97–137 (1938) (appendix listing and describing "Cases Holding State Action Invalid under the Fourteenth Amendment"). These sources, and others, are nicely summarized in MICHAEL J. PHILLIPS, THE *LOCHNER* COURT, MYTH AND REALITY: SUBSTANTIVE DUE PROCESS FROM THE 1890s TO THE 1930s, at 32–35 & 62 n.1 (2001).

8. PHILLIPS, *supra* note 7, at 5. Phillips reduces Frankfurter's list of 220 cases to 128 by eliminating cases he categorizes as having been decided on privileges or immunities, equal protection, or procedural due process grounds. After making some further adjustments to the list and then deleting what he classifies as "peripheral" and "borderline" substantive due process cases, he arrives at a list of only 56 "core" substantive due process cases. Of these 56, he identifies only 10 cases as liberty-of-contract decisions; that is, those in which the Court "used express freedom-of-contract reasoning to strike down government action." *Id.* at 35–58 & 86–87 n.210. Phillips's classification is far too restrictive, however; it omits many significant liberty-of-contract decisions—for example, *Meyers* and *Pierce*, which he classifies as cases involving "personal rights," *id.* at 48, and *Buchanan*, which he classifies as a "land-use" case, *id.* at 46–47, 157–58.

9. Adkins Children's Hospital, 261 U.S. 525, 546–54 (1923).

10. Bunting v. Oregon, 243 U.S. 426 (1917). Both Chief Justice Taft and Justice Holmes, in their dissents in *Adkins*, maintained that *Lochner* had been overruled by *Bunting*. *See Adkins*, 261 U.S. at 564 (Taft, C.J., dissenting, writing that he found it "impossible" to reconcile *Bunting* with *Lochner* and adding that he had "always supposed that the Lochner case was thus overruled sub silento") and at 570 (Holmes, J., dissenting, writing that he thought *Lochner* "would be allowed a deserved repose"). Many modern scholars agree. *See, e.g.*, DAVID P. CURRIE, THE CONSTITUTION IN THE SUPREME COURT: THE SECOND CENTURY, 1888–1986, 103 (1990) (maintaining that *Bunting* "buried *Lochner* without even citing it").

11. *Bunting*, 243 U.S. at 433–34, 437–38. Chief Justice White and Justices Van Devanter and McReynolds dissented, without opinion; Justice Brandeis took no part in deciding the case. Felix Frankfurter joined the attorney general of Oregon in briefing the Court in defense of the law, *id.* at 430, just as he would also cowrite the brief in defense of the District of Columbia minimum-wage law in *Adkins*.

12. Radice v. New York, 264 U.S. 292, 293–95 (1924) (following the *Muller* Court's recognition of "the physical limitations of women").

13. Jacobson v. Massachusetts, 197 U.S. 11, 29 (1905) (upholding mandatory smallpox vaccination and stating, "In every well-ordered society charged with the duty of conserving the safety of its members, the rights of the individual in respect of his liberty may at times, under the pressure of great dangers, be subjected to such restraint, to be enforced by reasonable regulations, as the safety of the general public may demand.").

14. *E.g.*, Second Employers' Liability Cases, 223 U.S. 1 (1912) (upholding federal law governing railroads' liability for the employees' on-the-job injuries); Chicago,

Burlington & Quincy Railroad v. McGuire, 219 U.S. 549 (1911) (upholding state law similarly governing railroads' liability for employees' injuries); New York Central Railroad v. White, 243 U.S. 199 (1917), and Mountain Timber v. Washington, 243 U.S. 219 (1917) (rejecting substantive due process challenges to workers' compensation laws for hazardous employments). This line of cases is nicely summarized by Michael Phillips, who concludes that the Court during the *Lochner*-era "in all, . . . probably rejected eighteen substantive due process attacks on workers' compensation provisions and kindred laws." Phillips, *supra* note 7, at 54–55. David Bernstein points to this line of cases in refuting Cass Sunstein's claim that *Lochner*-era jurisprudence involved preserving a supposed "baseline" of common–law rights; as he argues, "the Court did not see the common law as natural and prepolitical, but as manmade and mutable." David E. Bernstein, Lochner's *Legacy's Legacy*, 82 TEX. L. REV. 1, 26 (2003) [hereafter "Bernstein, *Legacy*"]. He also notes that, "after the landmark *White* decision, the Supreme Court consistently upheld federal and state workers' compensation statutes, including laws with novel features," and that most of these decisions were unanimous. *Id.* at 30–31.

15. *Adkins,* 261 U.S. at 547.

16. *Id. See* Atkin v. Kansas, 191 U.S. 207 (1903) (state law regulating wages and hours of laborers employed by municipal paving contractors); Heim v. McCall, 239 U.S. 175 (1915) (state law giving citizens a preference over aliens in employment on public works); Ellis v. United States, 206 U.S. 246 (1907) (federal statute limiting hours worked by federal workers or employees of federal contractors to eight per day).

17. *See* Knoxville Iron Co. v. Harbison, 183 U.S. 13 (1901) (state law requiring employer to redeem scrip in cash); McLean v. Arkansas, 211 U.S. 539 (1909) (state law requiring that, for payment purposes, coal produced by miners be weighed as it comes from the mine and before it is passed over a screen); Erie Railroad v. Williams, 233 U.S. 685 (1914) (state law requiring that railroads pay their employees semimonthly in cash).

18. Charles W. McCurdy, *The "Liberty of Contract" Regime in American Law, in* THE STATE AND FREEDOM OF CONTRACT 182–83 (Harry N. Scheiber ed., 1998). McCurdy sees the decisions upholding statutes regulating company-store scrip and coal-weighing procedures as transitional precedents, eventually permitting the Court generally to uphold social legislation of all types. In an additional wage-payment case he regards as "most revealing," *Keokee Consolidated Coke Company v. Taylor,* 234 U.S. 224 (1917), the Court unanimously rejected a liberty-of-contract challenge to a Virginia statute that forbade mining or manufacturing companies to pay wages in scrip redeemable only in company stores. Holmes's opinion for the Court originally recognized that employees were under "the power of duress," but when his colleagues objected, Holmes eventually produced a very brief opinion that limited the police power justification to the fraud-prevention rationale the Court used in *McLean.* McCurdy, *supra,* at 183.

19. *See* Tyson & Brother v. Banton, 273 U.S. 418 (1927) (resale of theater tickets); Ribnik v. McBride, 277 U.S. 350 (1928) (employment agency fees); Williams v. Standard Oil, 278 U.S. 235 (1929) (retail price of gasoline).

20. In *Tyson,* Stone found justification in the "virtual monopoly of the best seats" held by certain ticket brokers. More generally, he argued that price regulations should be constitutional where "a situation or a combination of circumstances materially restricting the regulative flow of competition" exists, "so that buyers or sellers are

placed at such a disadvantage in the bargaining struggle that serious economic consequences result to a very large number of members of the community." 273 U.S. at 450–52 (Stone, J., dissenting).

21. Chief Justice Taft was succeeded by Charles Evans Hughes in 1930; in the same year, Justice Sanford was succeeded by Owen J. Roberts; two years later, in 1932, Justice Holmes was succeeded by Benjamin Cardozo.

22. Nebbia v. New York, 291 U.S. 502, 536 (1934). The law clearly was designed to help protect the state's dairy farmers from the spiraling fall in milk prices. Nebbia, the proprietor of a grocery store in Rochester, sold two quarts of milk and a 5-cent loaf of bread for 18 cents; he was convicted for violating the board's order, which had fixed a minimum price of 9 cents for the retail sale of a quart of milk.

23. *Id.* at 537–39.

24. Bernstein, *Revisionism, supra* note 3, at 46 & n.255 (citing, inter alia, Champion v. Ames, 188 U.S. 321 (1903) (upholding a federal law banning lotteries); Hennington v. Georgia, 163 U.S. 299 (1896) (upholding a Sunday law); Butler v. Perry, 240 U.S. 328 (1916) (upholding the ancient practice of requiring citizens to work on road projects for the common good)).

25. Adkins v. Children's Hospital, 261 U.S. 525, 561 (1923).

26. ERNST FREUND, THE POLICE POWER: PUBLIC POLICY AND CONSTITUTIONAL RIGHTS iii (1904).

27. *Id.* at 6 (emphasis omitted). In a footnote, Freund cited the opinion of Chief Baron Fleming of the English Exchequer Court, in *Bate's Case* (1606), that the king had absolute power to do that which is *salus populi*, or applied to the general benefit of the people. *Id.* at 6 n.7. While Freund thus saw the police power as concerned with policy (the promotion of the public welfare) and executive in its function, Tiedeman and Cooley had seen it as concerned with justice (the maintenance of private rights) and thus judicial in function.

28. *Id.* at 3.

29. As Charles McCurdy notes, a leading proponent of social legislation, economist Henry W. Farnam, was influenced by another work of Freund's, his *Standards of American Legislation*, published in 1917, which advocated essentially a "public welfare" standard for the courts in reviewing constitutionality. McCurdy, *supra* note 18, at 192–93.

30. On this shift generally, see Herbert Hovenkamp, *The Political Economy of Substantive Due Process*, 40 STAN. L. REV. 379, 381–82 (1988); David N. Mayer, *The Jurisprudence of Christopher G. Tiedeman: A Study in the Failure of Laissez-Faire Constitutionalism*, 55 MO. L. REV. 93, 151–52 (1990) [hereafter "Mayer, *Tiedeman*"].

31. Mayer, *Tiedeman, supra*, at 151. Ironically, Tiedeman also was a student of the German sociological school, led by German jurist Rudolf von Jhering. Tiedeman based his laissez-faire constitutionalism not on formalist, or "mechanical," rules but rather on a sociological conception of the law. *Id.* at 102–25.

32. Hadley Arkes's biography of George Sutherland, for example, reproduces on its frontispiece a page from Sutherland's commonplace book, written when he was studying the law in 1882 (when he was 20), which quotes a passage from Burlamaqui's treatise on natural law, defining "natural liberty" and "civil liberty." HADLEY ARKES, THE RETURN OF GEORGE SUTHERLAND: RESTORING A JURISPRUDENCE OF NATURAL RIGHTS (1994) (frontispiece). As the title of the book suggests, Arkes's study of Sutherland's jurisprudence emphasizes its foundations in natural rights theory.

33. *See, e.g.*, Michael Les Benedict, The Blessings of Liberty: A Concise History of the Constitution of the United States 280–82 (2d ed. 2006); Kermit L. Hall, The Magic Mirror: Law in American History 281–82 (1989). Bruce Ackerman has described the New Deal Revolution as one of the "three great turning points of constitutional history"; like the other two turning points he identifies—the Founding and Reconstruction—it involved "a total repudiation of the preexisting constitutional tradition and its replacement. . . with a new comprehensive synthesis." Bruce Ackerman, We the People: Foundations 58, 114 (1991). Professor Ackerman nevertheless notes that the new synthesis merely began in 1937, and he emphasizes the Court's famous footnote in its *Caroline Products* opinion the following year as the critical watershed, thus suggesting that the real "revolution" occurred the year after 1937. *Id*. at 119.

34. It should be noted that Justice Roberts was the author of the majority opinion in the 1934 decision of *Nebbia v. New York*; Chief Justice Hughes was the author of the majority opinions in *Home Building & Loan Assn. v. Blaisdell*, 290 U.S. 398 (1934) (upholding the Minnesota debt moratorium law against an Article I, Section 10, contract clause challenge), and *Ashwander v. Tennessee Valley Authority*, 297 U.S. 288 (1936) (upholding the constitutionality of the TVA as an exercise of Congress's power, under Article IV, Section 3, "to dispose of and make all needful Rules and Regulations respecting the Territory or other Property belonging to the United States"). Their stance in these cases anticipated the two justices' eventual permanent alignment with the three liberals on the Court.

35. *See, e.g.*, 2 Alfred H. Kelly, Winfred A. Harbison, & Herman Belz, The American Constitution: Its Origins and Development 488 (7th ed. 1991); Currie, *supra* note 10, at 236.

36. West Coast Hotel v. Parrish, 300 U.S. 379 (1937) (upholding a Washington State minimum wage law); National Labor Relations Bd. v. Jones and Laughlin Steel Corp., 301 U.S. 1 (1937) (upholding the National Labor Relations Act); National Labor Relations Bd. v. Friedman-Harry Marks Clothing Co., 301 U.S. 58 (1937) (upholding the NLRA as applied to a small manufacturer with only a negligible effect on interstate commerce); Associated Press v. National Labor Relations Bd., 301 U.S. 103 (1937) (upholding the NLRA as applied to the labor relations of newspapers and press associations); Stewart Machine Co. v. Davis, 301 U.S. 548 (1937) (upholding the Social Security Act's unemployment excise tax on employers); Helvering v. Davis, 301 U.S. 619 (1937) (upholding the Social Security Act's old-age tax and benefit provisions).

37. On this profound shift in the Court's reading of the Tenth Amendment, see David N. Mayer, *Justice Clarence Thomas and the Supreme Court's Rediscovery of the Tenth Amendment*, 25 Capital U. L. Rev. 339, 379–86 (1996). For decisions illustrating the Court's pre-1937 application of the Tenth Amendment, see, for example, *Hammer v. Dagenhart*, 247 U.S. 251 (1918) (striking down a federal law banning from interstate commerce goods produced by child labor); *Bailey v. Drexel Furniture Co.*, 259 U.S. 20 (1922) (striking down a federal law imposing a prohibitive tax on goods produced by child labor); *United States v. Butler*, 291 U.S. 1 (1936) (striking down the Agricultural Adjustment Act, the first congressional attempt to limit agricultural production). In *United States v. Darby*, 312 U.S. 100 (1941), the Court unanimously upheld the Fair Labor Standards Act of 1938, overruling *Hammer v. Dagenhart*. In his opinion for the Court, Justice Stone reduced the Tenth Amendment to the mere statement of "a truism that all is retained which has not been surrendered," which became a mere tau-

tology as the Court declined to enforce the amendment as a limitation on Congress's commerce or spending powers. Not until the emergence of what scholars have called the "new federalism" of the Rehnquist Court would the Court again cite the Tenth Amendment in decisions limiting federal power.

38. *West Coast Hotel,* 300 U.S. at 397 (overruling *Adkins v. Children's Hospital* and upholding legislation setting minimum wages and/or maximum hours as reasonable exercises of the police power, not violating the due process clauses of the Fifth and Fourteenth Amendments). As legal historian James Ely notes, the decision in *West Coast Hotel* "effectively repudiated the liberty of contract doctrine" and "marked the virtual end of economic due process as a constitutional norm." JAMES W. ELY JR., THE GUARDIAN OF EVERY OTHER RIGHT: A CONSTITUTIONAL HISTORY OF PROPERTY RIGHTS 127 (1992).

39. United States v. Carolene Products Co. 304 U.S. 144 (1938) (rejecting a due process challenge to a federal law prohibiting interstate shipment of "filled" milk). The most famous part of Justice Stone's opinion for the majority of the Court in *Carolene Products Co.* is his footnote 4—called by Professor Ackerman "the most famous [footnote] in Supreme Court history." ACKERMAN, *supra* note 33, at 119. As discussed more fully later in this chapter, the footnote suggested a standard of review with "more exacting judicial scrutiny" for legislation falling within "a specific prohibition of the Constitution, such as those of the first ten amendments," or for legislation disadvantaging "discrete and insular minorities," or obstructing "political processes which can ordinarily be expected to bring about repeal of undesirable legislation." 304 U.S. at 152–53 n.4. As Professor Currie notes, Justice Stone's footnote "established the Court's agenda for the next fifty years." CURRIE, *supra* note 10, at 244.

40. The new standard of review announced in *Carolene Products* for "regulatory legislation affecting ordinary commercial transactions" is discussed more fully *infra,* text at notes 55–56.

41. On the constitutional double standard, see ELY, *supra* note 38, at 133; PHILLIPS, *supra* note 7, at 185–92; BERNARD H. SIEGAN, THE SUPREME COURT'S CONSTITUTION 41–42 (1987).

42. *West Coast Hotel,* 300 U.S. at 399 (1937); Richard A. Epstein, *The Mistakes of 1937,* 11:2 GEORGE MASON U. L. REV. 5, 18–19 (1988). As many modern economists argue, minimum-wage laws actually harm the very groups of persons they purportedly help. *See generally* GEORGE REISMAN, CAPITALISM: A TREATISE ON ECONOMICS 382–84, 659–60 (1996) (explaining how minimum-wage laws cause unemployment and create legal barriers to entry, or monopolize the market, against the less able and the disadvantaged).

43. 300 U.S. at 402–04 (Sutherland, J., dissenting). Sutherland's stance was reminiscent of Justice Story's admonition, in his *Commentaries on the Constitution,* "not to enlarge the construction of a given power beyond the fair scope of its terms, merely because the restriction is inconvenient, impolitic, or even mischievous." JOSEPH STORY, COMMENTARIES ON THE CONSTITUTION OF THE UNITED STATES 144 (Ronald D. Rotunda & John E. Novak eds., Carolina Academic Press 1987) (abridged ed. 1833).

44. *E.g.,* EARL M. MALTZ, RETHINKING CONSTITUTIONALISM: ORIGINALISM, INTERVENTIONISM, AND THE POLITICS OF JUDICIAL REVIEW 3 (1994) ("[A] principle that the Court should defer generally to legislative judgments has no obvious political bias and therefore fits comfortably within the basic framework of neutral principles.").

45. Indeed, one of Farnam's books, *The Economic Utilization of History* (1913), may have furnished the idea that "the states are laboratories for social experiments," which Justice Brandeis pronounced in his famous dissent in *New State Ice Co. See* McCurdy, *supra* note 18, at 189.

46. Michael Phillips discusses "the myth of the modern Court's economic neutrality," arguing persuasively that the post-1937 substantive due process jurisprudence embodied in the opinions of Justices Black and Douglas has not been neutral in practice but rather has sanctioned a particular political/economic theory. He describes that theory as "corporatism: a fusion of public and private power in which large groups dominate society, government serves their interests, and individuals count for relatively little as individuals." He also follows Hadley Arkes in seeing corporatism as "the New Deal's main economic philosophy." "Where that philosophy prevails, moreover, legislatures are not completely free to adopt whatever social or economic theory they desire. In particular, they are not completely free to institute laissez-faire policies that would prevent private interests from using government to defeat competitors." PHILLIPS, *supra* note 7, at 164–65, 166. Similarly, Richard Epstein has identified the economic policy behind the Progressive movement and the New Deal as one based on government-created and -regulated cartels, in lieu of free, competitive markets. *See* RICHARD A. EPSTEIN, HOW PROGRESSIVES REWROTE THE CONSTITUTION 77–100 (2006).

47. For example, in a series of decisions in the first two decades of the 20th century the Court expanded the commerce power to give Congress, in effect, general police powers to regulate health, safety, or morality, rather than purely commercial matters. *See, e.g.*, Champion v. Ames, 188 U.S. 321 (1903) (upholding a ban on lottery tickets in interstate commerce); Hipolite Egg Co. v. United States, 220 U.S. 45 (1911) (upholding the federal Pure Food and Drug Act); Hoke v. United States, 227 U.S. 308 (1913) (upholding the so-called White Slave Act, criminalizing the transportation of women across state lines "for immoral purposes"). That expansion could not be justified under the basic rationale for the commerce power—to ensure a national market free from state interference.

48. *Nebbia*, 291 U.S. at 537.

49. Barry Cushman has argued persuasively that *Nebbia* marks the Court's abandonment of its *Lochner*-era jurisprudence. *See* BARRY CUSHMAN, RETHINKING THE NEW DEAL COURT: THE STRUCTURE OF A CONSTITUTIONAL REVOLUTION 7 (1998).

50. Home Building & Loan Ass. v. Blaisdell, 290 U.S. 398 (1934).

51. These pre-1937 decisions include *Schechter v. United States*, 295 U.S. 495 (1935) (unanimously striking down the National Industrial Recovery Act); *United States v. Butler*, 297 U.S. 1 (1936) (striking down the Agricultural Adjustment Act); and *Carter v. Carter Coal Co.*, 298 U.S. 238 (1936) (striking down the Coal Conservation Act of 1935).

52. In 1937, Justice Van Devanter retired and was replaced by former senator Hugo Black, the "ultra-radical of the Senate" and a strident populist. The following year, Justice Sutherland retired and was replaced by Stanley Reed, former solicitor general of Kentucky and an advocate of the modern regulatory state. Justice Cardozo died also in 1938; Roosevelt replaced him with Felix Frankfurter, a Harvard Law School professor who was a protégé of and political collaborator with Justice Brandeis in reform causes (and who had written the briefs defending the Oregon maximum-hours law in *Bunting* and the D.C. minimum-wage law in *Adkins v. Children's Hospital*). In 1939, Justice Butler died; he was replaced the following year by former attorney general and Michigan governor Frank Murphy, a friend of organized labor. Also in 1939, Jus-

tice Brandeis retired, replaced by William O. Douglas, chairman of the Securities and Exchange Commission and a former professor. In 1941, Justice McReynolds retired and was replaced by Robert H. Jackson, another attorney general. The same year, Charles Evens Hughes stepped down as chief justice, succeeded by Associate Justice Harlan F. Stone. The vacancy created by Stone's elevation to chief was filled, first by South Carolina senator James F. Byrnes and later by former professor and circuit judge Wiley Rutledge. Thus, by World War II all but one of the justices on the Court were Roosevelt appointees. In 1945, President Truman appointed Ohio senator Harold H. Burton to replace Justice Roberts, the last holdover from the mid-1930s. CURRIE, *supra* note 10, at 277–79; 2 KELLY, HARBISON, & BELZ, *supra* note 35, at 489.

53. Perhaps the most glaring example of the Court's ignoring the text of the Constitution and its own prior decisions in order to reach a result favorable to the Roosevelt administration is the infamous decision in *Korematsu v. United States*, 323 U.S. 214 (1944), upholding the executive order that authorized the relocation of Japanese Americans to concentration camps. In his opinion for the majority, Justice Black conceded that under the *Carolene Products Co.* analysis, the racial classification was "immediately suspect" and therefore must be subjected to "the most rigid scrutiny"; nevertheless, he was loath to second-guess the Roosevelt administration's national security actions during wartime. In the words of dissenting Justice Murphy, the majority permitted the government "to infer that examples of individual disloyalty prove group disloyalty," a fundamental denial of due process. For other examples of "victims of the judicial New Deal," see CURRIE, *supra* note 10, at 239–44.

54. Carolene Products Co., 304 U.S. 144 (1938); Geoffrey P. Miller, *The True Story of Carolene Products*, 1987 SUP. CT. REV. 397, 398, 399.

55. *Carolene Products Co.*, 304 U.S. at 152.

56. Timothy Sandefur, *The Right to Earn a Living*, 6 CHAPMAN L. REV. 207, 262 (2003).

57. *Carolene Products Co.*, 304 U.S. at 153 n.4. It should be noted that Justice Stone's reference to "a specific prohibition of the Constitution, such as those of the first ten amendments," if taken literally, would include the Ninth and Tenth Amendments and would not exclude provisions of the Bill of Rights that protect property rights and economic liberty, such as the Fifth Amendment's takings and due process clauses.

58. Palko v. Connecticut, 302 U.S. 419 (1937) (upholding a state criminal conviction, notwithstanding double jeopardy, because the Court held that the Fifth Amendment protection against double jeopardy was not so fundamental a right that its denial in state court would constitute a deprivation of due process). Since *Palko*, the Court has incorporated the Fifth Amendment double jeopardy provision as well as most of the other rights of accused persons guaranteed by the Fifth and Sixth Amendments; however, the Fifth Amendment right to a grand jury indictment along with a few other provisions of the Bill of Rights—such as the Seventh Amendment right to a jury trial in civil cases—have yet to be incorporated under the Fourteenth Amendment's due process clause. The Second Amendment guarantee of the right to bear arms was not incorporated into the Fourteenth Amendment until 2010, with the Court's decision in *McDonald v. City of Chicago*, 561 U.S. ___, 130 S. Ct. 3020 (June 28, 2010).

59. West Virginia State Board of Education v. Barnette, 319 U.S. 624, 640 (1943).

60. In his dissenting opinion in *Roe v. Wade*, 410 U.S. 113 (1973), for example, Justice William Rehnquist pointed out the inconsistency in modern liberal substantive due process jurisprudence when he observed: "I agree. . . that the 'liberty,' against deprivation of which without due process the Fourteenth Amendment protects, embraces

more than the rights found in the Bill of Rights. But that liberty is not guaranteed absolutely against deprivation, but only against deprivation without due process of law. The test traditionally applied in the area of social and economic legislation is whether or not a law such as that challenged has a rational relation to a valid state objective. . . . But the Court's sweeping invalidation of any restrictions on abortion during the first trimester is impossible to justify under that standard. . . ." *Id.* at 173 (Rehnquist, J., dissenting).

61. Griswold v. Connecticut, 381 U.S. 419, 482 (1965).

62. Planned Parenthood v. Casey, 505 U.S. 833, 861 (1992) (plurality opinion of Justices O'Connor, Kennedy, and Souter).

Conclusion

1. On the distinction between myths, on the one hand, and folktales or legends on the other, see Encyclopedia of Urban Legends 111–13, 279 (Jan Harold Brunvand ed., 2001) (entries on "Definition of 'Legend'" and "Myth").

2. How the Progressives "rewrote" American constitutional law—and, in the process, unfairly caricatured the Supreme Court's liberty of contract jurisprudence—is nicely discussed in Richard A. Epstein's aptly titled book, *How Progressives Rewrote the Constitution* (2006).

3. Chief among the proponents of this revisionist interpretation is political science professor Howard Gillman, whose 1993 book, *The Constitution Besieged: The Rise and Demise of Lochner Era Police Power Jurisprudence*, is critically discussed in chapter 1.

4. As briefly mentioned in the section on the Fourteenth Amendment in chapter 1, proponents of the proposed amendment during the congressional debates in 1866 maintained that the equal protection clause would "abolish all class legislation." See the discussion of Senator Howard's speech in chapter 1, the text at note 124, *supra*.

Index

About the Author

David N. Mayer is professor of law and history at Capital University in Columbus, Ohio, where he teaches courses in Anglo-American legal and constitutional history, among other subjects. Professor Mayer formerly taught at IIT Chicago-Kent College of Law, held a postdoctoral fellowship at the Institute for Humane Studies, and was an attorney in Washington, D.C. He has received degrees from the University of Virginia (Ph.D. and M.A. in history) and the University of Michigan (J.D. and A.B.). He has written *The Constitutional Thought of Thomas Jefferson* (Charlottesville: University of Virginia Press, 1994) and is the author of several articles in law, history, and political science journals.

Cato Institute

Founded in 1977, the Cato Institute is a public policy research foundation dedicated to broadening the parameters of policy debate to allow consideration of more options that are consistent with the traditional American principles of limited government, individual liberty, and peace. To that end, the Institute strives to achieve greater involvement of the intelligent, concerned lay public in questions of policy and the proper role of government.

The Institute is named for *Cato's Letters*, libertarian pamphlets that were widely read in the American Colonies in the early 18th century and played a major role in laying the philosophical foundation for the American Revolution.

Despite the achievement of the nation's Founders, today virtually no aspect of life is free from government encroachment. A pervasive intolerance for individual rights is shown by government's arbitrary intrusions into private economic transactions and its disregard for civil liberties.

To counter that trend, the Cato Institute undertakes an extensive publications program that addresses the complete spectrum of policy issues. Books, monographs, and shorter studies are commissioned to examine the federal budget, Social Security, regulation, military spending, international trade, and myriad other issues. Major policy conferences are held throughout the year, from which papers are published thrice yearly in the *Cato Journal*. The Institute also publishes the quarterly magazine *Regulation*.

In order to maintain its independence, the Cato Institute accepts no government funding. Contributions are received from foundations, corporations, and individuals, and other revenue is generated from the sale of publications. The Institute is a nonprofit, tax-exempt, educational foundation under Section 501(c)3 of the Internal Revenue Code.

CATO INSTITUTE
1000 Massachusetts Ave., N.W.
Washington, D.C. 20001
www.cato.org